Cambridge School
Shakespeare

College

AS YOU LIKE IT

CAMBRIDGE
UNIVERSITY PRESS

Edited by Linzy Brady
Series editors: Richard Andrews and Vicki Wienand
Founding editor: Rex Gibson

CAMBRIDGE
UNIVERSITY PRESS

University Printing House, Cambridge CB2 8BS, United Kingdom

Cambridge University Press is part of the University of Cambridge.

It furthers the University's mission by disseminating knowledge in the pursuit of education, learning and research at the highest international levels of excellence.

www.cambridge.org
Information on this title: www.cambridge.org/9781107675124

Commentary and notes © Cambridge University Press 2000, 2015
Text © Cambridge University Press 2000, 2015

First published 2000
Second edition 2009
Third edition 2015

Printed in India by Replika Press Pvt. Ltd

A catalogue record for this publication is available from the British Library

ISBN 978-1-107-67512-4 Paperback

....

Cover image: The Old Vic Theatre 2010, © Geraint Lewis

Contents

Introduction

This *As You Like It* is part of the **Cambridge School Shakespeare** series. Like every other play in the series, it has been specially prepared to help all students in schools and colleges.

The **Cambridge School Shakespeare** *As You Like It* aims to be different. It invites you to lift the words from the page and to bring the play to life in your classroom, hall or drama studio. Through enjoyable and focused activities, you will increase your understanding of the play. Actors have created their different interpretations of the play over the centuries. Similarly, you are invited to make up your own mind about *As You Like It*, rather than having someone else's interpretation handed down to you.

Cambridge School Shakespeare does not offer you a cut-down or simplified version of the play. This is Shakespeare's language, filled with imaginative possibilities. You will find on every left-hand page: a summary of the action, an explanation of unfamiliar words, and a choice of activities on Shakespeare's stagecraft, characters, themes and language.

Between each act and in the pages at the end of the play, you will find notes, illustrations and activities. These will help to encourage reflection after every act and give you insights into the background and context of the play as a whole.

This edition will be of value to you whether you are studying for an examination, reading for pleasure or thinking of putting on the play to entertain others. You can work on the activities on your own or in groups. Many of the activities suggest a particular group size, but don't be afraid to make up larger or smaller groups to suit your own purposes. Please don't think you have to do every activity: choose those that will help you most.

Although you are invited to treat *As You Like It* as a play, you don't need special dramatic or theatrical skills to do the activities. By choosing your activities, and by exploring and experimenting, you can make your own interpretations of Shakespeare's language, characters and stories.

Whatever you do, remember that Shakespeare wrote his plays to be acted, watched and enjoyed.

Rex Gibson
Founding editor

This new edition contains more photographs, more diversity and more supporting material than previous editions, whilst remaining true to Rex's original vision. Specifically, it contains more activities and commentary on stagecraft and writing about Shakespeare, to reflect contemporary interest. The glossary has been enlarged too. Finally, this edition aims to reflect the best teaching and learning possible, and to represent not only Shakespeare through the ages, but also the relevance and excitement of Shakespeare today.

Richard Andrews and Vicki Wienand
Series editors

This edition of *As You Like It* uses the updated text of the play established by Michael Hattaway in **The New Cambridge Shakespeare**. Some minor editorial differences exist between this and the previous edition, although pagination and line numbering remain the same.

overthrown his brother and the kingdom's rightful ruler, Duke Senior, who now lives in exile in the Forest of Arden. Despite this conflict, the daughters of these two men – Rosalind, whose father has been exiled, and Celia, whose father now rules at court – are like sisters to each other.

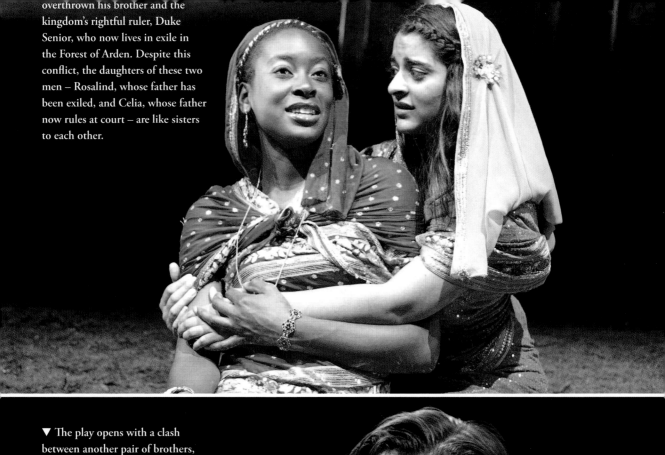

▼ The play opens with a clash between another pair of brothers, the sons of Sir Roland de Boys. Orlando is mistreated by his elder brother, Oliver, who plans to kill him.

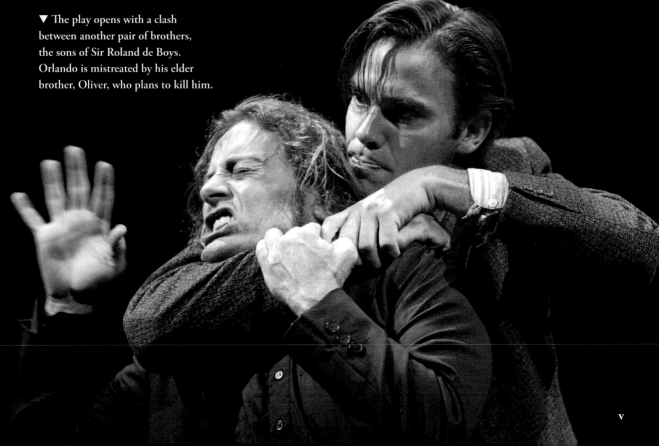

v

◀ Hoping that Orlando will be killed, Oliver persuades his brother to enter a wrestling match against Duke Frederick's dangerous star wrestler, Charles. Rosalind tries to dissuade Orlando from fighting, and they fall in love. She gives him a necklace to wear in her honour.

▼ Orlando defies all expectations by defeating Charles, but is dismissed as an enemy by Duke Frederick. Rosalind is also banished from the kingdom by her uncle, on pain of death, and she and Celia decide to run away together rather than be separated.

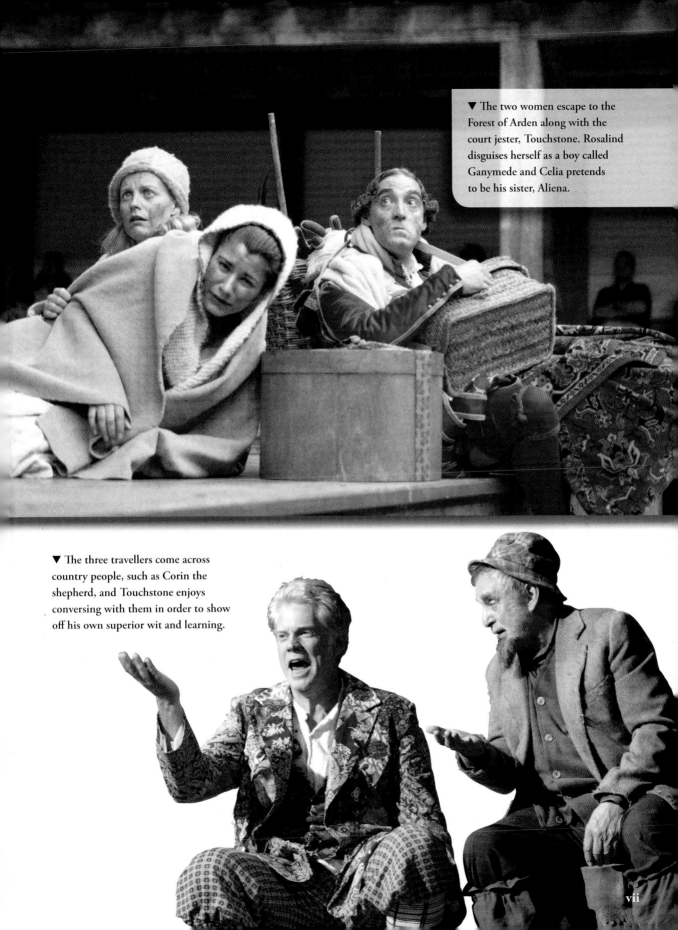

▼ The two women escape to the Forest of Arden along with the court jester, Touchstone. Rosalind disguises herself as a boy called Ganymede and Celia pretends to be his sister, Aliena.

▼ The three travellers come across country people, such as Corin the shepherd, and Touchstone enjoys conversing with them in order to show off his own superior wit and learning.

▼ In the Forest of Arden, Duke Senior enjoys a simple life, free from all the political manoeuvres and social ambitions of life at court. He is amused by Jaques, a melancholy and satirical courtier who reminds everyone that human folly and weakness exist even in the Forest of Arden.

In the forest, many kinds of love are in the air. Touchstone falls for Audrey, a simple goatherd, and plans to marry her. A shepherd named Silvius loves a disdainful shepherdess called Phoebe, but she rejects him and falls in love with Ganymede (who is really Rosalind in disguise).

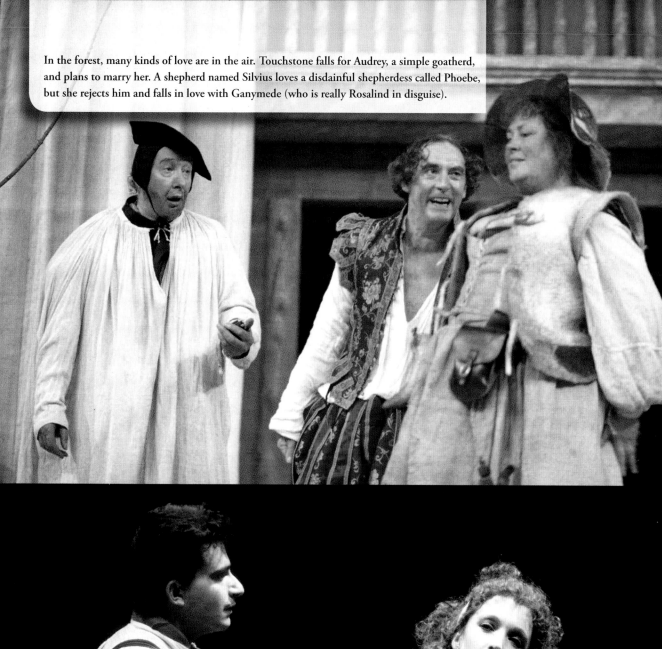

▲ Meanwhile, Orlando has also fled to the Forest of Arden to escape his brother's murderous intentions. He spends his time daydreaming about Rosalind and writing her second-rate love poems, which he hangs in the trees.

▼ Rosalind reads the poems and meets Orlando while disguised as Ganymede. She tries to cure Orlando's lovesick fantasies and teach him about real-life relationships, making him treat Ganymede as if he were Rosalind. In this way, Rosalind also tricks Orlando into 'marrying' her.

◀ Towards the end of the play, Orlando saves the life of his brother Oliver. This formerly evil character is converted to goodness and falls in love with Celia at first sight.

▼ Rosalind tires of all the complications that her disguise has caused. She promises Orlando, Silvius and Phoebe that they will all marry the right person if they do as she says.

▼ At the end of the play, all the complications seem resolved. Rosalind abandons her disguise and reveals her true identity, at which point Orlando keeps his promise to marry her and Phoebe keeps her promise to marry Silvius. As the weddings are about to take place, a messenger arrives with news that Duke Frederick has also converted to goodness and restored the kingdom to Duke Senior.

▼ The play ends as everyone except Jaques plans to return to the court. Rosalind takes centre stage to bid the audience goodbye in a witty epilogue.

List of characters

The court

The usurping court

DUKE FREDERICK younger brother to
  Duke Senior
CELIA his daughter (who disguises
  herself as Aliena)
ROSALIND daughter of Duke Senior
  (who disguises herself as Ganymede)
TOUCHSTONE a clown
CHARLES the Duke's wrestler
LE BEAU
FIRST LORD } courtiers
SECOND LORD

The de Boys household

OLIVER
JACQUES } sons of
ORLANDO Sir Roland de Boys
ADAM servant to Orlando
DENIS servant to Oliver

The Forest of Arden

The banished court

DUKE SENIOR the rightful duke
JAQUES
AMIENS
FIRST LORD } courtiers
SECOND LORD
FIRST PAGE } attendants on
SECOND PAGE the Duke

The people of Arden

CORIN a shepherd
SILVIUS a shepherd
PHOEBE a shepherdess
AUDREY a goatherd
WILLIAM a countryman
SIR OLIVER MARTEXT a priest
FORESTERS

HYMEN god of marriage

The action of the play takes place in Oliver's home, Duke Frederick's palace and the Forest of Arden

Orlando recounts how he inherited only £250. His father's will instructed the oldest son, Oliver, to educate Orlando. But Oliver treats him worse than the horses, and denies him status or education.

Stagecraft

Dramatic grammar (in pairs)

The play begins in the middle of a conversation between Orlando and his family's faithful servant, Adam, about the will left by Orlando's late father. Orlando is clearly agitated as he talks about the unfair treatment he has suffered at the hands of his own brother.

a Read Orlando's opening monologue aloud to yourself as you walk around the room. Pay particular attention to the grammar by changing direction as you walk:

- At each full stop, make a full 'about-turn' (180 degrees).
- At each comma, semi-colon and colon, make a half-turn (90 degrees to your right or left).
- Think of gestures to make at question marks, dashes and exclamation marks (such as stamping your foot or clicking your fingers).

b With your partner, discuss how the grammatical structure of the monologue reflects Orlando's feelings and experiences. How would you enact these lines to convey his motivations at this point?

c How does the grammar of Orlando's speech change at line 24 compared with the monologue above? Why do you think this might be? Take turns to explore different styles of speaking Orlando's response to his brother in this line. Decide which style of speaking you think best expresses Orlando's inner thoughts at this point.

d Imagine you are planning to direct a production of *As You Like It*. Make notes on the set, the costumes and the general impression you would wish to create of Orlando, Oliver and Adam. These notes could form the first part of a Director's Journal in which you can record your ideas about staging the play as you read on.

upon this fashion in this manner

by will (in my father's will)

poor a a mere

crowns gold coins

charged ordered

breed educate

keeps at school supports financially through university

profit progress

rustically like a peasant

stays keeps

unkept uncared for, uneducated

stalling sheltering

manège paces, stylish behaviour

riders trainers

dearly hired paid well

something social status

countenance attitude

hinds farm labourers

bars denies

mines my gentility undermines my good birth

avoid get rid of

Go apart stand aside

shake me up abuse me violently

make (Oliver's question means 'What are you doing?' but Orlando deliberately misunderstands 'make' to mean 'fashion' or 'create something')

mar spoil

1 Invent a scene (in small groups)

a Stage your own scene in which Sir Roland de Boys, on his deathbed, tells his three sons, Oliver, Jacques and Orlando, what is in his will and what he wants each of them to do.

b Alternatively, you could write the will of Sir Roland and perform a scene in which it is read aloud to the sons. All three sons should react to the will using facial expressions and physical gestures.

As You Like It

Act 1 Scene 1
The orchard of Oliver's house

Enter ORLANDO *and* ADAM

ORLANDO As I remember, Adam, it was upon this fashion bequeathed
me by will but poor a thousand crowns and, as thou say'st, charged
my brother, on his blessing, to breed me well: and there begins my
sadness. My brother Jacques he keeps at school, and report speaks
goldenly of his profit. For my part, he keeps me rustically at home   5
or, to speak more properly, stays me here at home unkept – for call
you that 'keeping' for a gentleman of my birth, that differs not from
the stalling of an ox? His horses are bred better for, besides that they
are fair with their feeding, they are taught their manège, and to that
end riders dearly hired. But I, his brother, gain nothing under him   10
but growth – for the which his animals on his dunghills are as much
bound to him as I. Besides this nothing that he so plentifully gives
me, the something that Nature gave me his countenance seems to
take from me: he lets me feed with his hinds, bars me the place of a
brother, and, as much as in him lies, mines my gentility with my   15
education. This is it, Adam, that grieves me, and the spirit of my
father, which I think is within me, begins to mutiny against this
servitude. I will no longer endure it, though yet I know no wise
remedy how to avoid it.

Enter OLIVER

ADAM   Yonder comes my master, your brother.   20
ORLANDO Go apart, Adam, and thou shalt hear how he will shake me
up.
[*Adam withdraws*]
OLIVER   Now sir, what make you here?
ORLANDO Nothing: I am not taught to make anything.
OLIVER   What mar you then, sir?   25

Oliver is angered by Orlando's protest at being kept in poverty. He threatens to strike Orlando, but Orlando seizes Oliver and demands his share of the will. Oliver seems to consent.

1 Brother against brother (in threes)

a Take parts as Orlando, Oliver and Adam, and rehearse lines 20–67 to experiment with how you would portray these characters on stage. Explore the points below to refine your ideas about the performance, and make notes in your Director's Journal on the most successful elements.

- **Language** Discuss why you think Orlando often echoes his brother's words. For example, the brothers call each other 'sir', but in what tones of voice and with what gestures? Locate each instance of Orlando's repetitions and decide how he might say them, and what he might mean by them. Try out a few different ways of speaking the lines to see what works best.

- **Status** Orlando appeals to his brother as a gentleman to treat him also as a gentleman. How would you show the difference in their status at this point? Think about the positions and postures of the actors.

- **Violence** Orlando is the younger brother, but he proves he is better at fighting than Oliver. Work out how you would stage the fight in a way that reveals the personality of each brother. The stage directions at lines 41, 42 and 59 suggest that Oliver begins the physical violence – but does he? Read the script without considering the stage directions, then discuss this point. Remember that the stage directions were not written by Shakespeare, but were inserted by the editors of later editions of the play.

b Write an **aside** for Adam at each question mark in lines 20–67, to allow him to voice his opinion on the conversation from his hiding place. Perform the scene again, with Adam speaking these asides aloud.

Marry by the Virgin Mary

be naught awhile clear off!
husks scraps
prodigal wastefully lavish
penury poverty

knows acknowledges
in ... blood because of our noble breeding
so know me know me as a brother
The courtesy of nations social custom
allows you my better says you are superior
blood rank or spirit
is nearer to his reverence makes you his legitimate heir
boy (an insult to provoke Orlando)
thou (this pronoun was used to speak to people of lower status, so it is a calculated insult here)
villein serf, lowest-status person (pun on 'villain')
railed on insulted
be patient calm down
accord peace

qualities accomplishments, manners

exercises acquired skills
allottery share, bequest
testament will

ORLANDO	Marry, sir, I am helping you to mar that which God made, a poor unworthy brother of yours, with idleness.
OLIVER	Marry, sir, be better employed, and be naught awhile.
ORLANDO	Shall I keep your hogs and eat husks with them? What prodigal portion have I spent that I should come to such penury?
OLIVER	Know you where you are, sir?
ORLANDO	O, sir, very well: here in your orchard.
OLIVER	Know you before whom, sir?
ORLANDO	Aye, better than him I am before knows me: I know you are my eldest brother, and in the gentle condition of blood you should so know me. The courtesy of nations allows you my better in that you are the first-born, but the same tradition takes not away my blood, were there twenty brothers betwixt us. I have as much of my father in me as you, albeit I confess your coming before me is nearer to his reverence.
OLIVER	[*Raising his hand*] What, boy!
ORLANDO	[*Seizing his brother*] Come, come, elder brother, you are too young in this.
OLIVER	Wilt thou lay hands on me, villain?
ORLANDO	I am no villein: I am the youngest son of Sir Roland de Boys; he was my father, and he is thrice a villain that says such a father begot villeins. Wert thou not my brother, I would not take this hand from thy throat till this other had pulled out thy tongue for saying so: thou hast railed on thyself.
ADAM	[*Coming forward*] Sweet masters, be patient, for your father's remembrance, be at accord.
OLIVER	Let me go, I say.
ORLANDO	I will not till I please. You shall hear me. My father charged you in his will to give me good education: you have trained me like a peasant, obscuring and hiding from me all gentleman-like qualities. The spirit of my father grows strong in me – and I will no longer endure it. Therefore allow me such exercises as may become a gentleman or give me the poor allottery my father left me by testament: with that I will go buy my fortunes.

[*He releases Oliver*]

| OLIVER | And what wilt thou do? Beg when that is spent? Well, sir, get you in. I will not long be troubled with you: you shall have some part of your 'will'; I pray you leave me. |

30
35
40
45
50
55
60

Oliver resolves to get rid of Orlando. Charles tells of Duke Senior's banishment, Rosalind and Celia's great friendship, and of many courtiers joining Duke Senior in the Forest of Arden.

Characters

Oliver's soliloquies (in pairs)

Oliver shows the unpleasant side of his nature, calling the loyal servant Adam 'old dog'. He then has two short **soliloquies**, at lines 68–9 and line 75. The stage convention is that in a soliloquy a character speaks the truth, showing their true personality and intentions.

- Experiment with different ways of speaking the soliloquies. Use tone, gesture and dramatic pauses to convey Oliver's character and motivations. Decide how to deliver each soliloquy and share your interpretations with the rest of the class.

1 Setting the scene for the play (in small groups)

Charles's news helps to establish the play's context, relationships and themes. But how does the news relayed by Charles link to the story so far, and to the history of Oliver and Orlando?

- Use the list of characters on page 1 to help you draw a character web. Devise symbols or a colour code to show the status of characters you have met so far and the relationships between them. You could also include sketches of the characters and additional notes about their apparent temperaments and motivations. As you become familiar with more of the play's characters, add to your character web so that it serves as a useful 'who's who' of As You Like It.

Write about it

Who, what, where, when, why?

Write a newspaper article about the Duke's banishment, using the details of Charles's account in lines 79–95. Embellish the article with features such as eye-witness accounts, quotes from the characters involved and language that is suitable for either a tabloid or a broadsheet newspaper.

grow upon me become troublesome to me

physic your rankness cure your fast-growing insolence

Holla come here

importunes begs

way (way of killing Orlando)

morrow morning

old Duke (Duke Senior)

good leave cheerful permission

the Duke's daughter, her cousin (Celia, who is Duke Frederick's daughter and Rosalind's cousin)

bred brought up

to stay by staying

of by

merry (this term was often used to denote social equality)

fleet the time carelessly pass the time without a care

golden world first age of the world or ideal, carefree existence described in ancient Greek and Latin texts

ORLANDO I will no further offend you than becomes me for my good.

OLIVER [*To Adam*] Get you with him, you old dog.

ADAM Is 'old dog' my reward? Most true, I have lost my teeth in your   65
service. God be with my old master: he would not have spoke such
a word.

Exeunt Orlando [and] Adam

OLIVER Is it even so, begin you to grow upon me? I will physic your
rankness, and yet give no thousand crowns neither. – Holla, Denis.

Enter DENIS

DENIS Calls your worship?   70

OLIVER Was not Charles, the Duke's wrestler, here to speak with me?

DENIS So please you, he is here at the door, and importunes access to
you.

OLIVER Call him in.

[Exit Denis]

'Twill be a good way, and tomorrow the wrestling is.   75

Enter CHARLES

CHARLES Good morrow to your worship.

OLIVER Good Monsieur Charles, what's the new news at the new
court?

CHARLES There's no news at the court, sir, but the old news: that is, the
old Duke is banished by his younger brother, the new Duke, and   80
three or four loving lords have put themselves into voluntary exile
with him, whose lands and revenues enrich the new Duke; therefore
he gives them good leave to wander.

OLIVER Can you tell if Rosalind, the Duke's daughter, be banished
with her father?   85

CHARLES O no; for the Duke's daughter, her cousin, so loves her, being
ever from their cradles bred together, that she would have followed
her exile or have died to stay behind her; she is at the court and no
less beloved of her uncle than his own daughter, and never two
ladies loved as they do.   90

OLIVER Where will the old Duke live?

CHARLES They say he is already in the Forest of Arden, and a many
merry men with him; and there they live like the old Robin Hood of
England. They say many young gentlemen flock to him every day,
and fleet the time carelessly as they did in the golden world.   95

Charles says he is reluctant to injure Orlando. Oliver falsely describes Orlando's character and intentions, and urges Charles to kill him. Alone on stage, Oliver expresses envy of Orlando's character and reputation.

Characters

Charles: a pompous wrestler? (in pairs)

Charles is Duke Frederick's wrestler. He is very proud of his reputation, and warns of what may happen if Orlando insists on fighting him. He speaks formally, often using long words and unnatural word order where a simpler style would do.

a Discuss what effect Charles's overblown speaking style might have on a listener. Think about the audience's impression, as well as how the other characters might react.

b Take turns to read aloud lines 97–107, then construct a verbal or written version of the speech that uses clearer wording and sentence structure. What difference does this make to the message? Why do you think Charles employs such complicated language?

1 A false brother (in pairs)

Oliver's descriptions of Orlando are often descriptions of himself. Psychoanalysts call this 'projection' – that is, attributing your own feelings or characteristics to others. Keep this in mind as you complete the following activities.

a One person speaks lines 108–23 in character as Oliver, pausing after every short section. In the pause, the other person judges whether or not Oliver is lying by proclaiming aloud 'True' or 'False'. Switch roles and see if there are any points in the speech when you disagree about whether or not he is being truthful.

b Take turns to read through Olivier's soliloquy at lines 127–34. Together, compile notes on Oliver's character and his behaviour towards Orlando. Write a psychoanalyst's report on Oliver, giving possible reasons why he might hate Orlando so much and why he might project so many of his own feelings and motivations onto his brother.

disposition intention

disguised (it was not becoming for a gentleman to fight with a common wrestler)

fall bout, round of fighting

credit reputation

loath to foil reluctant to defeat

brook endure

thing of his own search plan of his own devising

requite reward

underhand means secret methods

envious emulator jealous imitator

parts qualities

villainous contriver wicked plotter

as lief rather

disgrace disfigurement or injury

grace himself on thee gain credit at your expense

practise plot

device trick

anatomise him analyse his faults

go alone walks without aid

stir this gamester shake this upstart

noble device nobility

altogether misprized scorned by everyone

kindle the boy (incite Orlando to wrestle)

OLIVER   What, you wrestle tomorrow before the new Duke?

CHARLES   Marry, do I, sir; and I came to acquaint you with a matter. I
          am given, sir, secretly to understand that your younger brother
          Orlando hath a disposition to come in, disguised, against me to try
          a fall. Tomorrow, sir, I wrestle for my credit, and he that escapes   100
          me without some broken limb shall acquit him well. Your brother is but
          young and tender and, for your love, I would be loath to foil him, as
          I must for my own honour, if he come in; therefore, out of my love
          to you, I came hither to acquaint you withal, that either you might
          stay him from his intendment, or brook such disgrace well as he   105
          shall run into, in that it is a thing of his own search and altogether
          against my will.

OLIVER   Charles, I thank thee for thy love to me, which thou shalt find
          I will most kindly requite. I had myself notice of my brother's
          purpose herein, and have by underhand means laboured to dissuade   110
          him from it – but he is resolute. I'll tell thee, Charles, it is the
          stubbornest young fellow of France, full of ambition, an envious
          emulator of every man's good parts, a secret and villainous contriver
          against me, his natural brother. Therefore use thy discretion: I had
          as lief thou didst break his neck as his finger. And thou wert best   115
          look to't – for if thou dost him any slight disgrace or if he do not
          mightily grace himself on thee, he will practise against thee by
          poison, entrap thee by some treacherous device, and never leave
          thee till he hath ta'en thy life by some indirect means or other. For
          I assure thee – and almost with tears I speak it – there is not one so   120
          young and so villainous this day living. I speak but brotherly of him,
          but should I anatomise him to thee as he is, I must blush and weep,
          and thou must look pale and wonder.

CHARLES   I am heartily glad I came hither to you. If he come tomorrow,
          I'll give him his payment; if ever he go alone again, I'll never wrestle   125
          for prize more – and so God keep your worship.   *Exit*

OLIVER   Farewell, good Charles. – Now will I stir this gamester. I hope
          I shall see an end of him, for my soul – yet I know not why – hates
          nothing more than he. Yet he's gentle, never schooled and yet
          learned, full of noble device, of all sorts enchantingly beloved, and   130
          indeed so much in the heart of the world, and especially of my own
          people who best know him, that I am altogether misprized. But it
          shall not be so long this wrestler shall clear all: nothing remains but
          that I kindle the boy thither, which now I'll go about.

                                                                    Exit

Celia tries to cheer Rosalind, who thinks with sadness of her banished father. Responding to Celia's affection, Rosalind joins in witty wordplay about love, fortune and nature.

Themes

Fortune and her wheel (in small groups)

Fortune was commonly depicted as a blindfolded goddess who used her wheel to raise people into prosperity and happiness before plunging them down again into misery.

- Look at the wheel of Fortune illustrated below and have a go at drawing and colouring your own. Annotate where Rosalind and Celia are on this wheel of Fortune, and show the direction in which they might each – or both – be heading. Where on the wheel are the other characters?

1 Fortune, Nature and witty repartee

In lines 30–6, Celia says that Fortune bestows either virtue or beauty upon women, and that beautiful women ('fair') are rarely chaste ('honest'). Rosalind challenges her, as she believes that Fortune only affects 'gifts of the world' such as money and power. According to Rosalind, a person's looks, intelligence and moral qualities are 'the lineaments of Nature' – features given by Nature rather than Fortune. The theme of nature's relationship to fortune is central to the play, so keep it in mind as you read on.

- Rewrite lines 25–45 in your own words, to make the wit and wordplay intelligible and amusing to a modern audience. Some of the wordplay involves exploiting certain words' multiple definitions, so check the glossaries on this page and on page 12 to make sure that you have understood all the possible meanings.

Act 1 Scene 2
Duke Frederick's palace

Enter ROSALIND *and* CELIA

CELIA I pray thee, Rosalind, sweet my coz, be merry.

ROSALIND Dear Celia, I show more mirth than I am mistress of, and would you yet were merrier: unless you could teach me to forget a banished father, you must not learn me how to remember any extraordinary pleasure. 5

CELIA Herein, I see, thou lov'st me not with the full weight that I love thee; if my uncle, thy banished father, had banished thy uncle, the Duke my father, so thou hadst been still with me, I could have taught my love to take thy father for mine; so wouldst thou, if the truth of thy love to me were so righteously tempered as mine is to thee. 10

ROSALIND Well, I will forget the condition of my estate to rejoice in yours.

CELIA You know my father hath no child but I, nor none is like to have; and, truly, when he dies thou shalt be his heir: for what he hath taken away from thy father perforce I will render thee again in affection. By mine honour, I will, and when I break that oath, let me turn monster. Therefore, my sweet Rose, my dear Rose, be merry. 15

ROSALIND From henceforth I will, coz, and devise sports. Let me see, what think you of falling in love? 20

CELIA Marry, I prithee do, to make sport withal: but love no man in good earnest – nor no further in sport neither – than with safety of a pure blush thou mayst in honour come off again.

ROSALIND What shall be our sport then?

CELIA Let us sit and mock the good housewife Fortune from her wheel, that her gifts may henceforth be bestowed equally. 25

ROSALIND I would we could do so: for her benefits are mightily misplaced, and the bountiful blind woman doth most mistake in her gifts to women.

CELIA Tis true, for those that she makes fair she scarce makes honest, and those that she makes honest she makes very ill-favouredly. 30

ROSALIND Nay, now thou goest from Fortune's office to Nature's: Fortune reigns in gifts of the world, not in the lineaments of Nature.

Celia comments that fools are sent by nature to sharpen witty people's intelligence. Touchstone jokes about honour. He hints at corruption in Duke Frederick's court.

Language in the play

Language games (in small groups)

Like all Shakespeare's clowns, Touchstone loves playing with language in order to entertain his listeners and to criticise the follies of high-status people.

a Touchstone jokes to make a serious point, and seems to imply that Duke Frederick's court lacks honour. Read through his riddle-like story of the knight and the 'pancakes' in lines 50–65. Try to understand the meaning of the joke and how it relates to Duke Frederick.

b In lines 56–7, Touchstone tricks Celia and Rosalind into stroking their chins and swearing by their non-existent beards, in order to help illustrate his point. How might this affect the relationship and balance of power between the entertainer and his onstage audience?

c Find examples of Touchstone's puns, slapstick comedy, mimicry and other comic features in the script opposite. Do you think that humour can be an effective vehicle for communicating criticism or discussion on serious topics? Why? Think of some characters in television shows or of some comedians who do this, and compare them with Touchstone.

fall into the fire lose her virtue
wit (line 36) intelligence
flout at complain about, mock
argument theme, discussion
too hard more than a match
Nature's natural idiot, born fool
Peradventure perhaps
wits (line 42) mental faculties
reason of talk about
whetstone sharpening stone
away along

pancakes fritters, burgers
naught worthless
stand to it insist, swear
forsworn perjured, lying on oath
unmuzzle unleash, set free

Prithee I pray you (pardon)

taxation slander, criticism

By my troth honestly, upon my faith
wit (line 70) wisdom

Enter TOUCHSTONE

CELIA   No? When Nature hath made a fair creature, may she not by   35
           Fortune fall into the fire? Though Nature hath given us wit to flout
           at Fortune, hath not Fortune sent in this fool to cut off the
           argument?

ROSALIND Indeed there is Fortune too hard for Nature, when Fortune
           makes Nature's natural the cutter-off of Nature's wit.   40

CELIA   Peradventure this is not Fortune's work neither but Nature's
           who, perceiving our natural wits too dull to reason of such god-
           desses, hath sent this natural for our whetstone: for always the
           dullness of the fool is the whetstone of the wits. – How now, Wit,
           whither wander you?   45

TOUCHSTONE   Mistress, you must come away to your father.

CELIA   Were you made the messenger?

TOUCHSTONE   No, by mine honour, but I was bid to come for you.

ROSALIND Where learned you that oath, fool?

TOUCHSTONE   Of a certain knight that swore, by his honour, they were   50
           good pancakes, and swore, by his honour, the mustard was naught.
           Now, I'll stand to it, the pancakes were naught and the mustard
           was good – and yet was not the knight forsworn.

CELIA   How prove you that in the great heap of your knowledge?

ROSALIND Aye, marry, now unmuzzle your wisdom.   55

TOUCHSTONE   Stand you both forth now. Stroke your chins and swear,
           by your beards, that I am a knave.

CELIA   By our beards – if we had them – thou art.

TOUCHSTONE   By my knavery – if I had it – then I were. But if you
           swear by that that is not you are not forsworn: no more was this   60
           knight swearing by his honour, for he never had any; or if he had,
           he had sworn it away before ever he saw those pancakes or that
           mustard.

CELIA   Prithee, who is't that thou mean'st?

TOUCHSTONE   One that old Frederick, your father, loves.   65

CELIA   My father's love is enough to honour him. Enough! Speak no
           more of him; you'll be whipped for taxation one of these days.

TOUCHSTONE   The more pity that fools may not speak wisely what wise
           men do foolishly.

CELIA   By my troth, thou say'st true: for, since the little wit that fools   70
           have was silenced, the little foolery that wise men have makes a
           great show. – Here comes 'Monsieur the Beau'.

Celia, Rosalind and Touchstone all mock Le Beau for his affected speech. He brings news of how Charles has seriously injured an old man's three sons. The news dismays the women.

Stagecraft

Mocking Le Beau (in small groups)

Le Beau (French for 'the beautiful') is often played as an overdressed courtier who puts on airs and graces and uses elaborate gestures. He speaks with an affected accent (pronouncing 'sport' as 'spot') and is unable to keep up with witty wordplay of the other characters. Le Beau usually fails to see that Celia, Rosalind and Touchstone are mocking him.

- As a director, how you would advise actors to perform the script opposite for greatest comic effect? Discuss this in your group and write detailed notes in your Director's Journal, describing what you would want to see and hear on stage from each of the characters. Consider the following points in your actors' notes, then use your findings to perform lines 73–116 for another group. Try to make them laugh as much as possible!

Mimicry Celia speaks in French (line 76) and repeats Le Beau's words (line 79), while Rosalind and Touchstone use pompously exaggerated language (lines 81–2).

Imagery Celia uses an image from bricklaying (line 83), suggesting that Touchstone is thickly laying on the irony like a bricklayer slapping on a trowelful of mortar. Does Le Beau overhear her, and what is his response? Does he understand the joke?

Interruptions Le Beau's sad story of Charles defeating three sons of an old man at wrestling is interrupted in line 94 and lines 96–7. How does Le Beau react to the interruptions?

put on us force-feed us with

marketable valuable, saleable (because heavier)

lost missed

sport amorous fun and games

colour kind, nature

fortune good luck

destinies decree goddesses of fate enforce

rank social status (Rosalind replies with a pun on 'rank', meaning stinking)

loosest release

amaze confuse, bewilder

lost the sight of missed

match rival

proper honest, good-looking

growth stature

bills papers, writing

presents (Rosalind puns on Le Beau's use of the word 'presence' – bills were legal documents that often began 'Be it known unto all men by these presents')

dole sad weeping

Enter LE BEAU

ROSALIND	With his mouth full of news.
CELIA	Which he will put on us as pigeons feed their young.
ROSALIND	Then shall we be news-crammed. 75
CELIA	All the better: we shall be the more marketable. – *Bonjour,* Monsieur Le Beau, what's the news?
LE BEAU	Fair princess, you have lost much good sport.
CELIA	'Sport': of what colour?
LE BEAU	'What colour', madam? How shall I answer you? 80
ROSALIND	As wit and fortune will.
TOUCHSTONE	[*Imitating Le Beau*] Or as the destinies decree.
CELIA	Well said: that was laid on with a trowel.
TOUCHSTONE	Nay, if I keep not my rank –
ROSALIND	Thou loosest thy old smell. 85
LE BEAU	You amaze me, ladies! I would have told you of good wrestling which you have lost the sight of.
ROSALIND	Yet tell us the manner of the wrestling.
LE BEAU	I will tell you the beginning and, if it please your ladyships, you may see the end, for the best is yet to do; and here where you 90 are they are coming to perform it.
CELIA	Well, the beginning that is dead and buried.
LE BEAU	There comes an old man and his three sons –
CELIA	I could match this beginning with an old tale.
LE BEAU	Three proper young men, of excellent growth and presence – 95
ROSALIND	With bills on their necks: 'Be it known unto all men by these presents'.
LE BEAU	The eldest of the three wrestled with Charles, the Duke's wrestler, which Charles in a moment threw him and broke three of his ribs that there is little hope of life in him. So he served the 100 second and so the third: yonder they lie, the poor old man, their father, making such pitiful dole over them that all the beholders take his part with weeping.
ROSALIND	Alas!
TOUCHSTONE	But what is the sport, monsieur, that the ladies have 105 lost?
LE BEAU	Why, this that I speak of.
TOUCHSTONE	Thus men may grow wiser every day. It is the first time that ever I heard breaking of ribs was sport for ladies.
CELIA	Or I, I promise thee. 110

The court and the wrestlers enter. Duke Frederick says that Orlando insists on fighting, but Charles is certain to win the wrestling match. Celia and Rosalind try to persuade Orlando not to fight.

1 Why, Orlando? (in pairs)

Do you think Orlando volunteered to fight Charles, or did Oliver or others in the court force him? Conduct an interview with Orlando just before the fight, and try to determine what motivations or pressures were involved in his decision.

2 Friendly or menacing or something else? (in threes)

Duke Frederick greets Celia ('daughter'), then Rosalind ('cousin'). Rosalind is actually his niece, but in Shakespeare's time 'cousin' was used much more loosely than it is today.

a In what tone of voice does Frederick say '– and cousin'? Remember that he has banished Rosalind's father and seized his dukedom. Also consider why and how Frederick says 'crept' in line 122.

b Discuss the possible postures and gestures of Duke Frederick, Rosalind and Celia during this meeting. How might they physically interact with one another as they speak their lines? Write stage directions at lines 122–3 and 127–8, and take parts to perform lines 122–30.

▼ What do you think Orlando is really thinking as he responds politely to Celia and Rosalind? Is he distracted by their concern, impressed by their kindness or offended that they think he will not win?

any else longs anyone else who wishes

this broken music in his sides the sound of ribs being broken (like a smashed violin)

dotes upon foolishly loves

Flourish fanfare of trumpets to signify the presence of royalty or people in authority

forwardness rash bravery

successfully as if he might win

cousin (this term could refer to various relatives, such as nieces)

liege lord

odds in the man a strong advantage for Charles

fain gladly

is the general challenger offers to fight anybody

come but in merely enter the competition

try test

cruel proof (Charles's defeat of the old man's three sons)

misprized despised

suit plea, request

ROSALIND   But is there any else longs to see this broken music in his sides? Is there yet another dotes upon rib-breaking? Shall we see this wrestling, cousin?

LE BEAU   You must if you stay here, for here is the place appointed for the wrestling and they are ready to perform it.   115

CELIA   Yonder, sure, they are coming. Let us now stay and see it.

Flourish. Enter DUKE FREDERICK, LORDS, ORLANDO, CHARLES, *and* ATTENDANTS

DUKE FREDERICK   Come on; since the youth will not be entreated, his own peril on his forwardness.

ROSALIND   Is yonder the man?

LE BEAU   Even he, madam.   120

CELIA   Alas, he is too young; yet he looks successfully.

DUKE FREDERICK   How now, daughter – and cousin: are you crept hither to see the wrestling?

ROSALIND   Aye, my liege, so please you give us leave.

DUKE FREDERICK   You will take little delight in it, I can tell you: there   125
is such odds in the man. In pity of the challenger's youth, I would fain dissuade him, but he will not be entreated. Speak to him, ladies: see if you can move him.

CELIA   Call him hither, good Monsieur Le Beau.

DUKE FREDERICK   Do so; I'll not be by.   130

[*The Duke stands aside*]

LE BEAU   Monsieur the challenger, the princess calls for you.

ORLANDO   I attend them with all respect and duty.

ROSALIND   Young man, have you challenged Charles the wrestler?

ORLANDO   No, fair princess, he is the general challenger. I come but in as others do to try with him the strength of my youth.   135

CELIA   Young gentleman, your spirits are too bold for your years: you have seen cruel proof of this man's strength. If you saw yourself with your eyes or knew yourself with your judgement, the fear of your adventure would counsel you to a more equal enterprise. We pray you, for your own sake, to embrace your own safety and give   140
over this attempt.

ROSALIND   Do, young sir: your reputation shall not therefore be misprized. We will make it our suit to the Duke that the wrestling might not go forward.

Orlando says that he will lose nothing if he is defeated, because he is naturally unlucky and of no importance. Charles mocks him, but Rosalind and Celia support him. He defeats Charles.

Write about it
The Arden Mirror

In role as a sportswriter reporting on Charles and Orlando's wrestling match for *The Arden Mirror*, complete the following activities as you research and write your report:

- Describe in detail the highlights of the match. Include eye-witness accounts and comments from supporters on both sides.
- Add quotations from the script opposite for each character, styling these as quotes from Arden's celebrity set.
- Sketch an image of the wrestling match and write an appropriate caption to accompany it.

hard thoughts strict judgement

fair beautiful or favourable

trial test of strength

foiled defeated

gracious in favour with Fortune, or in favour politically

injury wrong

only merely

supplied occupied, made good

eke out add to

be deceived in you underestimate your strength

lie with his mother earth die

more modest working less ambitious aim

come your ways let's get under way

Hercules (in Greek mythology, the world's strongest man)

thunderbolt in mine eye (Celia craves the power to cast a thunderbolt at Orlando's opponent)

down fell, take down

not yet well breathed barely warmed up

ORLANDO   I beseech you, punish me not with your hard thoughts,   145
wherein I confess me much guilty to deny so fair and excellent
ladies anything. But let your fair eyes and gentle wishes go with me
to my trial, wherein if I be foiled, there is but one shamed that was
never gracious; if killed, but one dead that is willing to be so. I shall
do my friends no wrong, for I have none to lament me; the world no   150
injury, for in it I have nothing; only in the world I fill up a place,
which may be better supplied when I have made it empty.

ROSALIND   The little strength that I have, I would it were with you.

CELIA   And mine to eke out hers.

ROSALIND   Fare you well: pray heaven I be deceived in you.   155

CELIA   Your heart's desires be with you.

CHARLES   Come, where is this young gallant that is so desirous to lie
with his mother earth?

ORLANDO   Ready, sir, but his will hath in it a more modest working.

DUKE FREDERICK   You shall try but one fall.   160

CHARLES   No, I warrant your grace you shall not entreat him to a
second, that have so mightily persuaded him from a first.

ORLANDO   You mean to mock me after: you should not have mocked me
before. But come your ways.

ROSALIND   Now Hercules be thy speed, young man.   165

CELIA   I would I were invisible, to catch the strong fellow by the leg.

[They] wrestle

ROSALIND   O excellent young man.

CELIA   If I had a thunderbolt in mine eye, I can tell who should down.

[Charles is thrown to the ground.] Shout

DUKE FREDERICK   No more, no more!

ORLANDO   Yes, I beseech your grace, I am not yet well breathed.   170

DUKE FREDERICK   How dost thou, Charles?

LE BEAU   He cannot speak, my lord.

DUKE FREDERICK   Bear him away.

[Charles is carried out]

What is thy name, young man?

ORLANDO   Orlando, my liege, the youngest son of Sir Roland de Boys.   175

Duke Frederick is displeased to find that Orlando is the son of his old enemy. Rosalind and Celia offer comfort to Orlando, but he seems unable to reply.

Language in the play
From prose to verse (in small groups)

At line 176, for the first time in the play, the characters speak in verse rather than prose (see 'Verse and prose' on p. 183 for more information on these forms).

a Read lines 176–82 aloud together, concentrating on the beat of the **iambic pentameter** – the rhythm is 'da DUM da DUM da DUM da DUM da DUM'.

b Now read aloud Orlando's prose at lines 145–52. Can you hear the difference between the rhythms in the prose and the verse? Describe in your own words the difference between them.

c Discuss why you think the characters switch from prose to verse in this way. What effect does it have on how the characters' words come across?

Stagecraft
Exploring the script (in threes)

Lines 194–212 provide a wonderful chance to try out some of Shakespeare's lines as actors. Orlando has won the fight and, it seems, the heart of Rosalind (if not of Celia, too).

* Prepare a dramatic reading of the script opposite, paying particular attention to the following lines. In your Director's Journal, compose detailed stage directions based on your interpretations.

Line 198 'Wear this for me'. How does Rosalind hand over her chain, and how does Orlando receive it?

Line 200 In what ways could Celia's goodbye to Orlando show how much or how little she cares about him?

Line 204 'He calls us back.' This line often evokes audience laughter because Orlando has not called them back. Rosalind longs to speak to him again and, overhearing his aside, thinks he is talking to her. How might she show her desire to return to him?

Lines 206–7 'overthrown / More than your enemies.' How long do they 'gaze upon each other' before Celia calls Rosalind away?

Line 208 'Have with you' means 'I'm coming' or 'Hold on a minute'. How does Rosalind break her eye contact with Orlando?

---

house family

change exchange
calling name, birthright

given him tears unto entreaties wept as well as begged
Ere before
ventured put himself at risk
Gentle noble
envious malicious
Sticks me at heart deeply pains me
have well deserved are worthy of good reward
But justly exactly
mistress future wife (Celia probably means Rosalind)
out of suits with Fortune no longer enjoying success and happiness
hand power
better parts spirits or most human qualities
quintain wooden post used as a target for knights practising with lances on horseback
mere complete

Have with you I'm coming

DUKE FREDERICK   I would thou hadst been son to some man else;
      The world esteemed thy father honourable
      But I did find him still mine enemy.
      Thou shouldst have better pleased me with this deed
      Hadst thou descended from another house.   180
      But fare thee well. Thou art a gallant youth:
      I would thou hadst told me of another father.
      [Exeunt Duke Frederick, Le Beau, Touchstone, Lords, and Attendants]
CELIA   Were I my father, coz, would I do this?
ORLANDO I am more proud to be Sir Roland's son –
      His youngest son – and would not change that calling 185
      To be adopted heir to Frederick.
ROSALIND My father loved Sir Roland as his soul
      And all the world was of my father's mind;
      Had I before known this young man his son,
      I should have given him tears unto entreaties   190
      Ere he should thus have ventured.
CELIA   Gentle cousin,
      Let us go thank him and encourage him;
      My father's rough and envious disposition
      Sticks me at heart. – Sir, you have well deserved:
      If you do keep your promises in love   195
      But justly, as you have exceeded all promise,
      Your mistress shall be happy.
ROSALIND *[Giving him a chain from her neck]* Gentleman,
      Wear this for me: one out of suits with Fortune,
      That could give more, but that her hand lacks means. –
      Shall we go, coz?
CELIA   Aye. – Fare you well, fair gentleman. 200
          [They turn to go]
ORLANDO *[Aside]* Can I not say, 'I thank you'? My better parts
      Are all thrown down, and that which here stands up
      Is but a quintain, a mere lifeless block.
ROSALIND *[To Celia]* He calls us back. My pride fell with my fortunes,
      I'll ask him what he would. – Did you call, sir?   205
      Sir, you have wrestled well and overthrown
      More than your enemies.
          [They gaze upon each other]
CELIA   Will you go, coz?
ROSALIND Have with you. – Fare you well.
         Exeunt [Rosalind and Celia]

Orlando suspects he has fallen in love with Rosalind. Le Beau urges him to leave the court and so avoid Duke Frederick's malice, which is also directed at Rosalind.

1 'The Duke is humorous'

Today, to say that someone is 'humorous' means that they are amusing, with a lively sense of humour. But in Shakespeare's day it meant moody, unbalanced, unpredictable. That is because Elizabethans believed that a person's nature was governed by four 'humours' (see p. 132). These humours corresponded to different moods – anger, melancholy, bravery and calmness. If the humours were not properly balanced, it resulted in mood swings and extreme behaviour.

- How would you describe the temperament and balance of emotions in each character in the play so far? Make notes on every character as if you are a medical practitioner in Shakespeare's day, describing their emotions and behaviour and then relating it to the four humours.

2 How to play Le Beau? (in pairs)

Compare Le Beau's message and delivery here to his appearance earlier in the scene. Does he represent, after all, the kinder and more benign side of the court, or is he lying in order to get Orlando out of the court?

a Read the dialogue in two ways: with Le Beau acting as a trusted friend to Orlando; then as if he is trying to deceive Orlando.

b Discuss which interpretation seems more believable in the context of the script and the characters as you understand them so far.

> ## Write about it
> ### Disliking Rosalind, disliking Orlando (in small groups)
>
> **a** Compare Le Beau's lines 229–33 with how Oliver explains his hatred for Orlando in Scene 1, lines 128–32. What similarities can you find?
>
> **b** What advice would you give to Orlando and Rosalind, both of whom find themselves discriminated against because of circumstances and attributes over which they have no control?
>
> **c** Compose three or four proverbs to help these characters make sense of their situation and find the courage to face the difficulties that come their way.

passion strong feeling
urged conference wished us to talk

Or either
something weaker (a woman – that is, Rosalind)
Albeit although
deserved acquired

misconsters misconstrues (misinterprets)

More suits you to conceive is better for you to imagine

indeed in reality
taller more spirited or handsome

whose (this refers to both Celia and Rosalind)

gentle well-born
Grounded based

knowledge friendship
much bounden greatly indebted

from the smoke … smother out of the frying pan, into the fire

ORLANDO	What passion hangs these weights upon my tongue?
	I cannot speak to her, yet she urged conference. 210

Enter LE BEAU

	O poor Orlando! thou art overthrown:
	Or Charles or something weaker masters thee.
LE BEAU	Good sir, I do in friendship counsel you
	To leave this place. Albeit you have deserved
	High commendation, true applause, and love, 215
	Yet such is now the Duke's condition
	That he misconsters all that you have done.
	The Duke is humorous: what he is indeed
	More suits you to conceive than I to speak of.
ORLANDO	I thank you, sir; and pray you tell me this: 220
	Which of the two was daughter of the Duke,
	That here was at the wrestling?
LE BEAU	Neither his daughter, if we judge by manners,
	But yet indeed the taller is his daughter;
	The other is daughter to the banished Duke 225
	And here detained by her usurping uncle
	To keep his daughter company, whose loves
	Are dearer than the natural bond of sisters.
	But I can tell you that of late this Duke
	Hath ta'en displeasure 'gainst his gentle niece, 230
	Grounded upon no other argument
	But that the people praise her for her virtues
	And pity her for her good father's sake;
	And, on my life, his malice 'gainst the lady
	Will suddenly break forth. Sir, fare you well, 235
	Hereafter, in a better world than this,
	I shall desire more love and knowledge of you.
ORLANDO	I rest much bounden to you: fare you well.

[*Exit Le Beau*]

	Thus must I from the smoke into the smother,
	From tyrant duke unto a tyrant brother. 240
	But heavenly Rosalind! *Exit*

Celia tries to cheer Rosalind, who seems downcast and love-sick for Orlando. She asks if Rosalind really has fallen in love so quickly, and jokes at her evasive reply. Duke Frederick enters, angry.

1 A melancholy lover (in pairs)

The opening of Scene 3, where Rosalind appears so unhappy, contrasts sharply with Orlando's elation at the end of Scene 2. Both moods spring from the same cause: falling in love.

a Discuss how serious Rosalind's dejection is. Consider the following questions when coming to your judgement:

- Are her replies to Celia spoken in genuine sadness, and is she melancholy (depressed, dejected) because of love-sickness?
- Are her responses playful and light hearted, amusing both Celia and the audience as a parody of the stereotypical melancholy lover?
- Does she want to shock Celia by referring to Orlando as the future father of her children (see line 8)?

b Role-play a conversation between a director and a costume and props designer, suggesting how you might interpret and visually present the opening of the scene. Describe what the characters might wear or carry in order to indicate their moods and emotions, and how they could use costume and props to emphasise certain lines or illustrate particular images in the script. It may be useful for you to have a look at an early seventeenth-century study of love-sickness – Robert Burton's *Anatomy of Melancholy*.

Language in the play
Wrestling as a metaphor

a After the wrestling match, Celia urges Rosalind to 'wrestle with thy affections' (line 16). Identify other moments in the play so far where wrestling seems to be an underlying **metaphor** (see p. 182).

b How might you suggest the metaphor of wrestling in this scene? Are there any particular words that could be emphasised and accompanied by gestures in order to bring this to the fore? Are the characters simply wrestling with depressed feelings, or is there perhaps some tension between them, too?

reasons observations, remarks
laid up made ill

briars thorny branches, difficulties and trials
working-day world world of toil and trouble
burs prickly seed heads
holy-day foolery holiday play, fun
walk not in the trodden paths walk down a different road that others have not chosen
coat petticoat
Hem cough them up to get rid of the choking feeling or sew them up like the hem on a dress
cry 'hem' and have him cough to attract Orlando's attention
turning … service leaving this joking
ensue follow as a logical conclusion
kind of chase course of argument

faith in truth

that his virtues

Act 1 Scene 3
A room in Duke Frederick's palace

Enter CELIA *and* ROSALIND

CELIA	Why, cousin; why, Rosalind – Cupid have mercy, not a word?
ROSALIND	Not one to throw at a dog.
CELIA	No, thy words are too precious to be cast away upon curs: throw some of them at me. Come, lame me with reasons.
ROSALIND	Then there were two cousins laid up, when the one should be lamed with reasons, and the other mad without any.
CELIA	But is all this for your father?
ROSALIND	No, some of it is for my child's father – O how full of briars is this working-day world!
CELIA	They are but burs, cousin, thrown upon thee in holy-day foolery: if we walk not in the trodden paths, our very petticoats will catch them.
ROSALIND	I could shake them off my coat: these burs are in my heart.
CELIA	Hem them away.
ROSALIND	I would try, if I could cry 'hem' and have him.
CELIA	Come, come, wrestle with thy affections.
ROSALIND	O they take the part of a better wrestler than myself.
CELIA	O, a good wish upon you: you will try in time in despite of a fall. But turning these jests out of service, let us talk in good earnest. Is it possible, on such a sudden, you should fall into so strong a liking with old Sir Roland's youngest son?
ROSALIND	The Duke my father loved his father dearly.
CELIA	Doth it therefore ensue that you should love his son dearly? By this kind of chase I should hate him for my father hated his father dearly; yet I hate not Orlando.
ROSALIND	No, faith, hate him not, for my sake.
CELIA	Why should I not? Doth he not deserve well?

Enter DUKE FREDERICK *with* LORDS

ROSALIND	Let me love him for that, and do you love him because I do. Look, here comes the Duke.
CELIA	With his eyes full of anger.

Line numbers: 5, 10, 15, 20, 25, 30

Duke Frederick banishes Rosalind on pain of death. She protests that neither she nor her father is a traitor. Celia supports her, saying that she and Rosalind have been inseparable friends.

1 Banishment or death (in large groups)

Duke Frederick's reasons for banishing Rosalind from court are that he does not trust her (line 45) and that she is her father's daughter (line 48).

a Create a mind-map of all the possible emotions that Rosalind might be feeling at this tense moment, showing how her feelings might change throughout her exchange with Duke Frederick.

b Take turns to speak Rosalind's responses in the script opposite in a way that expresses one of the emotions featured in your mind-map. Which response tells you most about her state of mind and her reaction to her banishment? Which emotion seems most fitting for each response?

c From what you know of the play so far, improvise an imagined monologue for Rosalind about her suffering and her dilemma. Every member of the group should say a sentence or two in turn, and you should keep going until you feel you have explored all the relevant aspects of Rosalind's difficult situation.

dispatch you … haste go away as quickly as you value your safety

you/thou (the change to the singular pronoun indicates increasing disdain)
public general, common

fault offence
If with … hold intelligence if I understand myself

dear noble
in a thought unborn subconsciously

purgation purification
grace itself virtue, goodness

whereon on what
likelihoods indications

stayed her let her stay
ranged along also been banished
pleasure will, choice
remorse compassion
Juno's swans (in Roman mythology, the swans draw the chariot of the queen of the gods)

DUKE FREDERICK   Mistress, dispatch you with your safest haste
                And get you from our court.
ROSALIND   Me, uncle?
FREDERICK   You, cousin.
                Within these ten days if that thou be'st found
                So near our public court as twenty miles,
                Thou diest for it.
ROSALIND   I do beseech your grace   35
                Let me the knowledge of my fault bear with me:
                If with myself I hold intelligence,
                Or have acquaintance with mine own desires,
                If that I do not dream or be not frantic
                (As I do trust I am not) then, dear uncle,   40
                Never so much as in a thought unborn,
                Did I offend your highness.
DUKE FREDERICK   Thus do all traitors:
                If their purgation did consist in words,
                They are as innocent as grace itself.
                Let it suffice thee that I trust thee not.   45
ROSALIND   Yet your mistrust cannot make me a traitor;
                Tell me whereon the likelihoods depends?
DUKE FREDERICK   Thou art thy father's daughter, there's enough.
ROSALIND   So was I when your highness took his dukedom,
                So was I when your highness banished him;   50
                Treason is not inherited, my lord,
                Or if we did derive it from our friends,
                What's that to me? My father was no traitor.
                Then, good my liege, mistake me not so much
                To think my poverty is treacherous.   55
CELIA   Dear sovereign, hear me speak.
DUKE FREDERICK   Aye, Celia, we stayed her for your sake,
                Else had she with her father ranged along.
CELIA   I did not then entreat to have her stay,
                It was your pleasure – and your own remorse.   60
                I was too young that time to value her,
                But now I know her: if she be a traitor,
                Why so am I. We still have slept together,
                Rose at an instant, learned, played, eat together,
                And wheresoe'er we went, like Juno's swans,   65
                Still we went coupled and inseparable.

Duke Frederick rebukes Celia, saying that Rosalind steals her good reputation. He again banishes Rosalind with threats of death. Celia proposes that she and Rosalind go to the Forest of Arden.

1 Standing up to tyranny (in groups of five or more)

a Read through lines 28–79 and discuss the following questions:

- Do you think this scene, where Duke Frederick banishes his niece and rebukes Celia, should be played intimately or in front of the court? What difference does it make?
- How might you best portray Duke Frederick's sentencing of Rosalind? Think about the actors' positioning and any props you might use.
- Suggest how the lords attending on Duke Frederick behave as they watch and hear his angry words to his daughter and his niece.
- How does Celia 'entreat' her father to let Rosalind stay with her? Is she on her knees? Does she hold Rosalind's hand or perhaps her father's hand?

b Prepare a tableau to represent one or two significant moments in the script opposite. Set your scenes in the court, and make sure that they capture the dramatic tension and the main character's emotions and relationships. Don't forget to include the lords of the court, as the positioning and expressions of these spectators are instrumental in creating the mood of the scene.

c When in position for the tableau, take it in turns to 'unfreeze' for a minute in order to describe your characters' thoughts and feelings at this moment.

Characters

Celia's role (in pairs)

In deciding to hatch a plan for her and Rosalind, Celia begins to take on a more important role in the play.

a Look back at her speeches and interventions so far and discuss in pairs what characteristics she shows. Which of the following adjectives best describe her: loyal, impulsive, humorous, brave, rebellious, resentful, bossy, supportive?

b Make a list of character traits for Celia and put them in order of priority. Try to match these traits with moments in the play where she has demonstrated them.

c Take turns to sit in the hot-seat as Celia and answer questions about her relationship with her father, with the court, with other characters and with Rosalind. The interviewer should make notes on Celia's character while listening to her answers.

subtle crafty, cunning
smoothness plausibility

name reputation
show appear

doom sentence, judgment

provide yourself prepare to leave

greatness power

sundered separated

devise … fly plan together our escape

change change of fortunes

at our sorrows pale dimmed in sympathy with our grief

DUKE FREDERICK   She is too subtle for thee, and her smoothness,
                Her very silence, and her patience
                Speak to the people and they pity her.
                Thou art a fool: she robs thee of thy name   70
                And thou wilt show more bright and seem more virtuous
                When she is gone.
                              [Celia starts to speak]
                        Then open not thy lips!
                Firm and irrevocable is my doom
                Which I have passed upon her: she is banished.

CELIA   Pronounce that sentence then on me, my liege,   75
                I cannot live out of her company.

DUKE FREDERICK   You are a fool. – You, niece, provide yourself:
                If you outstay the time, upon mine honour
                And in the greatness of my word, you die.

                                Exeunt Duke and Lords

CELIA   O my poor Rosalind, whither wilt thou go?   80
                Wilt thou change fathers? I will give thee mine!
                I charge thee be not thou more grieved than I am.

ROSALIND   I have more cause.

CELIA   Thou hast not, cousin:
                Prithee be cheerful. Know'st thou not the Duke
                Hath banished me, his daughter?

ROSALIND   That he hath not.   85

CELIA   No? 'Hath not'? Rosalind lacks then the love
                Which teacheth thee that thou and I am one;
                Shall we be sundered, shall we part, sweet girl?
                No, let my father seek another heir!
                Therefore devise with me how we may fly,   90
                Whither to go, and what to bear with us;
                And do not seek to take your change upon you,
                To bear your griefs yourself and leave me out:
                For, by this heaven, now at our sorrows pale,
                Say what thou canst, I'll go along with thee.   95

ROSALIND   Why, whither shall we go?

CELIA   To seek my uncle in the Forest of Arden.

ROSALIND   Alas, what danger will it be to us
                (Maids as we are) to travel forth so far?
                Beauty provoketh thieves sooner than gold.   100

To avoid harassment, Celia proposes to disguise herself as a country girl. Rosalind decides to dress as a young man. They plan to take Touchstone with them to the Forest of Arden.

1 Roman references (in pairs)

Rosalind's plan to disguise herself as a young man will result in all kinds of comic ambiguities. In Shakespeare's time, this effect was heightened by fact that the actor playing Rosalind would have been a boy acting as a girl (Rosalind) acting as a boy (Ganymede). More layers of comedy and confusion are added by the meanings of the names chosen by Rosalind and Celia in disguise.

In Roman mythology, Ganymede was a beautiful young man. Jupiter (Jove), king of the gods, fell in love with him and, disguised as an eagle, seized him and carried him off to Mount Olympus to become his cup-bearer ('page'). 'Ganymede' was also Elizabethan slang for a young gay man. 'Aliena' is Latin for 'the stranger'.

- Take turns to step into role as a young male actor in Shakespeare's theatre company. Describe your new role as Rosalind and how you feel about the disguises and 'sex-changes' in the play. Is it difficult to switch from acting like a woman to acting like a man? How do you expect the audience to respond to these disguises, and to the new names Rosalind and Celia have chosen?

2 Becoming a man (in pairs)

On the surface, Rosalind's image of a young man as having a 'gallant curtal-axe upon my thigh' and a 'boar-spear in my hand' refers to a romantic vision of hunting and nobility, rather than an everyday Elizabethan youth. It also has a second meaning that is a cheeky sexual joke – this kind of double meaning is known as a **double-entendre**. The description in lines 110–12 may also be Shakespeare's comment on the boastful frauds ('mannish cowards') who frequented London taverns. They had a swaggering, war-like appearance ('swashing and a martial outside'), and used it as a bluff ('outface') to sell false stories of their courage.

- Experiment with various ways of walking and talking 'like a man'. Advise each other on how to disguise 'feminine' traits and emulate 'masculine' traits. What kind of man are you trying to be?

mean attire lowly and unattractive dress

umber brown pigment to conceal their pale complexions

smirch make dirty

never stir assailants avoid harassments

suit me all points dress entirely

gallant fine

curtal-axe cutlass, short broadsword

boar-spear spear for killing wild pigs

swashing blustering

outside outer garments

semblances false or outward appearance

state new rank

assayed attempted

The clownish fool Touchstone

travail wearisome journey and hardships

woo persuade

CELIA	I'll put myself in poor and mean attire
	And with a kind of umber smirch my face;
	The like do you. So shall we pass along
	And never stir assailants.
ROSALIND	Were it not better,
	Because that I am more than common tall,
	That I did suit me all points like a man,
	A gallant curtal-axe upon my thigh,
	A boar-spear in my hand, and in my heart
	Lie there what hidden woman's fear there will.
	We'll have a swashing and a martial outside
	As many other mannish cowards have
	That do outface it with their semblances.
CELIA	What shall I call thee when thou art a man?
ROSALIND	I'll have no worse a name than Jove's own page,
	And therefore look you call me 'Ganymede'.
	But what will you be called?
CELIA	Something that hath a reference to my state:
	No longer 'Celia' but 'Aliena'.
ROSALIND	But, cousin, what if we assayed to steal
	The clownish fool out of your father's court:
	Would he not be a comfort to our travail?
CELIA	He'll go along o'er the wide world with me:
	Leave me alone to woo him. Let's away
	And get our jewels and our wealth together,
	Devise the fittest time and safest way
	To hide us from pursuit that will be made
	After my flight. Now go we in content,
	To liberty, and not to banishment.

105

110

115

120

125

Exeunt

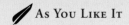

Looking back at Act 1
Activities for groups or individuals

1 Mapping the characters so far

Visual maps and diagrams can help you place the characters in relation to one another.

- Continue to develop the character web you started on page 6 and add more characters to it, using additional symbols and extending the colour code to show status and relationships between the people you have met so far.

2 Summary tableaux

Act 1 is full of lively and exciting action: the clash of brothers, a murderous plot, the wrestling match, love at first sight, Duke Frederick's anger, the death threat against Rosalind and her banishment, and a planned secret escape. There are dramatic contrasts, too, as despair and tyranny alternate with laughter and friendship.

- In large groups, discuss what you think are the most important and dramatic events of Act 1. Prepare a series of tableaux that portray these moments as clearly and vividly as possible. Take photographs of the tableaux and use them to create a display that visually summarises Act 1. You could even use the photos of the tableaux to draw panels that make up the first section of an *As You Like It* graphic novel.

3 Biblical references: the prodigal son

In Scene 1, lines 29–30, Orlando refers to a story in the Bible about 'the prodigal son'. This parable centres upon a kind father, a disdainful older brother and a younger brother who was so poor he lived with the pigs and ate their food. However, Orlando points out that he is not like this younger brother because he has not wasted his inheritance and dishonoured his family.

- Read the 'prodigal son' passage in the Bible (Luke 15:11–32) or look it up online. Make notes on the similarities and differences between the parable and Orlando's story so far in the play. What do you think

Orlando is trying to say about himself and his brother by referring to this story? Predict how the feud between Oliver and his brother will end.

4 As you like it?

The title of this play might be interpreted as an invitation to the audience to make of the play what they will. It might also refer to the way that the characters seem to do as they like in spite of difficulties or conventional proprieties.

- List the ways in which the different characters you have met so far have done as they like, rather than what has been expected of them. Think about the villainous characters as well as Orlando, Rosalind and Celia.
- Predict what each of the characters would most 'like' to happen in the rest of the play. Write a social media update for each character, capturing their different perspectives at the end of Act 1.

5 Utopia

In Act 1 Scene 1, lines 92–5, Charles mentions the 'golden world' (from Classical literature) and the figure of Robin Hood (from English folklore).

- Research both of these concepts of what constitutes a utopia (an ideal world), and make notes in a two-column table. What common ideas start to emerge? What differences are there? Do you think it is possible to have a utopia on Earth?

6 Banishment or liberty?

The first act ends, as the acts in Shakespeare's plays often do, with a **rhyming couplet** (see page 184):

> *Now go we in content,*
> *To liberty, and not to banishment.*

- Look at the images opposite and make notes in your Director's Journal about how you would stage the end of this act. Would you focus on the exciting prospect of liberty or show the characters' optimism in the face of exile and homelessness?

33

Duke Senior claims that life in the forest is far superior to life at court. Even its hardships are beneficial, and moral lessons are everywhere. He regrets that the deer are hunted and killed.

Stagecraft

First sight of Arden (in pairs)

The Forest of Arden has been depicted in a number of very different ways in productions of the play. It is contrasted with the corruption and tyranny of the court, and is clearly a rural retreat in opposition to the location of the court in the city.

- How do you imagine the forest? How would you stage it if you were an artistic director and set designer? Discuss the possibilities, then draw an initial sketch of your design in your Director's Journal. Use lines from the script, both here and in Act 1 Scene 1, lines 92–5, to guide your imagination. Compare your sketches with those of others in the class, and discuss the similarities and differences.

1 'Sweet are the uses of adversity' (in small groups)

Duke Senior claims that misfortunes ('adversity') are valuable, that good can come out of afflictions. He uses an image from an old myth: the ugly toad that has 'a precious jewel in his head'.

- Do you believe that troubles are good for you? Talk together about what you think of Duke Senior's claim, using practical examples from your own experience.
- What images or metaphors can you think of to express your beliefs about overcoming adversity? Compile a list of existing proverbs or meaningful sayings on the subject, or make up your own using some of Duke Senior's words in this speech (such as 'peril', 'chiding' or 'haunt').

2 Learning from nature (in pairs)

Lines 15–17 express the belief that humans can learn from nature, and that there are moral lessons in the landscape itself ('Sermons in stones'). Duke Senior even sees the bitter winter wind as a helpful 'counsellor' that does not flatter or lie to him.

- Take turns to speak Duke Senior's lines in different styles, and give feedback on your partner's readings. Then write detailed actors' notes to clearly instruct the actor playing Duke Senior how to perform these lines. Include an explanation for the actor detailing why you would like the lines spoken in that particular way.

co-mates companions
old custom long-standing practice
painted pomp false ceremony of the court

churlish rude, violent

feelingly by experience, intensely

jewel (this fabled 'toadstone' was reputed to serve as an antidote to the toad's venom)
exempt from public haunt not visited by people
tongues language, meaning

irks troubles, distresses
native burghers citizens from birth
desert city remote place
confines boundaries, territory
forkèd heads arrows
gored pierced, made bloody
melancholy (a fashionable condition thought to be caused by too much black bile – see page 110)
along at full length

Act 2 Scene 1
The Forest of Arden

Enter DUKE SENIOR, AMIENS, *and two or three*
LORDS *dressed as foresters*

DUKE SENIOR	Now, my co-mates and brothers in exile,
	Hath not old custom made this life more sweet
	Than that of painted pomp? Are not these woods
	More free from peril than the envious court?
	Here feel we not the penalty of Adam, 5
	The seasons' difference, as the icy fang
	And churlish chiding of the winter's wind –
	Which when it bites and blows upon my body
	Even till I shrink with cold, I smile and say,
	'This is no flattery' – these are counsellors 10
	That feelingly persuade me what I am.
	Sweet are the uses of adversity
	Which like the toad, ugly and venomous,
	Wears yet a precious jewel in his head,
	And this our life exempt from public haunt 15
	Finds tongues in trees, books in the running brooks,
	Sermons in stones, and good in everything.
AMIENS	I would not change it; happy is your grace
	That can translate the stubbornness of Fortune
	Into so quiet and so sweet a style. 20
DUKE SENIOR	Come, shall we go and kill us venison?
	And yet it irks me the poor dappled fools,
	Being native burghers of this desert city,
	Should, in their own confines, with forkèd heads
	Have their round haunches gored.
FIRST LORD	Indeed, my lord. 25
	The melancholy 'Jaques' grieves at that,
	And in that kind swears you do more usurp
	Than doth your brother that hath banished you.
	Today my lord of Amiens and myself
	Did steal behind him as he lay along 30
	Under an oak, whose antique root peeps out
	Upon the brook that brawls along this wood,

The First Lord describes how Jaques, watching a wounded deer, draws moral lessons about society from the stricken animal's plight. Duke Senior looks forward to debating with Jaques.

1 Learning more from nature (in pairs)

Duke Senior ends his first speech claiming that nature could teach all kinds of moral lessons about human life. Now he asks what lessons Jaques has drawn from the sight of a wounded stag, and the First Lord lists three of Jaques's conclusions that criticise society.

a Write out in your own words the three lessons, as described by the Lord in lines 46–57. They centre upon:

- the deer weeping into the stream
- the wounded deer abandoned by the herd
- the well-fed herd ignoring the wounded deer.

b Look back at what Duke Senior said about deer hunting in lines 21–5. Suggest how he now reacts to hearing himself so strongly criticised.

Themes

Usurping at court and in the forest

Jaques criticises Duke Senior and his lords (lines 60–3). He sees them as usurpers and tyrants who have robbed the deer of their natural rights to the forest by hunting and killing them.

- Do you agree with Jaques? If so, why? How is this relevant to the action of the play so far?
- Write two paragraphs describing the different instances of usurpation that have shaped the plot and ideas of the play so far.

2 'the melancholy Jaques' (in pairs)

Jaques is tagged with an **epithet** at line 41. An epithet is a term used to characterise a person or thing, such as in the title of 'Catherine the Great'.

a Create similar epithets for all the characters you have encountered in the play so far. Try to capture some aspect of their character in a single word.

b Write multiple epithets for each character, depending on how the other characters might see them. For example, Oliver might say 'dangerous Orlando', while Rosalind might see him as 'sweet Orlando'.

---

sequestered separated

leathern coat hide, skin

Much markèd of carefully watched by

Augmenting adding to

moralise this spectacle read the sight as a moral lesson

similes comparisons

needless stream stream that does not need more water

sum of more abundance (of tears)

velvet friend fallow deer

part / The flux of company bring divisions among friends

careless carefree

invectively vehemently, critically

usurpers illegal rulers

assigned and native God-given and natural

cope meet, talk with

matter good sense

To the which place a poor sequestered stag,
That from the hunter's aim had ta'en a hurt,
Did come to languish; and indeed, my lord,   35
The wretched animal heaved forth such groans
That their discharge did stretch his leathern coat
Almost to bursting, and the big round tears
Coursed one another down his innocent nose
In piteous chase; and thus the hairy fool,   40
Much markèd of the melancholy Jaques,
Stood on th'extremest verge of the swift brook,
Augmenting it with tears.

DUKE SENIOR   But what said Jaques?
Did he not moralise this spectacle?

FIRST LORD   O yes, into a thousand similes.   45
First, for his weeping in the needless stream:
'Poor deer', quoth he, 'thou mak'st a testament
As worldlings do, giving thy sum of more
To that which hath too much.' Then, being there alone,
Left and abandoned of his velvet friend: 50
''Tis right', quoth he, 'thus misery doth part
The flux of company.' Anon a careless herd,
Full of the pasture, jumps along by him
And never stays to greet him: 'Aye', quoth Jaques,
'Sweep on you fat and greasy citizens,   55
'Tis just the fashion. Wherefore do you look
Upon that poor and broken bankrupt there?'
Thus most invectively he pierceth through
The body of the country, city, court,
Yea, and of this our life, swearing that we   60
Are mere usurpers, tyrants, and what's worse,
To fright the animals and to kill them up
In their assigned and native dwelling-place.

DUKE SENIOR   And did you leave him in this contemplation?

SECOND LORD   We did, my lord, weeping and commenting   65
Upon the sobbing deer.

DUKE SENIOR   Show me the place;
I love to cope him in these sullen fits,
For then he's full of matter.

FIRST LORD   I'll bring you to him straight.

                                        Exeunt

Duke Frederick thinks some of his servants have assisted Rosalind and Celia to flee. Touchstone is reported missing. Frederick orders Orlando or Oliver be brought to him, and the refugees to be hunted down.

Stagecraft

Contrasts (in pairs)

Shakespeare ensures that each scene either contrasts with the one that precedes it, or follows on from it in order to offer comment. Imagine that you are co-directing the play with your partner, and carry out the following activities:

a Work out how to emphasise the dramatic contrasts between Scenes 1 and 2 with regard to each of the following:

- setting (the court versus the Forest of Arden)
- character (Duke Frederick versus Duke Senior)
- theme (both scenes have hunting as a theme).

b Consider how you would stage this short scene as dramatically as possible. You should think about giving the audience insight into character as well as information to advance the plot. Discuss the following questions and decide how you would show your ideas:

- Are the lords afraid of Duke Frederick?
- What does he do as the lords speak?
- How does he deliver his instructions in the final five lines?

c In your Director's Journal, compose detailed notes for the stage designer and the actors. Explain your ideas and give instructions for how they should be shown on stage. Remember to refer to costumes, scenery, props and blocking (the movements of actors in relation to one another on stage) in your notes.

villeins minor servants

Are of consent … in this supported and helped with the plot

untreasured bereft (of Celia)
roinish coarse, scurvy
clown jester
wont accustomed

parts and graces physical appearance and good manners
foil defeat

gallant young gentleman (Orlando)

inquisition investigation, enquiry
quail fail
again back
foolish runaways (Celia, Touchstone and possibly Rosalind)

Act 2 Scene 2
Duke Frederick's palace

Enter DUKE FREDERICK *with Lords*

DUKE FREDERICK	Can it be possible that no man saw them?	
	It cannot be: some villeins of my court	
	Are of consent and sufferance in this.	
FIRST LORD	I cannot hear of any that did see her;	
	The ladies, her attendants of her chamber,	5
	Saw her abed and, in the morning early,	
	They found the bed untreasured of their mistress.	
SECOND LORD	My lord, the roinish clown, at whom so oft	
	Your grace was wont to laugh, is also missing.	
	Hisperia, the princess' gentlewoman,	10
	Confesses that she secretly o'erheard	
	Your daughter and her cousin much commend	
	The parts and graces of the wrestler	
	That did but lately foil the sinewy Charles;	
	And she believes, wherever they are gone,	15
	That youth is surely in their company.	
DUKE FREDERICK	Send to his brother: 'Fetch that gallant hither.'	
	If he be absent, bring his brother to me –	
	I'll make him find him. Do this suddenly,	
	And let not search and inquisition quail	20
	To bring again these foolish runaways.	

Exeunt

Adam bemoans the fact that Orlando's good qualities have made him hated in the unnatural world of the court. He reveals that Oliver plots to kill Orlando, and urges Orlando to leave.

Language in the play
Dramatic language (in pairs)

There is a story that, when he was 30 years old, Shakespeare himself played Adam (who is almost 80 years old) at the Globe Theatre. If the story is true, how do you think he might have played the faithful old servant? Use the following activities to develop your ideas about this.

a   Find examples of the following language features in the script opposite (see pp. 180–5 for more detailed descriptions of these and other language features):

- repetition
- rhetorical questions
- **personification** (where something that is not human is endowed with personality and human characteristics)
- dramatic pauses
- **apostrophe** (where an abstract idea or absent person is addressed).

Write out each example you find and describe how it could best be exploited by an actor for dramatic effect on stage.

b   These language features might help create a stereotype of a fearful and pitiful old man, or they might produce a comically forgetful and befuddled character. Which portrayal do you favour – or have you devised another way of representing Adam?

c   Experiment with different ways of speaking Adam's first two speeches in this scene. Write three or four stage directions for the script opposite. Describe in detail the tone of voice, gestures, movements and props that you would want an actor to use.

1   A fallen world? (in small groups)

Orlando does not realise that his good qualities might make him hated in the envious and unnatural world of the court, or that his own house is dangerous because his brother wants him dead.

a   Do you think the Forest of Arden would be a safer place for 'virtuous' Orlando? Make a list of what seems immoral or unsavoury about the court, using quotes from the script where you can. Beside this, list your impressions – both positive and negative – of Arden.

b   Do you think there is a clear contrast between the court and Arden, or are the two worlds not so different after all? Divide your group in two and debate this question, using evidence from the script.

memory reminder

fond foolish
bonny stout, strapping
prizer champion prize-fighter
praise merit, reputation
graces virtues, fortunes
No more do yours yours do no less
sanctified blessed
comely beautiful, virtuous
Envenoms poisons

lives lives as

your praises you being praised
lodging dwelling place
fail of fails to do
cut you off kill you
practices plots, deceits
butchery slaughter-house

so as long as

Act 2 Scene 3
Outside Oliver's house

Enter ORLANDO

ORLANDO   Who's there?

[*Enter* ADAM]

ADAM   What, my young master! O my gentle master,
O my sweet master, O you memory
Of old Sir Roland, why, what make you here?
Why are you virtuous? Why do people love you?   5
And wherefore are you gentle, strong, and valiant?
Why would you be so fond to overcome
The bonny prizer of the humorous Duke?
Your praise is come too swiftly home before you.
Know you not, master, to some kind of men   10
Their graces serve them but as enemies?
No more do yours: your virtues, gentle master,
Are sanctified and holy traitors to you.
O what a world is this when what is comely
Envenoms him that bears it!   15

ORLANDO   Why, what's the matter?

ADAM   O unhappy youth,
Come not within these doors: within this roof
The enemy of all your graces lives
Your brother – no, no brother – yet the son –
Yet not the son, I will not call him son   20
Of him I was about to call his father –
Hath heard your praises, and this night he means
To burn the lodging where you use to lie
And you within it. If he fail of that,
He will have other means to cut you off: 25
I overheard him and his practices.
This is no place, this house is but a butchery:
Abhor it, fear it, do not enter it.

ORLANDO   Why whither, Adam, wouldst thou have me go?

ADAM   No matter whither, so you come not here.   30

Orlando prefers to face his murderous brother rather than become a beggar or highwayman. Adam offers his life savings and service to Orlando, who accepts and praises Adam's faithfulness.

Characters
Nobility (in small groups)

Both Orlando and Adam reveal signs of their nobility in this scene. Both are loyal, and would rather serve a higher cause than be forced to leave the court.

a Take turns in the hot-seat in role as each character, and question each other about your motivations.

b Discuss each character's reasons for their comments in lines 31–76. Which man is the nobler of the two, and what does this tell us about the world depicted in the play?

Write about it
God's providence (in pairs)

Adam offers his life savings to Orlando, saying that God will look after him.

a Look up the passage in the Bible that Adam refers to (Matthew 10:29 and Psalms 147:9). What is the significance of the ravens and sparrows? What does this show about Adam's willingness to give all his money to Orlando?

b Adam's actions remind Orlando of past times. Explain how this contrasts with Orlando's view of the modern world in lines 59–62.

c In role as Orlando, write up your ideas about the points above in a diary entry. In his writing, Orlando should reflect on Adam's faith in God, his selfless generosity and his loyalty.

1 How to play Adam? (in pairs)

a Some actors play Adam's lines for laughs in this scene. Discuss what you think of each of these examples from previous performances:

- **Line 45** 'Here is the gold' – he produces a huge bucket of coins.
- **Line 47** 'I am strong and lusty' – he almost faints as he speaks.
- **Lines 48–51** He uses gestures to illustrate his refusals.
- **Line 53** 'Frosty but kindly' – he taps his white-haired head.
- **Lines 54–5** 'I'll do the service of a younger man …' – he totters.

b Try playing the scene straight, and then for laughs. Which do you think works best?

---

base and boisterous lowly and violent

common public

do how I can whatever may befall me

a diverted blood an unnatural

bloody cruel, bloodthirsty

The thrifty hire … saved the wages I saved through frugality

foster-nurse retirement money

unregarded age disvalued old age

lusty vigorous

with unbashful forehead shamelessly

debility feebleness

the antique world past times

for duty because it was the right thing to do

not for meed not for dishonest reward

In lieu of in return for

husbandry careful management

youthful earned in youth

settled low content humble and contented way of living

ORLANDO	What, wouldst thou have me go and beg my food,
	Or with a base and boisterous sword enforce
	A thievish living on the common road?
	This I must do or know not what to do;
	Yet this I will not do, do how I can.
	I rather will subject me to the malice
	Of a diverted blood and bloody brother.
ADAM	But do not so: I have five hundred crowns,
	The thrifty hire I saved under your father,
	Which I did store to be my foster-nurse
	When service should in my old limbs lie lame
	And unregarded age in corners thrown;
	Take that, and He that doth the ravens feed,
	Yea providently caters for the sparrow,
	Be comfort to my age. Here is the gold:
	All this I give you; let me be your servant –
	Though I look old, yet I am strong and lusty;
	For in my youth I never did apply
	Hot and rebellious liquors in my blood,
	Nor did not with unbashful forehead woo
	The means of weakness and debility;
	Therefore my age is as a lusty winter,
	Frosty but kindly. Let me go with you:
	I'll do the service of a younger man
	In all your business and necessities.
ORLANDO	O good old man, how well in thee appears
	The constant service of the antique world,
	When service sweat for duty not for meed.
	Thou art not for the fashion of these times
	Where none will sweat but for promotion
	And, having that, do choke their service up
	Even with the having. It is not so with thee;
	But, poor old man, thou prun'st a rotten tree
	That cannot so much as a blossom yield,
	In lieu of all thy pains and husbandry.
	But come thy ways: we'll go along together
	And, ere we have thy youthful wages spent,
	We'll light upon some settled low content.

35

40

45

50

55

60

65

Adam resolves to be Orlando's faithful servant and bids goodbye to his old home, where he has lived for over sixty years. In Scene 4, Rosalind, Celia and Touchstone seem exhausted as they arrive in Arden.

Language in the play

Rhyming couplets (in pairs)

Shakespeare's scenes often end with a rhyming couplet, in order to give a sense of closure. However, at the end of Act 2 Scene 3, Adam has four rhyming couplets.

a Experiment with reading out lines 69–76 to emphasise the end rhymes and internal rhythm. Notice how the iambic pentameter is interrupted in line 76 by the emphasis on the two words 'die well'.

b Discuss what effect you think Shakespeare wanted to create here and what you predict will happen to Adam.

Stagecraft

Arriving in Arden (in threes)

The beginning of Scene 4 suggests that all three travellers are weary and that Touchstone is particularly disillusioned.

a Take parts and read aloud lines 1–13, then discuss where in this section the following actions might take place. Remember to look out for implicit stage directions in the script.
- Rosalind does something to help Celia.
- Celia collapses and refuses to carry on.
- Touchstone picks up Celia and carries her.

b Experiment with different ways of speaking Rosalind's line 11, 'Well, this is the Forest of Arden.' Choose your favourite of these, and describe the delivery in your Director's Journal. You should include stage directions as well as notes for the actor.

Jupiter (Jupiter, king of the gods in Roman mythology, was renowned for his cheerful disposition)

weaker vessel woman (Celia)
doublet and hose (jacket and breeches worn by men in Elizabethan times)

bear with consider, put up with
bear carry
cross burden or punishment (also the symbol on a coin – another of Touchstone's puns)
this is the Forest of Arden (Elizabethan playhouses did not have elaborate scenery or stage properties, so Rosalind's line is also a theatrical joke)

ADAM   Master, go on, and I will follow thee
            To the last gasp with truth and loyalty.   70
            From seventeen years till now almost fourscore
            Here lived I, but now live here no more.
            At seventeen years many their fortunes seek,
            But at fourscore it is too late a week;
            Yet Fortune cannot recompense me better   75
            Than to die well and not my master's debtor.

                                                   Exeunt

Act 2 Scene 4
The Forest of Arden

Enter ROSALIND *disguised as the boy* GANYMEDE,
CELIA *disguised as a shepherdess* ALIENA,
and the clown TOUCHSTONE *dressed in motley*

ROSALIND   O Jupiter, how merry are my spirits!

TOUCHSTONE   I care not for my spirits, if my legs were not weary.

ROSALIND   [*Aside*]   I could find in my heart to disgrace my man's
            apparel and to cry like a woman; but I must comfort the weaker
            vessel, as doublet and hose ought to show itself courageous to
            petticoat; therefore – courage, good Aliena!   5

CELIA   I pray you bear with me, I cannot go no further.

TOUCHSTONE   For my part, I had rather bear with you than bear you;
            yet I should bear no cross if I did bear you, for I think you have
            no money in your purse.   10

ROSALIND   Well, this is the Forest of Arden.

TOUCHSTONE   Aye, now am I in Arden, the more fool I! When I was
            at home I was in a better place; but travellers must be content.

                        Enter CORIN *and* SILVIUS

ROSALIND   Aye, be so, good Touchstone. Look you who comes here:
            A young man and an old in solemn talk.   15

CORIN   That is the way to make her scorn you still.

SILVIUS   O Corin, that thou knew'st how I do love her.

CORIN   I partly guess, for I have loved ere now.

1 A first encounter with pastoral (in pairs)

The travellers' meeting with Corin and Silvius is the court's first encounter with the pastoral tradition in the play (see pp. 165–6). Within this tradition, shepherds living out in the fields with their flocks are seen to inhabit an ideal world, away from the complexity and corruption of the city and the court. What do you think of the Forest of Arden so far in the play? Is it an ideal world, full of limitless possibilities – a place where dreams come true?

- Discuss whether the Forest of Arden is an idealised example of the pastoral tradition or whether it is a more complex place with its own dangers and disappointments. Find an example or a quotation from the play so far to support your views.

Themes
Unrequited love (in fives)

Silvius's expression of love reminds Rosalind of her own passionate feelings for Orlando.

- How would you want to stage this part of the scene? Should lines 16–37 be played straight or for laughs? Try them both ways. The three actors playing Rosalind, Celia and Touchstone should engage with each other as they react to the conversation with movements, gestures and facial expressions.

Write about it
Romantic advice

What advice might Rosalind, Celia or Touchstone have given to Silvius if he had not abruptly left? Write up one character's advice on solving his romantic problem as a letter, a scripted conversation or an agony aunt column. Try to capture the personality and speaking style of the character in your writing.

2 The foolishness of love

Touchstone makes fun of Silvius's words and tells how his love for a milkmaid, Jane Smile, made him behave foolishly. His comic conclusion is that it is inevitable that all lovers behave foolishly.

- Do you agree with Touchstone's conclusion? Write a paragraph about whether you think people behave strangely when they are in love.

fantasy imagination, desire

slightest folly smallest foolishness

Wearing wearying

broke from company run away from friends

passion pain in love

Phoebe (another name for Artemis, or Diana, the goddess of the moon and hunting)

hard adventure bad fortune

a-night at night

batler wooden paddle

dugs udder

chapped rough

peasecod peapod

run into strange capers do peculiar things

thou art ware of you know

ware aware or apprehensive

upon after

yond man yonder man (Corin)

Holla hello

clown country bumpkin

kinsman relative, fellow clown

SILVIUS	No, Corin, being old, thou canst not guess,	
	Though in thy youth thou wast as true a lover	20
	As ever sighed upon a midnight pillow.	
	But if thy love were ever like to mine –	
	As sure I think did never man love so –	
	How many actions most ridiculous	
	Hast thou been drawn to by thy fantasy?	25
CORIN	Into a thousand that I have forgotten.	
SILVIUS	O thou didst then never love so heartily.	
	If thou remembrest not the slightest folly	
	That ever love did make thee run into,	
	Thou hast not loved.	30
	Or if thou hast not sat as I do now,	
	Wearing thy hearer in thy mistress' praise,	
	Thou hast not loved.	
	Or if thou hast not broke from company	
	Abruptly as my passion now makes me,	35
	Thou hast not loved.	
	O Phoebe, Phoebe, Phoebe! *Exit*	
ROSALIND	Alas, poor shepherd, searching of thy wound,	
	I have by hard adventure found mine own.	
TOUCHSTONE	And I mine: I remember when I was in love, I broke my	40
	sword upon a stone and bid him take that for coming a-night to Jane	
	Smile; and I remember the kissing of her batler and the cow's dugs	
	that her pretty chapped hands had milked; and I remember the	
	wooing of a peasecod instead of her, from whom I took two cods	
	and, giving her them again, said with weeping tears, 'Wear these for	45
	my sake.' We that are true lovers run into strange capers; but as all	
	is mortal in Nature, so is all nature in love mortal in folly.	
ROSALIND	Thou speak'st wiser than thou art ware of.	
TOUCHSTONE	Nay, I shall ne'er be ware of my own wit till I break my shins	
	against it.	50
ROSALIND	Jove, Jove, this shepherd's passion	
	Is much upon my fashion.	
TOUCHSTONE	And mine, but it grows something stale with me.	
CELIA	I pray you, one of you question yond man	
	If he for gold will give us any food:	55
	I faint almost to death.	
TOUCHSTONE	Holla, you, clown!	
ROSALIND	Peace, fool; he's not thy kinsman.	

Rosalind asks where she may buy food and shelter. Corin says that his miserly employer's property is for sale, and offers help. He agrees to buy the sheep farm with Rosalind's and Celia's money.

1 'Your betters, sir'

Touchstone's instant response to Corin is sarcastic, but reveals the class differences between the court and the country folk.

a Add to the character web that you began on page 6. (Look at the list of characters on page 1, where the people of Arden are listed as a group).

b Do you think that there are significant differences between people who live in the cities and the countryside today? Is there any snobbery on one side – or perhaps both?

Stagecraft

Meeting Corin (in threes)

This meeting with Corin is the first time that Rosalind and Celia, disguised as Ganymede and Aliena, speak to a stranger. The travellers begin to learn more about what life is like in the Forest of Arden.

a Experiment with different ways of speaking Corin's line 63. Corin might have suspicions about this young person he calls 'gentle sir'. Or he might hesitate after his first three words, wondering just how to address this young boy who is so feminine in appearance. Would you want to show Rosalind being convincing as a boy, or perhaps as a ludicrous figure clumping around the stage? How else could she be perceived?

b In one production, to emphasise there was nothing suitable for the upper-class Rosalind and Celia to eat at the cottage, Corin fished in his pockets and pulled out the remains of an extremely stale loaf, which he broke in disgust as he emphasised 'you' in line 79. How would you advise the actor playing Corin to highlight the unpleasant aspects of the forest?

c Take parts and read aloud lines 68–93. Show through expressions and gestures what Corin thinks of Celia's plight, of his master, of Silvius and of the prospect of working for Rosalind and Celia. Then read through the scene twice more so that everyone has a chance to play Corin. Make notes in your Director's Journal, explaining how you came to your decisions about Corin's **stage business**.

Else if not

Good even (this phrase was used any time after noon)

entertainment food and shelter, hospitality

faints for succour will faint from distress if she doesn't receive help

churlish miserly
recks cares
hospitality generosity
cot cottage
bounds of feed all his pastures
sheepcote cottage
That you will feed on suitable for your refined tastes
in my voice as far as I am concerned
swain lover
but erewhile just now
stand with honesty is fair dealing or consistent with honour

mend increase
waste spend
time life

feeder shepherd, servant

CORIN	Who calls?
TOUCHSTONE	Your betters, sir.
CORIN	Else are they very wretched.
ROSALIND	[*To Touchstone*] Peace, I say –. Good even to you, friend.
CORIN	And to you, gentle sir, and to you all.
ROSALIND	I prithee, shepherd, if that love or gold

ROSALIND   I prithee, shepherd, if that love or gold
Can in this desert place buy entertainment,   65
Bring us where we may rest ourselves and feed.
Here's a young maid with travel much oppressed
And faints for succour.

CORIN   Fair sir, I pity her
And wish, for her sake more than for mine own,
My fortunes were more able to relieve her;   70
But I am shepherd to another man,
And do not shear the fleeces that I graze.
My master is of churlish disposition
And little recks to find the way to heaven
By doing deeds of hospitality.   75
Besides, his cot, his flocks, and bounds of feed
Are now on sale, and at our sheepcote now
By reason of his absence there is nothing
That you will feed on. But what is, come see,
And in my voice most welcome shall you be.   80

ROSALIND   What is he that shall buy his flock and pasture?

CORIN   That young swain that you saw here but erewhile,
That little cares for buying anything.

ROSALIND   I pray thee, if it stand with honesty,
Buy thou the cottage, pasture, and the flock,   85
And thou shalt have to pay for it of us.

CELIA   And we will mend thy wages. I like this place
And willingly could waste my time in it.

CORIN   Assuredly the thing is to be sold.
Go with me. If you like upon report   90
The soil, the profit, and this kind of life,
I will your very faithful feeder be,
And buy it with your gold right suddenly.

Exeunt

Amiens sings of the pleasure of forest life. Jaques asks for more singing, hoping it will add to his melancholy. He criticises the singing, politeness in general and Duke Senior.

Characters

Presenting Jaques (in small groups)

a Read this short scene, and think about what has been said about Jaques so far in the play. What is your opinion of him? Talk together about what each of the following quotations suggests about his personality.

- **Lines 11–12** He compares himself to a weasel (a small, quarrelsome, sharp-toothed animal).
- **Line 14** He criticises Amiens's singing (and often gets a laugh from the audience).
- **Line 17** He seems interested only in the names of people who owe him money.
- **Lines 27–9** He thinks Duke Senior too argumentative, and considers himself as intelligent as him but more humble.

b Count how many times Jaques asks Amien to sing for him. Discuss together how you think he asks each time – for example, increasingly annoyed or perhaps continuing to entreat him politely. What other evidence of his character is there in this scene?

c Write notes for the actor playing Jaques, describing your interpretation of the character and his behaviour in this scene.

greenwood in leaf
Who whoever
turn adapt, tune
note melody, tune
throat voice
Come let him come

Monsieur (French for 'sir' – to signify Jaques's high status, or perhaps to mock him)
weasel (this animal was known for its ferocity in Shakespeare's day)
stanzo stanza, verse

compliment politeness
dog-apes baboons

cover the while lay the table (the dialogue indicates that during this scene preparations are made for the picnic)
disputable argumentative

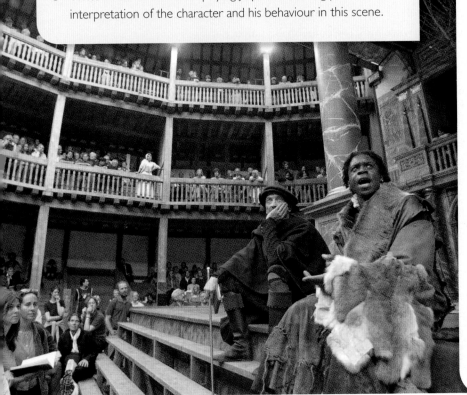

Act 2 Scene 5
The camp of Duke Senior

Enter AMIENS, JAQUES, *and other Lords dressed as foresters*

Song

AMIENS	Under the greenwood tree,
	Who loves to lie with me
	And turn his merry note
	Unto the sweet bird's throat:
	Come hither, come hither, come hither: 5
	Here shall he see
	No enemy
	But winter and rough weather.
JAQUES	More, more, I prithee more.
AMIENS	It will make you melancholy, Monsieur Jaques. 10
JAQUES	I thank it. More, I prithee more: I can suck melancholy out of a song as a weasel sucks eggs. More, I prithee more.
AMIENS	My voice is ragged: I know I cannot please you.
JAQUES	I do not desire you to please me, I do desire you to sing. Come, more, another stanzo – call you 'em 'stanzos'? 15
AMIENS	What you will, Monsieur Jaques.
JAQUES	Nay, I care not for their names; they owe me nothing. Will you sing?
AMIENS	More at your request than to please myself.
JAQUES	Well then, if ever I thank any man, I'll thank you; but that they 20 call 'compliment' is like th'encounter of two dog-apes. And when a man thanks me heartily, methinks I have given him a penny and he renders me the beggarly thanks. Come, sing; and you that will not, hold your tongues.
AMIENS	Well, I'll end the song. – Sirs, cover the while; the Duke will 25 drink under this tree. – He hath been all this day to look you.
JAQUES	And I have been all this day to avoid him: he is too disputable for my company: I think of as many matters as he, but I give heaven thanks and make no boast of them. Come, warble, come.

The exiled courtiers sing of the pleasures of leaving court and living simply in the country. Jaques's song mocks such pleasures and implies that Duke Senior's followers are fools.

1 Echoes of Duke Senior (in small groups)

Amiens's song echoes the theme of Duke Senior's first speech at the start of Act 2 ('Sweet are the uses of adversity').

- Re-read Duke Senior's speech and then read through the verses of Amiens's song in lines 1–8 and lines 30–8. Write another verse for Amiens's song, either in the style of Jaques's parody in lines 42–9 or following on from Amiens's original verses. Remember to incorporate ideas from Duke Senior's speech in the same way that the existing song does.

2 Jaques's singing

Jaques's parody of Amiens's song is typically flat and unsentimental. What do you think is the main point of this scene?

- to depict further the character of Jaques
- to show another side of Arden
- to provide some relief from the rest of the plot, which focuses on Rosalind, the court and the pastoral characters
- a critical commentary on the themes of the play as a whole
- another reason not listed above.

Write a paragraph to justify keeping this scene in the play, as opposed to just using the song as background music in your production.

Write about it

Two versions of Arden (in small groups)

In *As You Like It*, there is a big difference between life at the court and life in the forest. But even within the forest, there are different ideas about the life it offers.

- How is the Forest of Arden seen differently by Amiens, Jaques, Rosalind and Duke Senior? Write a diary entry for each character that describes what they have done that day and why they like (or hate) living in the forest, away from the world of the court.

Who doth ambition shun whoever gives up court life

i'th'sun a carefree life

in despite of my invention without using my imagination

A stubborn will to please to indulge his wilful fancies

Ducdame (a nonsense word, pronounced duc-da-me)

Gross palpable, obvious

And if if indeed

Greek nonsense (similar to the proverb 'it's all Greek to me')

rail against insult, criticise

the first-born of Egypt (in the Bible, a plague killed all of Egypt's first-born children; there was such wailing that no one could sleep)

banquet light meal, picnic

Song. All together here

Who doth ambition shun   30
And loves to live i'th'sun;
Seeking the food he eats
And pleased with what he gets:

Come hither, come hither, come hither:
   Here shall he see   35
    No enemy
But winter and rough weather.

JAQUES   I'll give you a verse to this note that I made yesterday in despite
of my invention.

AMIENS   And I'll sing it.   40

JAQUES   Thus it goes:

If it do come to pass
That any man turn ass,

Leaving his wealth and ease,
A stubborn will to please,   45

Ducdame, ducdame, ducdame.
   Here shall he see
    Gross fools as he,
And if he will come to me.

AMIENS   What's that 'ducdame'?   50

JAQUES   'Tis a Greek invocation to call fools into a circle. I'll go sleep if
I can: if I cannot, I'll rail against all the first-born of Egypt.

AMIENS   And I'll go seek the Duke: his banquet is prepared.

Exeunt

Wandering with Orlando in the forest, Adam fears he is near to death. Orlando comforts him and promises to find food and shelter. In Scene 7, Duke Senior is surprised at Jaques's cheerfulness.

Stagecraft

The end of the road (in pairs)

How would you bring Scene 6 to life on stage, despite its brief length? Study the two characters' lines, and work out what stage business you would have each actor perform to make the most of his part here. Consider the following:

- **Internal stage directions** Are there any hints in the script as to how the characters could enter or exit and what they could be doing as they speak their lines?
- **Dramatic language** Where can you find repetitions, rhetorical questions and **injunctions** (commands) in the script? How might you use them for dramatic effect?

heart courage
uncouth strange, wild
anything savage any wild animals
conceit imagination
powers physical strength
presently very soon

labour task
Well said (has Adam made some inarticulate response, or does Orlando mean 'Well done'?)
dinner meal in the middle of the day

1 How important is Scene 6? (in fours)

Some critics argue that Scene 6 adds little or nothing to the play, and could be cut in performance.

- Divide the group into two pairs. One pair will argue the case for dropping Scene 6 and the other will defend its inclusion in performances of the play. Prepare your case with your partner, then come together as a group to stage the debate. After the debate, tell the group whether you would include or delete the scene if you were directing the play, and give the main reason for your decision.

2 'discord in the spheres'

When Duke Senior hears that the melancholy Jaques was 'merry, hearing of a song', he expresses surprise (lines 5–6). His words 'discord in the spheres' echo the common belief of Shakespeare's times that Earth was at the centre of the universe, surrounded by crystal spheres on which the sun, moon and planets orbited. As the spheres moved, they created harmonious music. If Jaques has become happy, it will create chaos in that heavenly order.

he (Jaques)

compact of jars discordant, made up of jarring elements

- How would you advise Jaques to enter at line 8 to heighten Duke Senior's amazement?
- Consider possible scenarios for his entrance and try them out on one another.

you look merrily? (Duke Senior is amazed to see Jaques happy)

Act 2 Scene 6
The Forest of Arden

Enter ORLANDO *and* ADAM

ADAM   Dear master, I can go no further. O, I die for food. Here lie I down and measure out my grave. Farewell, kind master.

ORLANDO   Why, how now, Adam, no greater heart in thee? Live a little, comfort a little, cheer thyself a little. If this uncouth forest yield anything savage, I will either be food for it or bring it for food to   5
thee. Thy conceit is nearer death than thy powers. For my sake be comfortable; hold death a while at the arm's end. I will here be with thee presently, and if I bring thee not something to eat, I will give thee leave to die; but if thou diest before I come, thou art a mocker of my labour. Well said, thou look'st cheerly, and I'll be with thee   10
quickly. Yet thou liest in the bleak air. Come, I will bear thee to some shelter, and thou shalt not die for lack of a dinner if there live anything in this desert. Cheerly, good Adam.

Exeunt

Act 2 Scene 7
The camp of Duke Senior

Enter DUKE SENIOR, AMIENS, *and Lords dressed like outlaws*

DUKE SENIOR   I think he be transformed into a beast,
For I can nowhere find him like a man.

AMIENS   My lord, he is but even now gone hence;
Here was he merry, hearing of a song.

DUKE SENIOR   If he, compact of jars, grow musical,   5
We shall have shortly discord in the spheres.
Go seek him; tell him I would speak with him.

Enter JAQUES

AMIENS   He saves my labour by his own approach.

DUKE SENIOR   Why, how now, monsieur, what a life is this
That your poor friends must woo your company?   10
What, you look merrily?

Jaques recounts how he enjoyed meeting Touchstone and listening to his moralising. He praises Touchstone, and wishes he were a fool so that he could criticise whoever he wishes.

Language in the play
Meeting a fellow pessimist (in pairs)

Jaques is happy to have met another cynic like himself. Touchstone also takes a negative view of the 'miserable world' (line 13) in which growing old and becoming corrupt is inevitable ('And so, from hour to hour, we ripe and ripe, / And then, from hour to hour, we rot and rot'). Jaques may also be amused at the sexual innuendo in Touchstone's words – for example, in Elizabethan times 'hour to hour' was pronounced the same as 'whore to whore'.

a Touchstone's 'moral on the time' and his other observations in lines 19, 24–8 and 37–8 have a few different meanings. Use the glossary on this page to help you work out what these are. Write them out in modern English so that they could be understood by people today.

b Invent your own observation about time, or search the Internet to compile a list of pithy sayings and proverbs on this theme.

1 Jaques and Touchstone

If Touchstone is the fool of the court of Duke Frederick, then Jaques is the potential fool of Duke Senior's Arden court. Make comparisons between their roles in each realm by copying the table below and adding quotations where you can.

	Jaques	Touchstone
Entertainment		
Wit		
Social commentary		

motley (describes the costume of a professional jester, which was usually speckled or chequered)

good set terms elegant and precise language

dial watch, sundial
poke pocket or small sack
the world wags affairs are progressing

moral moralise
Chanticleer a crowing rooster

sans intermission without a break

dry (a dry brain was thought to possess a good memory but to be slow in understanding)
remainder biscuit (ships used to carry hard biscuits for sailors to eat, and at the end of a voyage any leftovers would be very dry indeed)
observation proverbs
In mangled forms in nonsense
suit request, garment
grows rank runs wild

Withal as well, also

gallèd offended, scarred

JAQUES   A fool, a fool: I met a fool i'th'forest,
              A motley fool – a miserable world –
              As I do live by food, I met a fool
              Who laid him down and basked him in the sun   15
              And railed on Lady Fortune in good terms,
              In good set terms, and yet a motley fool.
              'Good morrow, fool', quoth I. 'No, sir', quoth he,
              'Call me not fool till heaven hath sent me fortune.'
              And then he drew a dial from his poke   20
              And looking on it, with lack-lustre eye,
              Says, very wisely, 'It is ten o'clock.
              Thus we may see', quoth he, 'how the world wags:
              'Tis but an hour ago since it was nine,
              And after one hour more 'twill be eleven;   25
              And so, from hour to hour, we ripe and ripe,
              And then, from hour to hour, we rot and rot,
              And thereby hangs a tale.' When I did hear
              The motley fool thus moral on the time,
              My lungs began to crow like Chanticleer   30
              That fools should be so deep-contemplative;
              And I did laugh, sans intermission,
              An hour by his dial. O noble fool,
              O worthy fool: motley's the only wear.

DUKE SENIOR What fool is this?   35

JAQUES   A worthy fool: one that hath been a courtier
              And says, 'If ladies be but young and fair,
              They have the gift to know it'; and in his brain,
              Which is as dry as the remainder biscuit
              After a voyage, he hath strange places crammed   40
              With observation, the which he vents
              In mangled forms. O that I were a fool!
              I am ambitious for a motley coat.

DUKE SENIOR Thou shalt have one.

JAQUES   It is my only suit,
              Provided that you weed your better judgements   45
              Of all opinion that grows rank in them
              That I am wise. I must have liberty
              Withal, as large a charter as the wind,
              To blow on whom I please: for so fools have.
              And they that are most gallèd with my folly,   50
              They most must laugh. And why, sir, must they so?

Jaques claims that people hurt by clever criticism should acknowledge the humour. He wants to cleanse the world with his satire, but the Duke accuses him of hypocrisy. Jaques defends himself against the charge.

1 Would you laugh it off? (in small groups)

In lines 50–7, Jaques claims that the people he mocks would be wise to laugh rather than to ignore the criticism or feel hurt because of it.

a Talk about whether you think it is best to shrug off clever but hurtful remarks by joining in with the laughter, or to show that you are offended by confronting the person making the remarks.

b Improvise two different scenes: one in which catty jibes are diffused or ignored, and another in which the criticism is confronted and the target makes their feelings known.

2 Jaques: satirist or hypocrite? (in pairs)

Jaques wants to use his criticism like medicine, cleansing and curing the world's wrongs. He sees the 'motley' costume of a fool as the way he can speak his mind and confront his listeners with their own folly. Yet Duke Senior reveals Jaques's hypocrisy: he has been a lustful womaniser ('libertine') in the past, so it would be a sin for him to try to cure his own diseases in others.

a How does Jaques respond to Duke Senior's criticism? Use the glossary on this page to help you work out what his argument is. Then write out what he means in your own words and decide whether or not you agree with him.

b Discuss whether you agree with Duke Senior. Is Jaques simply a hypocrite who should be ignored?

▼ Decide who you think is Duke Senior and who is Jaques in this image. What are the reasons for your decision? If you imagined the characters differently to how they are shown here, what are the differences?

very wisely hit cleverly criticise
smart is hurt
seem senseless of the bob is unaware of the joke
anatomised laid bare
glances satirical hits

counter worthless coin

libertine one who follows his own extravagant inclinations
brutish sting animal lust
embossèd ... headed evils scabs and boils
licence of free foot utter freedom
disgorge vomit
cries out on denounces
tax any private party criticise a particular individual
the weary very means do ebb it exhausts itself
cost of princes most expensive clothes

basest function lowest office
bravery fine clothes
suits ... speech shows he is as foolish as I say he is

The why is plain as way to parish church:
He that a fool doth very wisely hit,
Doth very foolishly, although he smart,
If he seem senseless of the bob. If not, 55
The wise man's folly is anatomised
Even by the squand'ring glances of the fool.
Invest me in my motley; give me leave
To speak my mind, and I will through and through
Cleanse the foul body of th'infected world, 60
If they will patiently receive my medicine.

DUKE SENIOR Fie on thee! I can tell what thou wouldst do.

JAQUES What, for a counter, would I do but good?

DUKE SENIOR Most mischievous foul sin in chiding sin:
For thou thyself hast been a libertine, 65
As sensual as the brutish sting itself,
And all th'embossèd sores and headed evils
That thou with licence of free foot hast caught
Wouldst thou disgorge into the general world.

JAQUES Why, who cries out on pride 70
That can therein tax any private party?
Doth it not flow as hugely as the sea
Till that the weary very means do ebb?
What woman in the city do I name
When that I say the city-woman bears 75
The cost of princes on unworthy shoulders?
Who can come in and say that I mean her,
When such a one as she, such is her neighbour?
Or what is he of basest function
That says his bravery is not on my cost, 80
Thinking that I mean him, but therein suits
His folly to the mettle of my speech?
There then! How then? What then? Let me see wherein
My tongue hath wronged him. If it do him right,
Then he hath wronged himself; if he be free, 85
Why then my taxing like a wild goose flies
Unclaimed of any man. But who come here?

Enter ORLANDO [*with sword drawn*]

ORLANDO Forbear, and eat no more!

JAQUES Why, I have eat none yet.

Orlando's threats are met with kindly words from the Duke and scepticism by Jaques. Surprised by the Duke's invitation to eat, Orlando explains his menacing behaviour, asks for pity and is granted hospitality.

Stagecraft
Reaction to Orlando (in small groups)

Duke Senior and Jaques react very differently to Orlando's intrusion. Jaques seems to be mocking Orlando but Duke Senior is trying to understand why he is so desperate. Lines 102–3 change the atmosphere of the scene, as Duke Senior says 'Your gentleness shall force / More than your force move us to gentleness'.

a How would Duke Senior say this line? And how would Orlando respond? Think about the change in character and atmosphere. How would you stage this moment to emphasise the shift in tone?

b How might the rest of the camp, as a group, react to how Jaques and Duke Senior treat Orlando? Rehearse two versions of lines 87–104: one in which the others reflect Duke Senior's tone and appear disapproving of Jaques; the other in which they go along with Jaques's satirical humour by laughing at Orlando. Which version do you think works best?

Language in the play
Civility and gentleness (in pairs)

After bursting in on the peaceful scene with his sword drawn, Orlando asks that the others pardon his threatening appearance. He makes a gentle plea for help, appealing to Duke Senior to remember an earlier, better time. His appeal is made in formal, repetitive verse and Duke Senior replies in the same style.

- Discuss the mood that you would wish to create in lines 105–26. Take parts and perform the lines in ways that you think would evoke that atmosphere.

necessity be served really hungry people are fed
kind breed
distress (distress caused by hunger)
civility civilised behaviour
You touched my vein at first your first point was accurate
bare absolute
inland bred brought up in the city
nurture good manners
answerèd provided for

countenance appearance

melancholy dismal
Lose forget

knolled pealed, rung
goodman neighbour

engendered bred, caused
in gentleness courteously
upon command as you wish
wanting need

ORLANDO	Nor shalt not, till necessity be served.	90
JAQUES	Of what kind should this cock come of?	
DUKE SENIOR	Art thou thus boldened, man, by thy distress,	
	Or else a rude despiser of good manners	
	That in civility thou seem'st so empty?	
ORLANDO	You touched my vein at first: the thorny point	95
	Of bare distress hath ta'en from me the show	
	Of smooth civility; yet am I inland bred	
	And know some nurture. But forbear, I say;	
	He dies that touches any of this fruit	
	Till I and my affairs are answerèd.	100
JAQUES	And you will not be answerèd with reason, I must die.	
DUKE SENIOR	What would you have? Your gentleness shall force	
	More than your force move us to gentleness.	
ORLANDO	I almost die for food, and let me have it.	
DUKE SENIOR	Sit down and feed, and welcome to our table.	105
ORLANDO	Speak you so gently? Pardon me, I pray you:	
	I thought that all things had been savage here	
	And therefore put I on the countenance	
	Of stern commandment. But whate'er you are	
	That in this desert inaccessible,	110
	Under the shade of melancholy boughs,	
	Lose and neglect the creeping hours of time –	
	If ever you have looked on better days,	
	If ever been where bells have knolled to church,	
	If ever sat at any goodman's feast,	115
	If ever from your eyelids wiped a tear,	
	And know what 'tis to pity and be pitied,	
	Let gentleness my strong enforcement be,	
	In the which hope, I blush, and hide my sword.	
DUKE SENIOR	True is it that we have seen better days,	120
	And have with holy bell been knolled to church,	
	And sat at goodmen's feasts, and wiped our eyes	
	Of drops that sacred pity hath engendered:	
	And therefore sit you down in gentleness	
	And take upon command what help we have	125
	That to your wanting may be ministered.	
ORLANDO	Then but forbear your food a little while	
	Whiles, like a doe, I go to find my fawn	

Orlando leaves to fetch Adam. The Duke's comment that the world presents many sad scenes inspires Jaques to describe the seven ages of man.

Themes

The seven ages of man (in sevens)

Prepare and act out your own version of lines 139–66, using some or all of the following suggestions.

- One person speaks the lines while the others perform a mime or a simple collective gesture for each 'age'.
- Divide the speech into seven parts, with each person in the group taking responsibility for an 'age' and speaking it in role as a person in that stage in life. You should use posture, gesture and tone of voice to make each 'age' recognisably different.
- Work out a series of tableaux to illustrate the seven ages; the rest of the 'statues' stay perfectly still as each person in turn speaks the lines. They then change into the next 'age' tableau.
- Replace 'man' with 'woman' and 'he' with 'she' throughout, and think about how a man's life and a woman's life might differ in Shakespeare's time and today. Try one of the above activities again, with this new focus, and discuss any changes.

sufficed satisfied, fed

bit mouthful

waste consume

woeful pageants sad spectacles

merely actually

1 Jaques's tone (in pairs)

a Take turns reading Jaques's 'seven ages of man' speech (lines 139–66) in two different ways. Firstly, use a serious tone to provide a moment of reflection and stillness in the play. Secondly, try it in a more satirical and humorous style, make fun of humankind in its passage from cradle to grave. Which approach do you think works better? Why?

b Think about whom Jaques might be addressing as he speaks these lines. Does he fix on one person in particular or does he make eye contact with different characters as he goes on? Should Jaques mime the ages as he speaks? Consider how these elements might contribute to either the serious or the comic readings described above.

c In your Director's Journal, write up your ideas and opinions on how this speech should be performed.

2 All the world's a … what?

Compose a modern version of Jaques's speech, with a different central metaphor. Use the following prompts to help you:

All the world's a… circus
                     festival
                     city street
                     garden.

to his mistress' eyebrow (mimics the excessively descriptive love poems of Shakespeare's time)

strange foreign

pard leopard

Jealous in honour suspiciously careful of his reputation

good capon (a male chicken bred to be eaten)

wise saws moral sayings

modern instances trite examples or sayings

pouch purse

hose breeches

well saved carefully stored up

a world far

shrunk shank thin leg

mere oblivion complete forgetfulness

And give it food: there is an old poor man
Who after me hath many a weary step   130
Limped in pure love. Till he be first sufficed,
Oppressed with two weak evils, age and hunger,
I will not touch a bit.

DUKE SENIOR   Go find him out,
And we will nothing waste till you return.

ORLANDO   I thank ye, and be blest for your good comfort.   [*Exit*]   135

DUKE SENIOR Thou see'st we are not all alone unhappy:
This wide and universal theatre
Presents more woeful pageants than the scene
Wherein we play in.

JAQUES   All the world's a stage
And all the men and women merely players: 140
They have their exits and their entrances
And one man in his time plays many parts,
His acts being seven ages. At first the infant,
Mewling and puking in the nurse's arms;
Then the whining schoolboy with his satchel   145
And shining morning face, creeping like snail
Unwillingly to school; and then the lover,
Sighing like furnace, with a woeful ballad
Made to his mistress' eyebrow; then a soldier,
Full of strange oaths and bearded like the pard,   150
Jealous in honour, sudden, and quick in quarrel,
Seeking the bubble 'reputation'
Even in the cannon's mouth; and then the justice,
In fair round belly with good capon lined,
With eyes severe and beard of formal cut,   155
Full of wise saws and modern instances –
And so he plays his part; the sixth age shifts
Into the lean and slippered pantaloon,
With spectacles on nose and pouch on side,
His youthful hose well saved – a world too wide   160
For his shrunk shank – and his big manly voice,
Turning again toward childish treble, pipes
And whistles in his sound; last scene of all
That ends this strange eventful history
Is second childishness and mere oblivion,   165
Sans teeth, sans eyes, sans taste, sans everything.

Duke Senior invites Adam to eat. He calls for music. Amiens's song tells that nature, though harsh, is not so cruel as human ungratefulness; that most friendship is merely pretence and that most love is foolishness.

▲ How would you stage Adam's grateful eating of the food Duke Senior gives him? Should Adam be the focus of the onstage action as he eats and Amiens sings?

1 Amiens's song

Consider the following elements of Amiens's song and its staging:

- **Language** Identify repetition, rhyme, personification and apostrophe (see pp. 182–4) in Amiens's song. What effect does each of these poetic devices have on the listener?
- **Content** Amiens's song is about man's ingratitude. How does this fit with the plot of the play so far?
- **Staging** What are the other characters' responses to this song? What are they doing as they listen?
- **Music** What music would you choose to set the lyrics to in a performance? Find a suitable soundtrack, or write your own melody for the song. Devise a performance of the song, adding repetitions, echoes and sound effects (such as rustling leaves, bird noises, rough weather noises and so on).

venerable respected

for him on his behalf

fall to start eating
to question by questioning
cousin (this term could be used by a prince to address a lord)

unkind unnatural or ungenerous

keen sharp

rude rough

holly (a symbol of joy and friendship at Christmas)
feigning pretending
folly foolishness, infatuation

nigh deeply
benefits forgot ingratitude, forgetting of good deeds
warp freeze, shrivel

Enter ORLANDO *with* ADAM [*on his back*]

DUKE SENIOR	Welcome. Set down your venerable burden,
	And let him feed.
ORLANDO	I thank you most for him.
ADAM	So had you need: I scarce can speak
	To thank you for myself. 170
DUKE SENIOR	Welcome; fall to: I will not trouble you
	As yet to question you about your fortunes. –
	Give us some music, and, good cousin, sing.

Song

AMIENS

    Blow, blow, thou winter wind,
    Thou art not so unkind   175
    As man's ingratitude;
    Thy tooth is not so keen,
    Because thou art not seen,
    Although thy breath be rude.
        Hey-ho, sing hey-ho   180
        Unto the green holly,
        Most friendship is feigning,
        Most loving mere folly.
        The hey-ho, the holly,
        This life is most jolly.   185

    Freeze, freeze, thou bitter sky,
    That dost not bite so nigh
    As benefits forgot;
    Though thou the waters warp,
    Thy sting is not so sharp   190
    As friend remembered not.
        Hey-ho, sing hey-ho
        Unto the green holly,
        Most friendship is feigning,
        Most loving mere folly.   195
        The hey-ho, the holly,
        This life is most jolly.

Duke Senior sees in Orlando's face the likeness of his old friend Sir Roland de Boys. He proposes that Orlando tells him the rest of his story later.

Stagecraft

An unexpected ending (in pairs)

The end of Act 2 is full of dramatic possibilities for a director, and different productions have interpreted it in different ways. Most productions show Orlando and Adam eating and gaining new strength after their ordeal in the forest. However, in the 1996 Royal Shakespeare Company (RSC) production, the scene ended unexpectedly. As Duke Senior spoke his final line, all the characters moved towards Adam only to find that he had quietly passed away. Everyone stared, frozen in dismay at the sight of Adam's body, and the lights faded as the scene ended.

- Discuss these two options for staging the end of this scene, then suggest how you would direct it yourself. Think about the different ways the characters could exit at the final stage direction, 'Exeunt', which means that everybody leaves the stage.

Characters

Orlando: past and future (in pairs)

a Duke Senior proposes to hear the rest of Orlando's story later. Take turns to step into role as Orlando and recount what has happened to you up to this moment in the play. One person can begin, then give a signal to the other when they are ready for them take over.

b Write a paragraph predicting what you think will happen to Orlando from this point on. In role as Orlando, write another paragraph describing your plans for the future – these can differ from what you think will actually happen to him.

whispered communicated

faithfully convincingly, confidently

effigies likeness, image

limned
painted, colourfully depicted

residue of your fortune
rest of your story

Exeunt everyone leaves the stage

DUKE SENIOR   If that you were the good Sir Roland's son,
As you have whispered faithfully you were,
And as mine eye doth his effigies witness   200
Most truly limned and living in your face,
Be truly welcome hither. I am the Duke
That loved your father. The residue of your fortune
Go to my cave and tell me. – Good old man,
Thou art right welcome as thy master is. –   205
[*To Orlando*] Support him by the arm. [*To Adam*] Give me
   your hand,
And let me all your fortunes understand.

                                             Exeunt

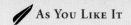

Looking back at Act 2
Activities for groups or individuals

1 Contrasts and juxtapositions

Act 2 continues Shakespeare's dramatic practice of inviting audience members to consider how the scene they are watching contrasts with and comments on the preceding scene. Some themes that run through this act – and are therefore a clear focus for such internal criticism and analysis – include court versus country, virtue versus evil and love versus enmity.

- Look back through the seven scenes of Act 2 and examine how each one is juxtaposed with the one before. For example, Scene 1 is set in the forest with the banished Duke Senior, whereas the last scene of Act 1 was set in Duke Frederick's corrupt court.
- Draw a diagram to show how the scenes in Act 2 are linked together. Annotate it with comments, images and quotations from the script.

2 Opportunities for design

The exiled lords appear dressed as 'foresters' or 'outlaws', and Amiens sings of 'the greenwood tree'.

- Sketch your designs for costumes for the 'outlaws' and the set for the forest. Would you want a modern setting or a historical one? This could be something other than Elizabethan England, such as ancient Rome or the old American West. Would you want the action to take place in winter, spring, summer or autumn? Maybe you want to create a more symbolic set rather than a naturalistic one? Your decisions will affect the mood you create through your designs, and therefore the interpretation of the play that the audience takes away.

3 Learning from nature

At the start of Act 2, Duke Senior claims that nature has a lot to teach humans about moral conduct.

- Do you agree that experiences in the Forest of Arden can teach more about good, evil, courage, honour and love than life in the 'civilised' city? Remember that Arden, as well as being an ideal world away from the corruptions of the court, is also a place of danger, hardship and personal struggles. Write at least one paragraph for each side of the argument. Remember to use examples and quotations from the script.

4 Different perspectives on Act 2

In Scene 2, Hisperia, Celia's lady-in-waiting, appears to answer Duke Frederick's questions about Rosalind and Celia. She is not mentioned again.

- Stage an interview with a partner. Take turns to step into role as Hisperia and tell all you know about events at the court up to the moment that Rosalind and Celia ran away. You might like to present the interview as if it is taking place under duress, as Hisperia 'confesses' to Duke Frederick's lords.

5 Wearing motley

In Scene 7, Jaques longs to play the clown and therefore be able to mock people's shortcomings and pretensions. He says 'motley's the only wear' and envies the freedom Touchstone has to hide his critical comments in his foolish remarks.

a Research the status and role of a court jester or an Elizabethan clown in your library or on the Internet. Write notes on how what have you learnt helps you to better understand the character of Touchstone.

b Look at the photographs of Touchstone opposite, then discuss how you would want to present him in a modern production of the play. Would you keep his 'motley' costume? Or would you think of some other way to represent his unique status in the play?

In Scene 1, Duke Frederick threatens Oliver and orders him to capture Orlando dead or alive. In Scene 2, Orlando praises Rosalind and hangs his love poems to her on trees.

1 What has just happened? (in small groups)

Scene 1 opens in the middle of a conversation, with Duke Frederick echoing what Oliver has just said: "'Not see him since?'"

a What do you think is happening in this scene? Read the two possible interpretations below and discuss the context to the characters' lines.

- In some productions, a bleeding and battered Oliver is thrown in by the lords. He has obviously been tortured.
- In other productions, Oliver and Duke Frederick are having a secret conversation out of hearing of the lords. There is no physical violence, but their interaction is full of tension.

b Improvise a short scene that might have taken place just before the beginning of Act 3, in which Duke Frederick and Oliver talk about Orlando. Make sure you include the declaration 'Not see him since' in Oliver's last speech.

Write about it

Poems in the trees

Orlando has written poems about Rosalind and hung them on trees around the forest so that everyone will read of her beauty and virtue.

a Write your own short poem(s) as if from Orlando to Rosalind, and/or from Rosalind to Orlando. Try to include some striking visual images, or use an extended metaphor to describe the object of the author's affection. Read the suggestions below to get you started:

- You could research the conventions of Elizabethan love sonnets, and use some of the ideas and phrases of love poetry from Shakespeare's day.
- You might choose to look at modern love poetry – for example, by reading through the lyrics of some of your favourite songs.

b When you have finished your poem(s), explain to the rest of the class which love poem or genre influenced your poem and why.

---

the better part made mercy so inclined to mercy

absent argument missing subject (Orlando)

seizure confiscating

quit acquit

brother's mouth (Orlando's testimony)

of such a nature fit for the task

Make an extent upon seize hastily

turn him going send him packing

thrice-crownèd queen of night in ancient Roman and Greek mythology, this goddess ruled three worlds: Earth as Diana (or Artemis), goddess of chastity and hunting; the underworld as Proserpina (or Persephone or Hecate); and heaven as Luna (or Selene), goddess of the moon

survey see

huntress' name (this refers to Rosalind but is also an allusion to Diana, the Roman goddess of hunting)

sway rule

character write, carve

virtue witnessed excellent qualities attested to

unexpressive she indescribable woman

Act 3 Scene 1
Duke Frederick's palace

Enter DUKE FREDERICK, *Lords, and* OLIVER

DUKE FREDERICK 'Not see him since'? Sir, sir, that cannot be!
              But were I not the better part made mercy,
              I should not seek an absent argument
              Of my revenge, thou present. But look to it:
              Find out thy brother, wheresoe'er he is;   5
              Seek him with candle; bring him dead or living
              Within this twelvemonth, or turn thou no more
              To seek a living in our territory.
              Thy lands and all things that thou dost call thine
              Worth seizure, do we seize into our hands   10
              Till thou canst quit thee by thy brother's mouth
              Of what we think against thee.
OLIVER   O that your highness knew my heart in this:
              I never loved my brother in my life.
DUKE FREDERICK   More villain thou. [*To Lords*] Well, push him out of doors   15
              And let my officers of such a nature
              Make an extent upon his house and lands.
              Do this expediently and turn him going.

                                Exeunt

Act 3 Scene 2
The Forest of Arden

Enter ORLANDO *with a sheet of paper in his hand*

ORLANDO   Hang there, my verse, in witness of my love;
              And thou, thrice-crownèd queen of night, survey
              With thy chaste eye, from thy pale sphere above,
              Thy huntress' name that my full life doth sway.
              O Rosalind, these trees shall be my books,   5
              And in their barks my thoughts I'll character
              That every eye which in this forest looks
              Shall see thy virtue witnessed everywhere.
              Run, run, Orlando, carve on every tree
              The fair, the chaste, and unexpressive she.   *Exit*

Touchstone, using clever-sounding language, says that he likes and dislikes country life. Corin replies in the same empty manner. Touchstone claims that Corin is damned for not having been at court.

1 Touchstone's wit

Touchstone's lines 2–9 are a series of statements saying that he both likes and dislikes country life.

a Draw up a table with two columns to list your own likes and dislikes of your school or college.

b Write a similar description of your school or college using the same style: 'in respect that it is … but in respect that …' Try to capture Touchstone's style and his ability to hide witty observations in seemingly foolish talk.

2 Empty talk – court versus country (in pairs)

Scene 3 begins with a conversation about one of the major themes of the play: the comparison of country life with court life. To gain a first impression of how Shakespeare mocks the pretentious conversations that often took place among his own contemporaries, take parts as Touchstone and Corin and speak lines 1–64. Then use some of the activities below to help you work out how you would stage the dialogue.

a Does Touchstone treat Corin as an equal or as an inferior? How would this be shown on stage?

b Touchstone dresses up his empty language by calling it 'philosophy'. Corin answers him in the same high-sounding but superficial style, saying banal things ('the property of rain is to wet', and so on). Is Corin mocking Touchstone or is he serious about what he says?

c Touchstone makes a number of digs at Corin. For example, 'a natural philosopher' could mean a foolish thinker, and 'an ill-roasted egg, all on one side' could be Touchstone's way of calling Corin half-baked. Decide whether Touchstone should share his sly humour with the audience. How could he show what he really means through his non-verbal actions?

d Write a few detailed stage directions to accompany this scene, so that the actors playing Touchstone and Corin understand how you want them to interact with each other. Remember to advise them on voice (volume, pace, tone), body movements (gesture, posture) and space (where they position themselves on stage or how they move around it).

in respect of with regard to
in respect that considering
private lonely

spare frugal
humour disposition
stomach inclination

wants lacks
means employment

wit knowledge
nature or art birth or education
complain of good breeding protest he has had a poor upbringing
natural philosopher student of science or fool
Wast were you
Nay, I hope I hope not

good courtly, or morally correct

parlous perilous

Act 3 Scene 3
The Forest of Arden

Enter CORIN *and* TOUCHSTONE

CORIN   And how like you this shepherd's life, Master Touchstone?

TOUCHSTONE   Truly, shepherd, in respect of itself, it is a good life; but
in respect that it is a shepherd's life, it is naught. In respect that it
is solitary, I like it very well; but in respect that it is private, it is a
very vile life. Now in respect it is in the fields, it pleaseth me well;   5
but in respect it is not in the court, it is tedious. As it is a spare life,
look you, it fits my humour well; but as there is no more plenty in
it, it goes much against my stomach. Hast any philosophy in thee,
shepherd?

CORIN   No more but that I know the more one sickens, the worse at ease   10
he is; and that he that wants money, means, and content is without
three good friends; that the property of rain is to wet and fire to
burn; that good pasture makes fat sheep; and that a great cause of
the night is lack of the sun; that he that hath learned no wit by
nature nor art may complain of good breeding, or comes of a very   15
dull kindred.

TOUCHSTONE   Such a one is a natural philosopher. – Wast ever in
court, shepherd?

CORIN   No, truly.

TOUCHSTONE   Then thou art damned.   20

CORIN   Nay, I hope.

TOUCHSTONE   Truly thou art damned: like an ill-roasted egg, all on one
side.

CORIN   For not being at court? Your reason.

TOUCHSTONE   Why, if thou never wast at court, thou never saw'st good   25
manners; if thou never saw'st good manners, then thy manners
must be wicked, and wickedness is sin, and sin is damnation. Thou
art in a parlous state, shepherd.

Corin argues that to adopt court behaviour in the country would be foolish. Touchstone mocks the examples Corin gives. Corin expresses his contentment with country life, but Touchstone remains cynical.

1 Court and country matters: a debate (in pairs)

Verbal jousting is much loved by fools in Shakespeare; they enjoy argument for its own sake, and often follow an absurd logic. Corin denies that he is damned for not being at court and he claims that it would be foolish to adopt court manners in the country. Touchstone rejects Corin's example, but his rejection is also a criticism of court manners.

a As you first read through this exchange, discuss whether Touchstone or Corin seems to 'win' the argument. Or is it a draw?

b As you read it the second time, stand opposite your partner. Take a step forward every time you think your character has an advantage over the other character in the debate (the other person takes a step back).

2 Elizabethan jokes, modern audiences
(in small groups)

Elizabethans loved jokes about adultery, particularly where the unsuspecting husband did not realise what his wife was up to. Men with unfaithful wives were ridiculed as 'cuckolds' and were said to have horns growing out of their head that were visible to everyone but them. Touchstone criticises breeding sheep as a sin, and calls Corin a pimp who brings together a young female sheep and a lustful, horned old ram.

a Compile a list of questions to ask Touchstone about his attitude and behaviour towards Corin. Is he winding him up? What response does Touchstone hope to get? What does he mean in lines 61–2 when he says, 'If thou be'st not damned for this, the devil himself will have no shepherds'?

b Take turns to sit in the hot-seat in role as Touchstone and answer the questions asked by the rest of the group.

salute greet
courtesy usage

Instance give an example
fells fleeces (sheep's woolly coats)

grease sweat

tar (used to heal wounds on sheep)
civet (perfume from the anal glands of civet cats)
worms' meat corpse
respect of comparison with
perpend consider
baser birth lower origin
flux secretion, discharge
Mend the instance improve your argument
make incision in cut (to let knowledge enter)
raw unlearned, immature
true trustworthy
earn that work for what
content with my harm accepting my hardships
bawd pimp
bell-wether lead sheep of the flock, which wears a bell
crooked-pated twisted-horned

CORIN   Not a whit, Touchstone: those that are good manners at the
         court are as ridiculous in the country as the behaviour of the coun-   30
         try is most mockable at the court. You told me you salute not at the
         court but you kiss your hands: that courtesy would be uncleanly if
         courtiers were shepherds.

TOUCHSTONE   Instance, briefly; come, instance.

CORIN   Why, we are still handling our ewes, and their fells, you know,   35
         are greasy.

TOUCHSTONE   Why, do not your courtier's hands sweat, and is not the
         grease of a mutton as wholesome as the sweat of a man? Shallow,
         shallow! A better instance, I say – come.

CORIN   Besides, our hands are hard.   40

TOUCHSTONE   Your lips will feel them the sooner. Shallow again: a
         more sounder instance, come.

CORIN   And they are often tarred over with the surgery of our sheep,
         and would you have us kiss tar? The courtiers' hands are perfumed
         with civet.   45

TOUCHSTONE   Most shallow man! Thou worms' meat in respect of a
         good piece of flesh, indeed! Learn of the wise and perpend: civet is
         of a baser birth than tar, the very uncleanly flux of a cat. Mend the
         instance, shepherd.

CORIN   You have too courtly a wit for me; I'll rest.   50

TOUCHSTONE   Wilt thou rest damned? God help thee, shallow man.
         God make incision in thee, thou art raw.

CORIN   Sir, I am a true labourer: I earn that I eat, get that I wear, owe no
         man hate, envy no man's happiness, glad of other men's good,
         content with my harm; and the greatest of my pride is to see my   55
         ewes graze and my lambs suck.

TOUCHSTONE   That is another simple sin in you: to bring the ewes and
         the rams together and to offer to get your living by the copulation of
         cattle; to be bawd to a bell-wether and to betray a she-lamb of a
         twelvemonth to a crooked-pated old cuckoldly ram out of all rea-   60
         sonable match. If thou be'st not damned for this, the devil himself
         will have no shepherds. I cannot see else how thou shouldst 'scape.

CORIN   Here comes young Monsieur Ganymede, my new mistress's
         brother.

Enter ROSALIND [*as* GANYMEDE]

Rosalind reads Orlando's poem in praise of her beauty. Touchstone composes a parody of the poem, full of sexual innuendo. Rosalind's reply puns jokingly at Touchstone's expense.

1 True love or trite verses? (in pairs)

Orlando's attempts at poetry demonstrate how difficult it is to say anything 'new' about love. Strong feelings of love can come across as ridiculous when set to rhymes that, according to Touchstone, sound like women trotting to the market! Touchstone is quick to mock Orlando's poetry, but what is Rosalind thinking?

a Write a few asides to insert into this scene, showing Rosalind's private responses to the poems she has just read or heard. Include her reaction to Touchstone's parody.

b Take turns to step into role as Rosalind and practise how you would say these asides. Then use them as the basis for Rosalind's diary entry at the end of the day, in which she reveals her deepest thoughts about Orlando and her hopes and fears for the future.

2 Touchstone's parody (in small groups)

How do your versions of Orlando's and Rosalind's love poems (see p. 70) compare with the example that Rosalind reads out here? You might notice the simple rhythm and the number of words that rhyme with 'Rosalind'. Touchstone picks up on this and criticises the jogging, jerky rhythm of Orlando's verses.

• Write another love poem (from Rosalind to Orlando or from Orlando to Rosalind) in the style of Touchstone's parody. Note that Touchstone makes up a **burlesque** (a comically exaggeration imitation) in the same simple rhythm ('false gallop') as Orlando's poem, and focusing on the physical aspects of love.

Write about it
'let the forest judge'

A well-known proverb states that 'many a wise word is said in jest'. What truth might be hidden in Touchstone's jests? What might he be trying to say about Orlando's romantic exaggerations?

• Write a letter from Touchstone to Rosalind describing the problems Rosalind might encounter in a marriage to Orlando if he expects her to be as perfect as his poem describes.

Western Inde West Indies

fairest lined beautifully sketched or painted

black to foul compared to

fair beauty

eight years together for eight years without stopping

the right butter-women's rank to market the jogging, jerky rhythm of women riding to the market

after kind chase a female cat

Wintered old

lined stuffed, padded out

sheaf and bind collect up and tie

to cart (the harvest was transported by cart – and prostitutes were punished by being paraded through the village in a cart)

false gallop simple rhythm

graft (Rosalind uses a gardening term to mean 'combine' or 'integrate')

medlar a type of apple best eaten when rotten, or an interfering busybody

right virtue true quality

ROSALIND   [*Reading from a paper*]

          'From the East to Western Inde   65

             No jewel is like Rosalind;

          Her worth, being mounted on the wind,

             Through all the world bears Rosalind;

          All the pictures fairest lined

             Are but black to Rosalind;   70

          Let no face be kept in mind

             But the fair of Rosalind.'

TOUCHSTONE I'll rhyme you so eight years together, dinners and suppers and sleeping-hours excepted. It is the right butter-women's rank to market.   75

ROSALIND Out, fool!

TOUCHSTONE For a taste:

          If a hart do lack a hind,

             Let him seek out Rosalind;

          If the cat will after kind,   80

             So be sure will Rosalind;

          Wintered garments must be lined,

             So must slender Rosalind;

          They that reap must sheaf and bind,

             Then to cart with Rosalind;   85

          Sweetest nut hath sourest rind,

             Such a nut is Rosalind;

          He that sweetest rose will find,

             Must find love's prick – and Rosalind.

    This is the very false gallop of verses: why do you infect yourself   90

with them?

ROSALIND Peace, you dull fool. I found them on a tree.

TOUCHSTONE Truly, the tree yields bad fruit.

ROSALIND I'll graft it with you, and then I shall graft it with a medlar; then it will be the earliest fruit i'th' country, for you'll be rotten ere you be half ripe, and that's the right virtue of the medlar.   95

TOUCHSTONE You have said – but whether wisely or no, let the forest judge.

Enter CELIA [*as* ALIENA] *with a writing*

ROSALIND Peace, here comes my sister, reading. Stand aside.

Celia reads Orlando's poem, which tells of the brevity of human life and of broken promises, but is mainly about how Rosalind embodies all beauty and grace. Rosalind calls it a boring sermon.

1 Echoes of Acts 1 and 2 (in pairs)

Orlando's poem says he will people the forest with proclamations ('Tongues') on every tree, containing wise sayings about society. Some will tell how human life is as short as the distance enclosed by a handspan, others will tell of broken promises between friends.

a Compile a list of any events, situations or lines in Acts 1 and 2 that might be echoed in Orlando's poem.

b Would you expect to find social commentary in love poems? Discuss what you expect from love poetry.

2 Heavenly Rosalind (in threes)

Orlando's praise of Rosalind compares her with famous women in ancient Greek and Roman mythology and history:

- She has Helen of Troy's beauty, but not her unfaithfulness.
- She has the majesty of Cleopatra, queen of Egypt.
- She has Atalanta's swiftness of movement – in Greek mythology, this beautiful huntress was given the gift of speed and vowed that any suitor who could not outrun her would be executed.
- She has Lucretia's faithfulness – in Roman mythology, this woman killed herself to prove her honesty and devotion to her husband.

a Identify the references to these women in Orlando's poem. Then discuss whether you think these comparisons really suit Rosalind or if you think they are just poetic, and fairly impersonal, exaggerations.

b What do you think Celia, Rosalind and Touchstone are each thinking as they hear this poem? Take parts and, as Celia experiments with different styles of reading (for example, mocking, passionate, thoughtful), the two listeners should react to the words with gestures and facial expressions.

c Rewrite lines 120–3 of the poem as a modern parody, using four examples of well-known female figures from today.

Stagecraft
Touchstone's exit

How would you direct Touchstone to speak the two lines before his exit (lines 135–6)? In your Director's Journal, make notes on all the possible elements of stage business that the actor could use, including how Touchstone could physically interact with Corin.

erring pilgrimage wandering or sinful journey
That so that
Buckles in his sum of age limits a man's length of life
violated vows broken promises

sentence pithy saying

quintessence purest essence
sprite soul, spirit
in little in miniature (in Rosalind)
Nature charged gave orders to nature

heavenly synod God's parliament or assembly of divinities

touches qualities, features

tedious homily boring sermon

Backfriends eavesdroppers, traitors

scrip shepherd's purse
scrippage (a nonsense word made up by Touchstone from the words 'scrip' and 'baggage')

CELIA   'Why should this a desert be?   100
                 For it is unpeopled? No:
             Tongues I'll hang on every tree,
                 That shall civil sayings show:
             Some how brief the life of man
                 Runs his erring pilgrimage   105
             That the stretching of a span
                 Buckles in his sum of age;
             Some of violated vows
                 'Twixt the souls of friend and friend;
             But upon the fairest boughs   110
                 Or at every sentence end
             Will I "Rosalinda" write,
                 Teaching all that read to know
             The quintessence of every sprite
                 Heaven would in little show.   115
             Therefore Heaven Nature charged
                 That one body should be filled
             With all graces wide-enlarged;
                 Nature presently distilled
             Helen's cheek but not her heart,   120
                 Cleopatra's majesty,
             Atalanta's better part,
                 Sad Lucretia's modesty.
             Thus Rosalind of many parts
                 By heavenly synod was devised,   125
             Of many faces, eyes, and hearts,
                 To have the touches dearest prized.
             Heaven would that she these gifts should have,
                 And I to live and die her slave.'

ROSALIND [*Coming forward*] O most gentle Jupiter, what tedious   130
          homily of love have you wearied your parishioners withal, and never
          cried, 'Have patience, good people!'

CELIA   How now? Backfriends! – Shepherd, go off a little. – Go with
          him, sirrah.

TOUCHSTONE Come, shepherd, let us make an honourable retreat,   135
          though not with bag and baggage, yet with scrip and scrippage.
                                    Exeunt Touchstone and Corin

CELIA   Didst thou hear these verses?

Rosalind and Celia joke about the lack of skill in the poems. Celia expresses amazement that Rosalind cannot guess who has written the verses. Rosalind begs to be told the poet's name.

1 But who is it? (in pairs)

The exchange between Rosalind and Celia is full of high spirits, teasing and excitement.

a Read the passage to yourself, then take parts and speak lines 137–212.

b Find the following examples in the script opposite, then discuss in detail how you would want to stage this witty exchange:

- In lines 137–42, Rosalind and Celia joke about Orlando's bad poetry, using puns on 'feet' and 'bear'.
- There is a series of quick-fire questions with no real answers in lines 149–57.
- Celia uses repetition in lines 160–1.
- Rosalind uses the metaphor of a corked bottle to show her eagerness to find out who Celia is talking about in lines 165–9.
- The metaphor backfires on Rosalind (line 170). Why might Rosalind be shocked? What is Celia implying here?

without outside
should be was

seven ... wonder nearly finished wondering (she was at the seventh day of a nine days' wonder).
palm-tree willow tree
Pythagorus (Greek philosopher who believed that a human spirit could migrate to beasts)
Trow you do you know

encounter come together in a loving embrace

petitionary vehemence urgent entreaties

out of all hooping beyond all astonishment
Good my complexion forgive my blushes
caparisoned dressed
disposition nature
South Sea of discovery incredibly long time
apace fast

of God's making a normal human being

ROSALIND	O yes, I heard them all, and more too, for some of them had in them more feet than the verses would bear.	
CELIA	That's no matter: the feet might bear the verses.	140
ROSALIND	Aye, but the feet were lame and could not bear themselves without the verse, and therefore stood lamely in the verse.	
CELIA	But didst thou hear without wondering how thy name should be hanged and carved upon these trees?	
ROSALIND	I was seven of the nine days out of the wonder before you came, for look here what I found on a palm-tree. I was never so berhymed since Pythagoras' time that I was an Irish rat – which I can hardly remember.	145
CELIA	Trow you who hath done this?	
ROSALIND	Is it a man?	150
CELIA	And a chain that you once wore about his neck? Change you colour?	
ROSALIND	I prithee, who?	
CELIA	O Lord, Lord, it is a hard matter for friends to meet, but mountains may be removed with earthquakes and so encounter.	155
ROSALIND	Nay, but who is it?	
CELIA	Is it possible?	
ROSALIND	Nay, I prithee now, with most petitionary vehemence, tell me who it is.	
CELIA	O wonderful, wonderful, and most wonderful wonderful, and yet again wonderful, and after that out of all hooping.	160
ROSALIND	Good my complexion, dost thou think, though I am caparisoned like a man, I have a doublet and hose in my disposition? One inch of delay more is a South Sea of discovery. I prithee tell me who is it – quickly, and speak apace. I would thou couldst stammer that thou might'st pour this concealed man out of thy mouth as wine comes out of a narrow-mouthed bottle: either too much at once or none at all. I prithee take the cork out of thy mouth that I may drink thy tidings.	165
CELIA	So you may put a man in your belly.	170
ROSALIND	Is he of God's making? What manner of man? Is his head worth a hat or his chin worth a beard?	
CELIA	Nay, he hath but a little beard.	
ROSALIND	Why, God will send more if the man will be thankful. Let me stay the growth of his beard, if thou delay me not the knowledge of his chin.	175

Celia reveals that Orlando wrote the poems. Rosalind's first thought is of her disguise as a man. She asks many eager questions and keeps interrupting Celia's story. They hide from Orlando and Jaques.

1 Quickfire questions (in pairs)

When Rosalind hears that Orlando is in the forest, she wonders what she will do about her disguise as a man, then launches into a flurry of questions.

a Take turns to speak lines 184–8. How quickly can you deliver the lines while still speaking every word perfectly clearly?

b How does it feel to be on the receiving end of this flurry of questions? Think of a different gesture or action for each question to show Celia's response. Is she confused, frustrated, amused or something else?

2 Rosalind's aside (in threes)

a How is it best to speak Rosalind's aside at line 197? Does she speak to herself, or to the audience? Think of three different ways Rosalind might say this aside, then discuss what each variation suggests.

b Take turns to step into role as Rosalind and speak these different variations. Try out different gestures or facial expressions to help communicate the intended meaning. The others in your group should give you feedback and direction.

c In your Director's Journal, write notes for the actor playing Rosalind to advise her on how best to interpret and perform the aside.

Characters

Conversations with the director (in pairs)

Imagine you are working on a new production of this play, and step into role as either the director or the actor playing Rosalind.

- The director thinks that in lines 179–210 Rosalind's tone should be pleading, breathless and self-tormenting.
- The actor thinks that Rosalind should comically exaggerate her speech, teasing Celia in order to hide her strong feelings about Orlando.

Prepare your case by finding words from the script that support your interpretation. Then improvise an argument between the director and the actor, in which each person tries to convince the other that their interpretation is correct and will create the greatest dramatic effect.

sad brow and true maid seriously and honestly

Wherein went he? what was he wearing?

Gargantua (a giant with an enormous appetite, featured in a sixteenth-century story by a French author named Rabelais)

catechism set of religious questions and answers

freshly healthy or shamelessly

atomies specks of dust

resolve answer

propositions questions

relish it … observance enjoy it by paying attention

Jove's tree (in ancient Roman mythology, the oak was sacred to Jupiter)

wounded knight (possibly wounded by Cupid's love arrows)

holla whoa (to stop a horse)

curvets prances

unseasonably in an ill-timed manner

furnished dressed

heart (a pun on 'hart', a young deer)

burden accompaniment

thou bring'st you put

bring me out make me forget my words

CELIA	It is young Orlando, that tripped up the wrestler's heels and your heart both in an instant.
ROSALIND	Nay, but the devil take mocking! Speak sad brow and true maid.
CELIA	I'faith, coz, 'tis he.
ROSALIND	Orlando?
CELIA	Orlando.
ROSALIND	Alas the day, what shall I do with my doublet and hose? What did he when thou saw'st him? What said he? How looked he? Wherein went he? What makes he here? Did he ask for me? Where remains he? How parted he with thee? And when shalt thou see him again? Answer me in one word.
CELIA	You must borrow me Gargantua's mouth first: 'tis a word too great for any mouth of this age's size. To say 'aye' and 'no' to these particulars is more than to answer in a catechism.
ROSALIND	But doth he know that I am in this forest and in man's apparel? Looks he as freshly as he did the day he wrestled?
CELIA	It is as easy to count atomies as to resolve the propositions of a lover; but take a taste of my finding him and relish it with good observance. I found him under a tree like a dropped acorn.
ROSALIND	[Aside] It may well be called Jove's tree when it drops such fruit.
CELIA	Give me audience, good madam.
ROSALIND	Proceed.
CELIA	There lay he stretched along like a wounded knight.
ROSALIND	Though it be pity to see such a sight, it well becomes the ground.
CELIA	Cry 'holla' to thy tongue, I prithee: it curvets unseasonably. He was furnished like a hunter.
ROSALIND	O ominous: he comes to kill my heart.
CELIA	I would sing my song without a burden; thou bring'st me out of tune.
ROSALIND	Do you not know I am a woman? When I think, I must speak. Sweet, say on.

Enter ORLANDO *and* JAQUES

CELIA	You bring me out. – Soft, comes he not here?
ROSALIND	'Tis he. Slink by, and note him.

[*Rosalind and Celia stand aside*]

180

185

190

195

200

205

210

Jaques and Orlando engage in a verbal fencing match, with Jaques criticising love. Orlando refuses to join Jaques in rebuking the world. They part, each mocking the other's folly: love and melancholy.

Language in the play

'you are full of pretty answers' (in pairs)

In the conversation between Orlando and Jaques, each man tries to score points off the other in politely phrased but insulting language. The exchange is a subversion of normal polite conversation, and Jaques finds Orlando's answers trite and sentimental. He implies that Orlando has made love to goldsmiths' wives and learned ('conned') his answers from the sentimental inscriptions that goldsmiths engraved inside rings. In reply, Orlando implies that Jaques spends his time in tavern bedrooms. These were hung with cheap imitation tapestries ('right painted cloth') with similar commonplace sayings painted on them.

- Take parts and speak the dialogue in the script opposite. Be superficially polite, but try to show up the other character with your wit and sharp delivery. Perform in front of another pair and ask them to judge when either character scores points in this way. The judges should pronounce a winner at the end of the exchange.

Stagecraft

Eavesdropping (in small groups)

Characters in Shakespeare's plays often eavesdrop on others, and at this point Rosalind and Celia have stood aside to observe Jaques and Orlando. This means that the audience can see the two women listening as well as the two men talking.

- Stage part of the script opposite, focusing on where you would place the characters in relation to each other and how they would interact with one another and with the audience. Think about the following points:

Positioning Where should the characters stand on the stage to show that they are (a) eavesdropping and (b) unaware of being overheard? 'Upstage' means the characters are further away from the audience; 'downstage' means that they are closer.

Movement Who should move around the stage? Who is most likely to talk to the audience with an aside or with gestures?

Stage design What props and scenery will you use to hide Rosalind and Celia from the other characters' view?

JAQUES   I thank you for your company, but, good faith, I had as lief have
           been myself alone.

ORLANDO   And so had I. But yet, for fashion sake, I thank you too for   215
           your society.

JAQUES   God buy you. Let's meet as little as we can.

ORLANDO   I do desire we may be better strangers.

JAQUES   I pray you mar no more trees with writing love-songs in their
           barks.   220

ORLANDO   I pray you mar no mo of my verses with reading them ill-
           favouredly.

JAQUES   'Rosalind' is your love's name?

ORLANDO   Yes, just.

JAQUES   I do not like her name.   225

ORLANDO   There was no thought of pleasing you when she was
           christened.

JAQUES   What stature is she of?

ORLANDO   Just as high as my heart.

JAQUES   You are full of pretty answers: have you not been acquainted   230
           with goldsmiths' wives and conned them out of rings?

ORLANDO   Not so; but I answer you right painted cloth, from whence
           you have studied your questions.

JAQUES   You have a nimble wit; I think 'twas made of Atalanta's heels.
           Will you sit down with me, and we two will rail against our mistress   235
           the world and all our misery.

ORLANDO   I will chide no breather in the world but myself, against
           whom I know most faults.

JAQUES   The worst fault you have is to be in love.

ORLANDO   'Tis a fault I will not change for your best virtue: I am weary   240
           of you.

JAQUES   By my troth, I was seeking for a fool, when I found you.

ORLANDO   He is drowned in the brook: look but in, and you shall see
           him.

JAQUES   There I shall see mine own figure.   245

ORLANDO   Which I take to be either a fool or a cipher.

JAQUES   I'll tarry no longer with you. Farewell, good Signor Love.

ORLANDO   I am glad of your departure. Adieu, good Monsieur
           Melancholy.

                                                            [*Exit Jaques*]

Rosalind, using her disguise as a young man, playfully tells Orlando how time moves at different speeds for different people. He expresses surprise at her refined accent.

1 First meeting (in pairs)

a To gain an initial impression of Rosalind's meeting with Orlando, take parts and speak from line 250 to the end of the scene. Keep in mind the following comment by an actor:

Rosalind now really tests her disguise. Will she be recognised by the man she loves? She has to speak and act like a man, but all the time she is teasing Orlando. Rosalind conceals her true feelings for Orlando. She hides them behind witty language and play-acting. But the audience knows how she feels, as does Celia.

b What advice would you give the actor playing Rosalind at this point in the play? Talk together with your partner about what Rosalind might be feeling, and how this could be most effectively conveyed by the actor. In your Director's Journal, write up your ideas in the form of actors' notes.

Themes

The passing of time (in small groups)

a Use quotes from Rosalind's speeches in lines 261–80 to fill in the first column of the table below, which shows how Rosalind understands the passing of time. In the second column, describe the way you experience time moving at different speeds in your own life – perhaps when you are excited, bored and so on.

Speed at which time passes	When? (according to Rosalind)	When? (according to you)
'ambles'		
'trots'		
'gallops'		
'stays it still'		

b Improvise a scenario that depicts one of Rosalind's portrayals of time passing.

c Discuss what insight you gain about Rosalind's feelings at this point in the play by considering her understanding of time.

---

saucy lackey cheeky or impertinent servant

under that habit in that disguise

play the knave pretend to be a boy, or put him down

swift foot of Time (the figure of Time was shown in engravings and proverbs as having wings on his feet)

ambles moves at a slow, easy pace

withal with

hard violently

between … solemnised during her betrothal (when she is engaged but not yet married)

sennight week (seven nights)

lacks is ignorant of

wasteful causing him to waste away

heavy tedious penury sad, painful poverty

softly leisurely

skirts outskirts, fringes

cony rabbit

kindled born

removed remote (from court)

ROSALIND I will speak to him like a saucy lackey, and under that habit 250
play the knave with him. [*To Orlando*] Do you hear, forester?

ORLANDO Very well. What would you?

ROSALIND I pray you, what is't o'clock?

ORLANDO You should ask me what time o'day: there's no clock in the
forest. 255

ROSALIND Then there is no true lover in the forest, else sighing every
minute and groaning every hour would detect the lazy foot of Time
as well as a clock.

ORLANDO And why not the swift foot of Time? Had not that been as
proper? 260

ROSALIND By no means, sir. Time travels in diverse paces with diverse
persons. I'll tell you who Time ambles withal, who Time trots
withal, who Time gallops withal, and who he stands still withal.

ORLANDO I prithee, who doth he trot withal?

ROSALIND Marry, he trots hard with a young maid between the con- 265
tract of her marriage and the day it is solemnised. If the interim be
but a sennight, Time's pace is so hard that it seems the length of
seven year.

ORLANDO Who ambles Time withal?

ROSALIND With a priest that lacks Latin, and a rich man that hath not 270
the gout; for the one sleeps easily because he cannot study, and the
other lives merrily because he feels no pain; the one lacking the
burden of lean and wasteful learning, the other knowing no burden
of heavy tedious penury. These Time ambles withal.

ORLANDO Who doth he gallop withal? 275

ROSALIND With a thief to the gallows; for though he go as softly as foot
can fall, he thinks himself too soon there.

ORLANDO Who stays it still withal?

ROSALIND With lawyers in the vacation; for they sleep between term
and term, and then they perceive not how Time moves. 280

ORLANDO Where dwell you, pretty youth?

ROSALIND With this shepherdess, my sister, here in the skirts of the
forest, like fringe upon a petticoat.

ORLANDO Are you native of this place?

ROSALIND As the cony that you see dwell where she is kindled. 285

ORLANDO Your accent is something finer than you could purchase in so
removed a dwelling.

Rosalind says she was taught to speak by a well-educated uncle who also taught her the folly of love. She accuses Orlando of not looking like a man in love.

1 The signs of love

Rosalind lists eight signs by which a man in love can be recognised. All are the marks of someone who does not give a thought to their appearance ('careless desolation').

a Write out, in your own words, the eight signs given in lines 312–18.

b Shakespeare gave another eight-item list of the marks of a lover in *The Two Gentlemen of Verona* (Act 2 Scene 1, lines 17–22):

to wreathe your arms like a malcontent; to relish a love-song like a robin-redbreast; to walk alone like one that had the pestilence; to sigh like a schoolboy that had lost his ABC; to weep like a young wench that had buried her grandam; to fast like one that takes diet; to watch like one that fears robbing; to speak puling like a beggar at Hallowmas.

Compare Shakespeare's list in lines 312–18 with the eight items from *The Two Gentlemen of Verona*.

c Make up your own list of eight items by which someone in love can be recognised. Try to use **similes** (comparisons using 'like' or 'as' – see p. 182).

2 Dramatic irony (in threes)

We, the audience, know what Rosalind knows, and a special relationship develops between us. This is an example of **dramatic irony**, where the audience knows more about what is happening on stage than other characters do, because we have access to all of the characters' experiences and perspectives.

a How is it best to play Rosalind's part in this situation? Cast yourselves as Rosalind, Orlando and an observer (representing the audience). Read through lines 251–357, with the person representing the audience speaking their thoughts out loud at suitable points.

b Discuss how to most effectively convey the dramatic irony of this episode, and work out how to find and exploit the potential humour of Orlando's ignorance and Rosalind's more knowing attitude. Take it in turns to act a few lines from the scene, putting some of your ideas into practice.

inland city
courtship courtly manners or wooing
touched infected
taxed accused

monstrous absurd

physic medicine, advice

elegies love poems
fancy-monger trader in love
quotidian fever that recurs every day

marks symptoms
cage of rushes weak prison

blue (with dark circles from grief)
unquestionable grumpy

your having … revenue your beard is as small as a younger brother's income

demonstrating exhibiting
careless uncared for
point-device … accoutrements neat and precise in your dress

still give … consciences always lie about their feelings
sooth truth
admired held up as an object for wonder

ROSALIND I have been told so of many; but indeed an old religious uncle of mine taught me to speak, who was in his youth an inland man, one that knew courtship too well, for there he fell in love. I have heard him read many lectures against it, and I thank God I am not a woman to be touched with so many giddy offences as he hath generally taxed their whole sex withal. 290

ORLANDO Can you remember any of the principal evils that he laid to the charge of women? 295

ROSALIND There were none principal; they were all like one another as halfpence are, every one fault seeming monstrous till his fellow-fault came to match it.

ORLANDO I prithee recount some of them.

ROSALIND No. I will not cast away my physic but on those that are sick. There is a man haunts the forest that abuses our young plants with carving 'Rosalind' on their barks; hangs odes upon hawthorns and elegies on brambles; all, forsooth, defying the name of Rosalind. If I could meet that fancy-monger, I would give him some good counsel, for he seems to have the quotidian of love upon him. 300 305

ORLANDO I am he that is so love-shaked. I pray you tell me your remedy.

ROSALIND There is none of my uncle's marks upon you. He taught me how to know a man in love, in which cage of rushes I am sure you are not prisoner. 310

ORLANDO What were his marks?

ROSALIND A lean cheek, which you have not; a blue eye and sunken, which you have not; an unquestionable spirit, which you have not; a beard neglected, which you have not – but I pardon you for that, for, simply, your having in beard is a younger brother's revenue. Then your hose should be ungartered, your bonnet unbanded, your sleeve unbuttoned, your shoe untied, and everything about you demonstrating a careless desolation. But you are no such man; you are rather point-device in your accoutrements, as loving yourself than seeming the lover of any other. 315 320

ORLANDO Fair youth, I would I could make thee believe I love.

ROSALIND Me believe it? You may as soon make her that you love believe it, which I warrant she is apter to do than to confess she does. That is one of the points in the which women still give the lie to their consciences. But, in good sooth, are you he that hangs the verses on the trees wherein Rosalind is so admired? 325

Rosalind tells how, as Ganymede, she once cured a lover by pretending to be his love and behaving capriciously. This drove the lover insane, and he became a monk. Orlando agrees to follow her cure.

1 The cure for madness (in pairs)

In Elizabethan times, mentally ill people were sometimes thought to be possessed by devils. They were cruelly locked in a dark room and whipped to drive out the evil spirits. Rosalind says 'Love is merely a madness', although she points out that even the people who whip the supposedly mad are themselves susceptible to the common insanity of falling in love. Shakespeare often made comparisons between lunatics and lovers, as in *A Midsummer Night's Dream*:

Love and madness
The lunatic, the lover, and the poet
Are of imagination all compact [composed].
One sees more devils than vast hell can hold,
That is the madman. The lover, all as frantic,
Sees Helen's beauty in a brow of Egypt

(Act 5 Scene 1, lines 7–17)

* Do you agree that love is a kind of madness? Discuss this proposition with your partner, then each prepare an argument either for or against it. To support your case, you should collect examples of people's behaviour when they are in love – think about historical figures as well as modern ones, and also consider how people you know have acted when they have been in love. Stage a debate with your partner and try to decide which argument is the most convincing.

2 Three staging decisions (in threes)

a At line 349 Orlando refuses to undergo a cure for love, but in line 352 he agrees. How does Rosalind get him to change his mind by how she speaks and behaves at lines 350–1? Practise different ways of saying these lines.

b In one production, Orlando gave Rosalind a hearty slap on the back at line 355, making her line 356 a kind of rebuke. Discuss how you would stage the final few lines of this scene.

c The 'Come, sister' in line 356 is addressed to Celia, who has not spoken a word throughout Rosalind's conversation with Orlando. What has she been doing? Does she approve of Rosalind's approach? Discuss how Celia reacts as she watches Rosalind's play-acting, and how she finally leaves the stage. Take parts as Celia, Rosalind and Orlando and try acting out some of your ideas to see what works best.

dark-house and a whip (supposed treatments for insanity in Shakespeare's time)

profess recommend

counsel advice

moonish changeable (like the moon)

effeminate gentle

fantastical capricious, temperamental

apish full of tricks, foolish

for every passion … anything showing all passions, but feeling none sincerely

cattle of this colour the same kind of creatures

forswear him break my promises to him

drave drove

nook, merely monastic remote place, as a monk

take upon me undertake

liver (this organ was thought to be the origin of love and violent passion)

faith truth, obligation

ORLANDO	I swear to thee, youth, by the white hand of Rosalind, I am that he, that unfortunate he.
ROSALIND	But are you so much in love as your rhymes speak?
ORLANDO	Neither rhyme nor reason can express how much.
ROSALIND	Love is merely a madness and, I tell you, deserves as well a dark-house and a whip as madmen do; and the reason why they are not so punished and cured is that the lunacy is so ordinary that the the whippers are in love too. Yet I profess curing it by counsel.
ORLANDO	Did you ever cure any so?
ROSALIND	Yes, one, and in this manner. He was to imagine me his love, his mistress, and I set him every day to woo me. At which time would I, being but a moonish youth, grieve, be effeminate, change-able, longing and liking, proud, fantastical, apish, shallow, incon-stant, full of tears, full of smiles; for every passion something, and for no passion truly anything, as boys and women are, for the most part, cattle of this colour; would now like him, now loathe him; then entertain him, then forswear him; now weep for him, then spit at him; that I drave my suitor from his mad humour of love to a living humour of madness, which was to forswear the full stream of the world and to live in a nook, merely monastic. And thus I cured him, and this way will I take upon me to wash your liver as clean as a sound sheep's heart, that there shall not be one spot of love in't.
ORLANDO	I would not be cured, youth.
ROSALIND	I would cure you if you would but call me Rosalind and come every day to my cot and woo me.
ORLANDO	Now, by the faith of my love, I will. Tell me where it is.
ROSALIND	Go with me to it and I'll show it you; and by the way you shall tell me where in the forest you live. Will you go?
ORLANDO	With all my heart, good youth.
ROSALIND	Nay, you must call me 'Rosalind'. – Come, sister, will you go?

Exeunt

Touchstone's literary jokes are lost on Audrey, although they amuse Jaques. Touchstone reflects that lovers and poets are both given to deception. He says he intends to marry Audrey.

Characters

Audrey and Touchstone (in small groups)

After the meeting of Rosalind and Orlando in Scene 3, Shakespeare now presents a lampoon (parody) of love.

a What is Audrey like? Many productions present her as simple-minded, dressed in old tattered clothes, speaking in a rustic accent and with her face covered in dirt. What evidence can you gather from the script about her appearance?

b In Shakespeare's time, 'goats' and 'Goths' (lines 5–6) had the same pronunciation. Ovid was a Roman poet (43 BC–AD 17) who was sent into exile among the Goths (an East Germanic people), perhaps because of his erotic poetry and sexual misbehaviour (for Elizabethans, 'capricious' meant goat-like or lustful). What do you think Touchstone is trying to say here? Look for clues in the script that show whether or not Audrey understands his jokes and allusions.

c How would you want Touchstone and Audrey to interact with each other? Is there some tenderness to the comedy here, or does Touchstone ruthlessly exploit Audrey's inferior wit and apparently placid nature?

Stagecraft

Jaques's unheard lines (in threes)

Presumably, Touchstone and Audrey do not hear Jaques's lines – they certainly do not seem to react or respond to them.

- How would you advise the actor playing Jaques to speak these lines? Think about how he relates to the audience at each line.

1 Relationships (in pairs)

a Discuss the couples that have come together in the play so far. How are the romantic relationships similar and different? Who is notably without a partner, and why?

b Draw up a list of the relationships in the play, then discuss the types of love represented in each one.

c Write a few notes on each relationship and predict how it will end.

Come apace hurry up
simple feature honest appearance

warrant protect

ill-inhabited miserably housed

seconded with supported by
forward clever
it strikes … little room
it is like paying a huge bill
for poor accommodation
(very disappointing)
poetical knowing about literature
(or about sex)
honest truthful or not sexually
experienced
feigning deceitful, imaginative
feign (line 14) pretend or desire
feign (line 16) lie

hard-favoured ugly

material practical

foul ugly, plain

place town square
couple marry

Act 3 Scene 4
The Forest of Arden

Enter TOUCHSTONE, AUDREY, *with* JAQUES *behind, watching them*

TOUCHSTONE Come apace, good Audrey; I will fetch up your goats, Audrey. And how, Audrey, am I the man yet? Doth my simple feature content you?

AUDREY Your features, Lord warrant us – what features?

TOUCHSTONE I am here with thee and thy goats as the most capricious   5
poet honest Ovid was among the Goths.

JAQUES O knowledge ill-inhabited, worse than Jove in a thatched house!

TOUCHSTONE When a man's verses cannot be understood, nor a man's good wit seconded with the forward child, understanding, it strikes a man more dead than a great reckoning in a little room. Truly, I   10
would the gods had made thee poetical.

AUDREY I do not know what 'poetical' is. Is it honest in deed and word? Is it a true thing?

TOUCHSTONE No, truly; for the truest poetry is the most feigning, and lovers are given to poetry; and what they swear in poetry may it be   15
said, as lovers, they do feign.

AUDREY Do you wish then that the gods had made me poetical?

TOUCHSTONE I do, truly; for thou swear'st to me thou art honest. Now if thou wert a poet, I might have some hope thou didst feign.

AUDREY Would you not have me honest?   20

TOUCHSTONE No, truly, unless thou wert hard-favoured: for honesty coupled to beauty is to have honey a sauce to sugar.

JAQUES A material fool.

AUDREY Well, I am not fair, and therefore I pray the gods make me honest.   25

TOUCHSTONE Truly, and to cast away honesty upon a foul slut were to put good meat into an unclean dish.

AUDREY I am not a slut, though I thank the gods I am foul.

TOUCHSTONE Well, praised be the gods for thy foulness: sluttishness may come hereafter. But be it as it may be, I will marry thee, and to   30
that end I have been with Sir Oliver Martext, the vicar of the next village, who hath promised to meet me in this place of the forest and to couple us.

JAQUES I would fain see this meeting.

Touchstone implies that all women are unfaithful, but says it is better to be a married man than a bachelor. Jaques warns against Sir Oliver, but Touchstone sees advantages in a bad priest.

1 Unfaithful wives and shamed husbands (in pairs)

Although it was a great insult for a man to be called a cuckold, Touchstone here jokes about it in an outrageous, comic way.

a What exactly is Touchstone saying? Find the points in lines 36–47 opposite where Touchstone makes the following statements:

- Many husbands are cuckolded but do not know it.
- All women are inevitably unfaithful.
- Rich men and poor men alike are cuckolded.
- Even a cuckold is better than a bachelor, just as a fortified city is better than a village.

b What is Audrey thinking and doing on stage during this speech? Does she understand what Touchstone is saying? Work out some suitable stage business for Touchstone's monologue and Audrey's reaction, and take parts to rehearse it.

▼ Do you think Audrey is listening to Touchstone as he talks on and on? Or is she distracted by something else entirely, as she appears to be in this image?

fearful anxious

stagger waver, hesitate

temple church

assembly congregation

horn-beasts forest stags or cuckolds

necessary inevitable

the dowry of brought about by

rascal an inferior deer or an impotent man

want lack

dispatch marry

on gift of any man (Touchstone does not want 'second-hand goods')

Monsieur What-Ye-Call't (Touchstone refers to Monsieur Jaques (jakes), which was the Elizabethan word for lavatory)

God'ild you God reward you

toy in hand trifle (Audrey? marriage?)

be covered put your hat on

bow curb yoke (restraints)

bells (worn by a falcon so it could be found and recaptured)

wainscot wood panelling

shrunk panel detached board

AUDREY   Well, the gods give us joy.   35

TOUCHSTONE   Amen. A man may, if he were of a fearful heart, stagger
in this attempt; for here we have no temple but the wood, no
assembly but horn-beasts. But what though? Courage! As horns are
odious, they are necessary. It is said, 'Many a man knows no end of   40
his goods.' Right: many a man has good horns and knows no end of
them. Well, that is the dowry of his wife, 'tis none of his own
getting. Horns? Even so. Poor men alone? No, no: the noblest deer
hath them as huge as the rascal. Is the single man therefore blessed?
No: as a walled town is more worthier than a village, so is the
forehead of a married man more honourable than the bare brow of   45
a bachelor. And, by how much defence is better than no skill, by so
much is a horn more precious than to want.

Enter SIR OLIVER MARTEXT

Here comes Sir Oliver. – Sir Oliver Martext, you are well met. Will
you dispatch us here under this tree, or shall we go with you to your
chapel?   50

MARTEXT   Is there none here to give the woman?

TOUCHSTONE   I will not take her on gift of any man.

MARTEXT   Truly, she must be given, or the marriage is not lawful.

JAQUES   [*Coming forward*] Proceed, proceed: I'll give her.

TOUCHSTONE   Good-even, good Monsieur What-Ye-Call't. How do   55
you, sir? You are very well met. God'ild you for your last company;
I am very glad to see you. Even a toy in hand here, sir.

[*Jaques removes his hat*]

Nay, pray be covered.

JAQUES   Will you be married, Motley?

TOUCHSTONE   As the ox hath his bow, sir, the horse his curb, and the   60
falcon her bells, so man hath his desires, and as pigeons bill, so
wedlock would be nibbling.

JAQUES   And will you, being a man of your breeding, be married under
a bush like a beggar? Get you to church, and have a good priest that
can tell you what marriage is. This fellow will but join you together   65
as they join wainscot, then one of you will prove a shrunk panel and,
like green timber, warp, warp.

TOUCHSTONE   I am not in the mind; but I were better to be married of
him than of another, for he is not like to marry me well and, not
being well married, it will be a good excuse for me hereafter to leave   70
my wife.

Touchstone's song mocks Sir Oliver, who claims he is not put off by such foolery. In Scene 5, Celia makes fun of Rosalind's distress over Orlando's non-appearance.

1 Reverse psychology (in pairs)

Celia mocks Rosalind's lovesick moodiness by exaggeratedly agreeing with whatever she says, even comparing Orlando with Judas – the disciple who, in the Bible, betrayed Jesus with a kiss.

a Take parts as Celia and Rosalind and speak lines 1–37. As you read through the lines a second time, stand a metre apart: whenever Rosalind and Celia seem to agree, take a step towards each other; when they disagree, take a step backwards. Which character seems to take the most steps forwards? Which character seems to take the most steps away from the other?

b What are Celia's strategies for dealing with Rosalind's mood swings? Do you think Rosalind is aware that she is being teased or indulged, or is she too absorbed in her own concerns to notice? Write notes in your Director's Journal advising the actors on how the two characters should interact with each other here.

2 Rosalind drops her disguise (in pairs)

In earlier scenes, Rosalind mocked the foolishness of love. However, here she seems to drop her disguise as Ganymede and give way to her feelings. What is the significance of Rosalind throwing off her disguise at this point in the play?

a In role as Celia, both you and your partner write a diary entry for that day. The writing should describe your response to seeing Rosalind behave as she has. Is she really revealing her true feelings or is she just performing another role?

b Exchange diary entries with your partner. In role as Rosalind, read through the entry and make notes on any parts that you feel are understanding, unfair, hurtful and so on. What do you remember thinking and feeling at the time? Do you have any criticisms of how Celia treated you? Take turns to act the part of Rosalind and confront Celia about the diary entry.

Stagecraft

Rosalind and Celia's cottage (in small groups)

Imagine you are set designers. Make a list of any items you could use to give the impression of a cottage in the forest, including props for the actors to use. Note down your ideas on how to use lighting, music, sounds – even smells! – to enhance your creation.

in bawdry immorally

brave fine, good

Wind go quickly

fantastical knave crazy villain
flout me out of my calling trick me out of my job

grace sense of propriety
become suit

dissembling deceiving
Something somewhat
Judas (the man who betrayed Jesus, who was sometimes depicted with red hair)

sanctity sacredness, purity
holy bread bread blessed in church
cast lips lips as cold as a statue's
Diana (the goddess of chastity in ancient Roman mythology)

JAQUES   Go thou with me and let me counsel thee.

TOUCHSTONE   Come, sweet Audrey, we must be married or we must
live in bawdry. – Farewell, good Master Oliver. Not

[*Sings*]   O sweet Oliver,   75

O brave Oliver,

Leave me not behind thee;

but [*Sings*]

Wind away,

Begone, I say,   80

I will not to wedding with thee.

MARTEXT   [*Aside*] 'Tis no matter; ne'er a fantastical knave of them all
shall flout me out of my calling.

Exeunt

Act 3 Scene 5
Outside the cottage of Rosalind and Celia

Enter ROSALIND *(disguised as* GANYMEDE*) and* CELIA *(disguised as* ALIENA*)*

ROSALIND   Never talk to me; I will weep.

CELIA   Do, I prithee; but yet have the grace to consider that tears do not
become a man.

ROSALIND   But have I not cause to weep?

CELIA   As good cause as one would desire: therefore weep.   5

ROSALIND   His very hair is of the dissembling colour.

CELIA   Something browner than Judas's: marry, his kisses are Judas's
own children.

ROSALIND   I'faith, his hair is of a good colour.

CELIA   An excellent colour: your chestnut was ever the only colour.   10

ROSALIND   And his kissing is as full of sanctity as the touch of holy
bread.

CELIA   He hath bought a pair of cast lips of Diana. A nun of winter's
sisterhood kisses not more religiously: the very ice of chastity is in
them.   15

ROSALIND   But why did he swear he would come this morning and
comes not?

Celia doubts whether Orlando is truly in love. Rosalind recounts how she met her father, Duke Senior, who failed to recognise her. Corin invites them to watch Silvius attempting to woo Phoebe.

Language in the play

Jousting

Renaissance tournaments included the aristocratic sport of jousting, where knights on horseback tried to hit one another with long lances (wooden poles). Tournaments were popular, and a knight would often compete for fame, and a lady's honour and attention.

a Celia uses imagery that relates to jousting in lines 33–7, but what does she suggest when using this metaphor? What does the metaphor itself imply? And is she being serious or ironic? Celia's teasing of Rosalind contains many opportunities for humour, so devise actions that would suit her lines here.

b What other imagery would you use to describe someone head over heels in love and eager to impress their beloved? Write a comic example like Celia's, as well as a more serious example. Use imagery drawn from the modern world and your own experiences.

1 From prose to poetry (in threes)

There is a shift from prose to poetry at line 38. When Corin enters speaking in verse, Rosalind and Celia switch from prose to verse. The characters use **blank verse**, which consists of unrhymed lines that have alternate stressed and unstressed syllables (see p. 183). Each line has five iambs (feet), each with an unstressed (×) and stressed (/) syllable that sounds like a heartbeat (da DUM, da DUM, da DUM, da DUM, da DUM):

```
×    /  ×   / ×   / ×  / ×   /
```
Who you saw sitting by me on the turf (line 40)

a Take parts and read aloud lines 38–50. Try to hear the rhythmic beat of the blank verse by tapping a beat on the table.

b Why do you think the play changes from prose to verse at line 38? Remember that Celia gives a very unflattering description of Orlando: as hollow as an empty wine glass or nutshell (lines 21–2), and a cheating bartender who adds up the bill wrongly (lines 26–8). In contrast, Corin invites them to 'see a pageant truly played' of rural lovers who could have featured in the common pastoral poetry of the day (see pp. 165–6).

pickpurse pickpocket
verity truthfulness, sincerity
concave hollow
covered goblet empty wine glass

tapster bartender
false reckonings untrue descriptions

brave fine, showy
traverse (when the jouster accidently breaks the spear against the body of his adversary)
puny tilter weak, inexperienced jouster
noble notable
goose simpleton
youth mounts young people get up to

pageant scene
pale complexion of true love (the sighs of lovers were thought to take the blood from the heart)

remove depart

CELIA	Nay, certainly, there is no truth in him.
ROSALIND	Do you think so?
CELIA	Yes, I think he is not a pickpurse nor a horse-stealer but, for his verity in love, I do think him as concave as a covered goblet or a worm-eaten nut.
ROSALIND	Not true in love?
CELIA	Yes, when he is in; but I think he is not in.
ROSALIND	You have heard him swear downright he was.
CELIA	'Was' is not 'is'; besides, the oath of a lover is no stronger than the word of a tapster: they are both the confirmers of false reckonings. He attends here in the forest on the Duke your father.
ROSALIND	I met the Duke yesterday and had much question with him; he asked me of what parentage I was. I told him of as good as he: so he laughed and let me go. But what talk we of fathers when there is such a man as Orlando?
CELIA	O that's a brave man: he writes brave verses, speaks brave words, swears brave oaths, and breaks them bravely, quite traverse, athwart the heart of his lover as a puny tilter that spurs his horse but on one side, breaks his staff like a noble goose. But all's brave that youth mounts and folly guides. – Who comes here?

Enter CORIN

CORIN	Mistress and master, you have oft enquired
	After the shepherd that complained of love
	Who you saw sitting by me on the turf,
	Praising the proud disdainful shepherdess
	That was his mistress.
CELIA	Well, and what of him?
CORIN	If you will see a pageant truly played
	Between the pale complexion of true love
	And the red glow of scorn and proud disdain,
	Go hence a little, and I shall conduct you
	If you will mark it.
ROSALIND	O come, let us remove,
	The sight of lovers feedeth those in love. –
	Bring us to this sight and you shall say
	I'll prove a busy actor in their play.

Exeunt

20

25

30

35

40

45

50

Silvius begs Phoebe to show him some kindness. She mocks the notion that her look might kill him. He warns that she might one day feel the pangs of love.

1 'I'll prove a busy actor' (in small groups)

Rosalind says she will 'prove a busy actor' as she eavesdrops on Silvius and Phoebe.

a Discuss to what extent Rosalind is 'a busy actor' throughout the play. Then compile a list of the different roles Rosalind plays (for example, daughter, traveller, relationship advisor). Discuss how convincingly you think she plays each of these roles.

b Remember that on Shakespeare's stage, Rosalind would have been played by a boy actor. Discuss the particular challenges faced by the actor. Do you think Rosalind is more or less comfortable in role as Ganymede than she is as herself? Why might this be?

2 If looks could kill (in pairs)

Elizabethans thought that the eyes were the 'windows to the soul', and that rejected lovers were wounded by the disdainful glances of the one they loved. Phoebe points out how ridiculous this idea is in lines 10–27.

- Take turns to read through these lines. Identify two moments of comedy that you would want to draw attention to in your own production of the play, and invent some stage business that would effectively emphasise it.

Themes

Love and passion

a Search in the library or on the Internet for the following two poems: Christopher Marlowe's 'The Passionate Shepherd to his Love' (1599) and Sir Walter Raleigh's reply, 'The Nymph's Reply to the Shepherd' (1600). One is an example of the pastoral tradition in literature, and the other is a parody of this tradition. (See pp. 165–6 for more information about these traditions).

b Consider how closely these poems evoke the behaviour of Silvius and Phoebe. Choose one of the poems and rewrite parts of it according to the perspective of either Silvius or Phoebe.

Falls drops
But first begs without begging
dies and lives gets his living (as an executioner)
bloody drops chopping people's heads off

fly thee for run from you because

'Tis pretty it's a nice idea
sure certainly
coward gates eyelids

counterfeit pretend
swoon faint

rush reed, straw
cicatrice scar-like mark
capable impressure visible impression or hollow darted shot

fresh cheek new face
power of fancy force of love
love's keen arrows Cupid's sharp darts

Act 3 Scene 6
The Forest of Arden

Enter SILVIUS *and* PHOEBE

SILVIUS | Sweet Phoebe, do not scorn me, do not, Phoebe.
Say that you love me not, but say not so
In bitterness. The common executioner,
Whose heart th'accustomed sight of death makes hard,
Falls not the axe upon the humbled neck   5
But first begs pardon. Will you sterner be
Than he that dies and lives by bloody drops?

Enter ROSALIND [*as* GANYMEDE], CELIA [*as* ALIENA],
and CORIN[*; they stand aside*]

PHOEBE | I would not be thy executioner;
I fly thee for I would not injure thee.
Thou tell'st me there is murder in mine eye,   10
'Tis pretty, sure, and very probable
That eyes, that are the frail'st and softest things,
Who shut their coward gates on atomies,
Should be called tyrants, butchers, murderers!
Now I do frown on thee with all my heart;   15
And if mine eyes can wound, now let them kill thee.
Now counterfeit to swoon, why, now fall down;
Or, if thou canst not, O for shame, for shame,
Lie not to say mine eyes are murderers.
Now show the wound mine eye hath made in thee.   20
Scratch thee but with a pin, and there remains
Some scar of it; lean upon a rush,
The cicatrice and capable impressure
Thy palm some moment keeps. But now mine eyes,
Which I have darted at thee, hurt thee not,   25
Nor I am sure there is no force in eyes
That can do hurt.

SILVIUS | O dear Phoebe,
If ever – as that 'ever' may be near –
You meet in some fresh cheek the power of fancy,
Then shall you know the wounds invisible   30
That love's keen arrows make.

Rosalind rebukes Phoebe for having no pity for Silvius, and criticises her looks and marriage prospects. Rosalind also censures Silvius for loving Phoebe. But Phoebe falls in love with the disguised Rosalind.

1 'Sell when you can' (in pairs)

Rosalind gives Phoebe a dose of her own medicine, pouring scorn on her upbringing and her beauty, and urging her to marry while she has the chance.

a Take turns to speak Rosalind's lines 35–63, trying to bring out the humour of her words and to make the insults strike home. The following explanations should help you to better understand what Rosalind says.

- **Line 39** 'Than without candle … bed' = 'your looks wouldn't exactly light up a room').
- **Lines 42–3** 'I see no more … sale-work' = 'you look like common, cheap goods'.
- **Lines 46–7** 'inky brows … eyeballs' – in Shakespeare's time, dark hair and features were not considered beautiful.
- **Line 54** ''Tis not her glass … her' = 'she thinks she's beautiful, not because of what she sees in the mirror but because you tell her she is'.
- **Line 60** 'Sell when you can … markets' – this is Rosalind's most cutting insult, so think about how to deliver it as a climactic line (it is followed by three less harsh lines of advice).

b Discuss why you think Rosalind launches into this long tirade against a complete stranger. Make predictions about how this episode might affect the future plot of the play.

Who might be your mother who do you think you are

exult rejoice, triumph
all at once and all the rest
wretched sad lover (Silvius)
What even

sale-work ready-made goods that are not of the highest quality
Od's may God save
tangle my eyes ensnare me with beauty
after for
bugle glassy black

foggy South the south wind
wind and rain sighs and tears
properer more handsome

out of because of
proper beautiful
lineaments features

fasting (don't eat anything while you pray)

Cry beg
Foul … scoffer ugliness is made worse by scorn
take her to thee take charge of her
chide a year together insult me for a year without interruption

PHOEBE   But till that time
Come not thou near me; and, when that time comes,
Afflict me with thy mocks, pity me not,
As till that time I shall not pity thee.

ROSALIND   [*Coming forward*] And why, I pray you? Who might be your mother   35
That you insult, exult, and all at once
Over the wretched? What though you have no beauty,
As, by my faith, I see no more in you
Than without candle may go dark to bed,
Must you be therefore proud and pitiless?   40
Why, what means this? Why do you look on me?
I see no more in you than in the ordinary
Of Nature's sale-work – Od's my little life,
I think she means to tangle my eyes too. –
No, faith, proud mistress, hope not after it;   45
'Tis not your inky brows, your black silk hair,
Your bugle eyeballs, nor your cheek of cream
That can entame my spirits to your worship. –
You, foolish shepherd, wherefore do you follow her
Like foggy South, puffing with wind and rain?   50
You are a thousand times a properer man
Than she a woman. 'Tis such fools as you
That makes the world full of ill-favoured children.
'Tis not her glass but you that flatters her,
And out of you she sees herself more proper   55
Than any of her lineaments can show her. –
But, mistress, know yourself. Down on your knees,
                          [*Phoebe kneels to Rosalind*]
And thank heaven, fasting, for a good man's love;
For I must tell you friendly in your ear,
Sell when you can: you are not for all markets.   60
Cry the man mercy, love him, take his offer,
Foul is most foul, being foul to be a scoffer. –
So take her to thee, shepherd; fare you well.

PHOEBE   Sweet youth, I pray you chide a year together;
I had rather hear you chide than this man woo.   65

Rosalind rejects Phoebe and tells her to be kinder to Silvius. Phoebe acknowledges that she loves Ganymede and proposes to use Silvius as a go-between. Silvius is grateful for anything from Phoebe.

1 To whom? (in pairs)

Rosalind has indeed proved 'a busy actor' in this episode with Silvius and Phoebe. Her final two speeches are especially 'busy', as they address both Phoebe and Silvius in turn. Her comments might also be addressed to the audience or muttered under her breath.

- As one person speaks Rosalind's part in lines 66–79, the other says to whom they think each line is addressed. Afterwards, discuss what might be achieved by addressing the audience directly.

Themes

Love at first sight (in small groups)

Lines 80–1 are probably a reference to the playwright Christopher Marlowe, who was killed in a tavern quarrel in 1593. One of his poems contained the line: 'Who ever loved that loved not at first sight?' Phoebe calls Marlowe 'Dead shepherd', and declares that she now finds his saying to be very true indeed.

Discuss the idea of love at first sight:

- Is there such a thing as love at first sight? Do you not have to know someone in order to really fall in love with them?
- Do you think you can you learn to love someone even when it is not love at first sight? Is it perhaps better to get to know someone as a friend before you begin a romantic relationship with them?
- Where does love come into a marriage that is (a) arranged by your family or (b) where the romance seems to have gone? How is new love different from seasoned love, and is one more valuable than the other?

Write about it

Phoebe/Silvius (in pairs)

Rosalind's intervention in the lovers' quarrel has an unexpected outcome: Phoebe falls in love with her, thinking her to be Ganymede – an attractive and forthright boy.

- In role as Phoebe, write out a diary entry. Describe your feelings about meeting this exciting new 'man'. What exactly has attracted you to him, and how do you compare him to Silvius?

---

sauce sharply taunt, rebuke

vows made in wine promises made when intoxicated

tuft of olives clump of olive trees
hard by nearby
ply her hard woo her vigorously

abused in sight deceived by what he sees

saw proverb, motto
might power, virtue

sorrow (line 85) sadness
sorrow (line 86) cry

extermined destroyed
neighbourly friendly

covetousness to desire wrongly

erst was irksome used to be irritating

glean the broken ears gather the remaining ears of corn
Loose set free
scattered random

ROSALIND	He's fallen in love with your foulness – [*To Silvius*] and she'll fall in love with my anger. If it be so, as fast as she answers thee with frowning looks, I'll sauce her with bitter words. – Why look you so upon me?
PHOEBE	For no ill will I bear you.

70

ROSALIND	I pray you do not fall in love with me

For I am falser than vows made in wine;
Besides, I like you not. – [*To Silvius*] If you will know my house,
'Tis at the tuft of olives, here hard by. –
Will you go, sister? – Shepherd, ply her hard. –

75

Come, sister. – Shepherdess, look on him better
And be not proud, though all the world could see,
None could be so abused in sight as he. –
Come, to our flock.   *Exeunt Rosalind, Celia, Corin*

PHOEBE	Dead shepherd, now I find thy saw of might:

80

'Who ever loved that loved not at first sight?'

SILVIUS	Sweet Phoebe, –
PHOEBE	Ha, what say'st thou, Silvius?
SILVIUS	Sweet Phoebe, pity me.
PHOEBE	Why I am sorry for thee, gentle Silvius.
SILVIUS	Wherever sorrow is, relief would be.

85

If you do sorrow at my grief in love,
By giving love your sorrow and my grief
Were both extermined.

PHOEBE	Thou hast my love: is not that neighbourly?
SILVIUS	I would have you.
PHOEBE	Why, that were covetousness.

90

Silvius, the time was that I hated thee,
And yet it is not that I bear thee love;
But since that thou canst talk of love so well,
Thy company, which erst was irksome to me,
I will endure – and I'll employ thee too.

95

But do not look for further recompense
Than thine own gladness that thou art employed.

SILVIUS	So holy and so perfect is my love,

And I in such a poverty of grace
That I shall think it a most plenteous crop

100

To glean the broken ears after the man
That the main harvest reaps. Loose now and then
A scattered smile, and that I'll live upon.

Phoebe's detailed description of Ganymede shows how much she loves him. But she denies that she does, and says she will write a taunting letter that Silvius will deliver.

Language in the play
Dramatic grammar (whole class)

Read through Phoebe's long speech by yourself as you walk around the room. Remember to use the following rules, as you did in the activity on page 2:

- At each full stop make a full 'about-turn' (180 degrees).
- At each comma, colon, semi-colon or dash make a half turn (90 degrees to your right or left).
- Devise a gesture to make at every question mark (such as stamping your foot or clicking your fingers).

Which words or lines stood out for you during this activity? How might the grammatical structure of the script reflect Phoebe's feelings at this point in the play?

2 Enjoy the language! (in pairs)

Phoebe's speech, which expresses the emotional turmoil that Ganymede has provoked in her, displays many of Shakespeare's characteristic language techniques.

a Use the following tips to help you speak lines 108–34 in a way that brings out the humour of the situation. Take turns to perform the speech to each other, and note down what works well in both readings.

- **Antithesis** A string of oppositions is created through the use of antithesis, where something is said and then contradicted.
- **Monosyllables** A long succession of monosyllables (single-sound words) helps the actor to speak each word sharply and emphatically. Shakespeare gives Phoebe long stretches of language full of monosyllables.
- **Lists** Shakespeare loved to pile up item on item to intensify meaning and dramatic effect. This speech is a long catalogue of how Phoebe has 'marked him / In parcels' (appraised him feature by feature).
- **Repetition** Shakespeare adds subtle repetition of words and phrases – such as 'yet' and 'he'/'his' – to capture Phoebe's confusion and gradual understanding of the situation and her own feelings.

b For each example of the language techniques listed above, write stage directions in your Director's Journal for an actor to follow. Make sure they are detailed enough to give the actor playing Phoebe inspiration about tone of voice, gesture and movement on stage.

erewhile just now

bounds pastures
carlot peasant, countryman

peevish irritating, foolish

complexion face, appearance

not very tall (that is, for a man she is not very tall, although as a woman she is 'more than common tall')
lusty luxuriant

mingled damask (the colour of a red and white rose)

parcels parts, items
gone near / To fall been on the point of falling

had he to do cause had he
black (the opposite of 'fair', which the Elizabethans thought was more beautiful)
answered not again did not retort
Omittance is no quittance not replying doesn't mean I pardon him

straight immediately
matter's contents are
passing short very sharp

PHOEBE	Know'st thou the youth that spoke to me erewhile?
SILVIUS	Not very well; but I have met him oft 105
	And he hath bought the cottage and the bounds
	That the old carlot once was master of.
PHOEBE	Think not I love him, though I ask for him;
	'Tis but a peevish boy – yet he talks well.
	But what care I for words? Yet words do well 110
	When he that speaks them pleases those that hear.
	It is a pretty youth – not very pretty;
	But sure he's proud – and yet his pride becomes him;
	He'll make a proper man. The best thing in him
	Is his complexion; and faster than his tongue 115
	Did make offence, his eye did heal it up;
	He is not very tall, yet for his years he's tall;
	His leg is but so-so, and yet 'tis well;
	There was a pretty redness in his lip,
	A little riper and more lusty red 120
	Than that mixed in his cheek: 'twas just the difference
	Betwixt the constant red and mingled damask.
	There be some women, Silvius, had they marked him
	In parcels as I did, would have gone near
	To fall in love with him: but, for my part, 125
	I love him not nor hate him not – and yet
	Have more cause to hate him than to love him.
	For what had he to do to chide at me?
	He said mine eyes were black, and my hair black,
	And, now I am remembered, scorned at me. 130
	I marvel why I answered not again;
	But that's all one. Omittance is no quittance.
	I'll write to him a very taunting letter
	And thou shalt bear it – wilt thou, Silvius?
SILVIUS	Phoebe, with all my heart.
PHOEBE	I'll write it straight: 135
	The matter's in my head and in my heart;
	I will be bitter with him and passing short.
	Go with me, Silvius.

Exeunt

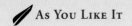

Looking back at Act 3
Activities for groups or individuals

1 Staging Arden

At the beginning of Act 3, the play leaves the court for the last time and establishes itself in Arden. What characteristics of this new setting would you want to represent on stage? Look at the examples of sets from other productions on the page opposite and elsewhere in this edition as you think about your own ideas.

◆ Imagine that you are part of the set design team for a new production of the play. Make initial sketches and/or detailed drawings of how you would like to stage Arden. Then present your plans to the class, and explain why you would want to represent the Forest of Arden in this way.

2 Life in Arden

Critics have had many different opinions about what Arden represents. Here are a few of them:

- Arden is the complete antithesis of the court.
- Arden is a kind of Eden, just as the court is akin to a fallen world.
- The characters undergo a positive transformation when they live in or travel to Arden.
- Arden represents an upside-down world where the usual conventions and hierarchies of social and political life are overturned.
- The people of Arden are all of a kind: rustic, simple and lacking in refined feelings.

◆ Arrange the statements above in order of preference, and be prepared to justify your arrangement to a partner.

◆ Write a short article about Arden for the programme of a new production of *As You Like It*, using one of the above observations as the title. Develop the central idea in the title and refer to characters, events and quotations from the play.

3 Parallel relationships

◆ How do the romantic relationships that emerge in the play – Rosalind/Orlando, Phoebe/Silvius and Audrey/Touchstone – show different forms of 'love' and different kinds of relationships between men and women?

◆ If you were directing the play and had to shorten Act 3 because of time constraints, which couple you would drop from the play? Discuss in groups whether you think any of the couples are an unnecessary distraction from the main plot, and which of them are absolutely crucial to the play's themes. Give reasons for your choices.

4 Time and time again

Time is a recurring theme in Shakespeare's work, both in his plays and his sonnets. The word 'time' is mentioned on eighty occasions in Shakespeare's 154 sonnets.

◆ Find a sonnet by Shakespeare that explores the theme of time. (You might like to choose sonnets 18, 19, 60, 64 or 73). What ideas about time are developed here?

◆ Write two paragraphs about how time is a theme that is developed in *As You Like It*. Remember to refer to the following passages as you do so:

- Adam's reflection on the passing of time in his life from hard-working youth to strong old age (Act 2 Scene 3, lines 38–55)
- Jaques's description of the seven ages of man (Act 2 Scene 7, lines 139–66)
- Rosalind's example of the way times moves at different speeds for different people (Act 3 Scene 3, lines 265–80).

Rosalind says that extremes of both melancholy or merriness are detestable. Jaques claims that his melancholy is more complex than anyone else's. Rosalind mocks his pretentiousness. She ignores Orlando.

1 Melancholic manifestations (in pairs)

Today, the word 'melancholy' is usually used to describe someone who is sad, but in Shakespeare's time it included other meanings: serious, cynical, world-weary, neurotic. Elizabethans used the theory of the four humours to explain people's behaviour, personalities or moods (see p. 132), and 'melancholy' was one of these humours.

a Discuss the difference between Jaques's melancholy and Orlando's melancholy. Would you describe Rosalind as melancholy? If so, how does how her mood differ from Jaques's and Orlando's. Look again at Act 3 Scene 3, as well as the script opposite, and select particular words or phrases that illustrate your interpretation.

b Imagine how a costume designer for a modern production might use costume to portray these different kinds of melancholy. Describe or sketch the costumes and props for each of the characters above.

Language in the play
Blank verse of a melancholic lover (in pairs)

Jaques thinks that Orlando is going to speak to Rosalind (Ganymede) 'in blank verse' (see p. 183), but in fact he speaks to her in prose.

a What is different about Orlando's greeting that makes Jaques think he is speaking verse? What else about Orlando's diction might make Jaques think he will speak in blank verse?

b Imagine that Orlando was going to speak in verse to Rosalind, but Jaques made him self-conscious and he changed his mind. Write out what he might have said to Rosalind if Jaques had not interrupted him. Use rhythms, rhymes, diction and imagery that would be suitable to a lover addressing his mistress.

2 Playing the melancholic

Jaques is perhaps the most famous stage depiction of 'the melancholy man'. Many Elizabethan gentlemen affected his pose: the world-weary cynic who feels that he has seen it all.

• Read lines 26–30 as Rosalind teases Jaques about his melancholic disposition. Then write a paragraph of your own advice to Jaques. Decide whether you will write in the same light-hearted manner as Rosalind or in a more serious style to try to help him deal with his emotions.

in extremity of either either extremely melancholic or joyful

abominable unnatural

modern censure common or ordinary criticism

emulation envy

fantastical imaginative

politic cunning

nice nit-picking

simples ingredients

sundry contemplation of various reflections on

often rumination frequent thinking

humorous fantastic

travel (a pun on 'travail', which means hard work)

Look you make sure you

lisp (an affectation of speech, perhaps acquired abroad)

disable disparage

nativity birthplace

countenance dignity, appearance, person

swam in a gondola floated in a gondola (been abroad and visited Venice)

Act 4 Scene 1
The Forest of Arden

Enter ROSALIND [*as* GANYMEDE], *and* CELIA [*as* ALIENA] *and* JAQUES

JAQUES   I prithee, pretty youth, let me be better acquainted with thee.

ROSALIND   They say you are a melancholy fellow.

JAQUES   I am so: I do love it better than laughing.

ROSALIND   Those that are in extremity of either are abominable
fellows, and betray themselves to every modern censure worse than   5
drunkards.

JAQUES   Why, 'tis good to be sad and say nothing.

ROSALIND   Why then, 'tis good to be a post.

JAQUES   I have neither the scholar's melancholy, which is emulation;
nor the musician's, which is fantastical; nor the courtier's, which is   10
proud; nor the soldier's, which is ambitious; nor the lawyer's, which
is politic; nor the lady's, which is nice; nor the lover's, which is all
these; but it is a melancholy of mine own, compounded of many
simples, extracted from many objects, and indeed the sundry contemplation of my travels, in which my often rumination wraps me   15
in a most humorous sadness.

ROSALIND   A traveller! By my faith, you have great reason to be sad. I
fear you have sold your own lands to see other men's. Then to have
seen much and to have nothing is to have rich eyes and poor hands.

JAQUES   Yes, I have gained my experience.   20

Enter ORLANDO

ROSALIND   And your experience makes you sad. I had rather have a fool
to make me merry than experience to make me sad – and to travel
for it too!

ORLANDO   Good day, and happiness, dear Rosalind.

JAQUES   Nay then, God buy you, and you talk in blank verse!   25

ROSALIND   Farewell, Monsieur Traveller. Look you lisp and wear
strange suits; disable all the benefits of your own country; be out of
love with your nativity, and almost chide God for making you that
countenance you are, or I will scarce think you have swam in a
gondola.   30

[*Exit Jaques*]

Rosalind berates Orlando for his lateness, and doubts whether he is truly in love. She jokes about deceived husbands, then demands that Orlando woo her and teases him about tongue-tied lovers.

1 The wooing scene (in small groups)

Lines 31–176 are often called 'the wooing scene', in which Rosalind tricks Orlando into wooing her. He thinks he is talking to a young man, Ganymede, who has promised to act as Rosalind to cure him of his love. But it really is Rosalind – and she loves the deception!

a Discuss whether you think Orlando really believes that this exercise will cure him of his love for Rosalind. Does he actually think that 'Ganymede' is a man?

b Compile a list of questions to ask Orlando in order to find out what he is thinking. Then take turns to sit in the hot-seat in role as Orlando, and answer the questions that the rest of the group asks.

Language in the play
Many-layered meaning (in pairs)

The script opposite has many opportunities for comic moments because of the different meanings of the words Rosalind uses as she talks with Orlando. Her language is both playful and funny.

a Find the two following examples in the script opposite and note down the different meanings that Rosalind uses. What effect do Rosalind's witty speeches have on Orlando?

- Rosalind says that she would rather be wooed by a snail, but she does not just mean to reprimand Orlando for being late. She refers to ideas of cuckoldry to make a comment on relationships and trust between men and women.
- Rosalind says that a lover should kiss his mistress when he runs out of things to say; and Orlando asks who could be lost for words in front of his mistress. Rosalind's reply in lines 66–7 could mean different things, because for Elizabethans the word 'ranker' had two different meanings (see the glossary).

b Which interpretation of 'ranker' seems most appropriate for this section of the play? Discuss how easy you think it would be for an audience to understand these different meanings. How would you advise the actors to help make the meanings clearer?

clapped him o'th'shoulder grabbed him by the shoulder in order to arrest him

heart-whole unwounded in the heart (not really in love)

tardy late

jointure marriage settlement

are fain … your wives for might expect such behaviour from your wives if you behave like this in love

leer appearance
holiday humour festive mood

very true, real

gravelled stuck (like a grounded ship)
matter small talk
cleanliest shift best thing to do

puts you to entreaty makes you beg
out self-conscious and out of his depth or lost for words
ranker fouler or greater
wit intelligence, attractiveness
suit pleading, wooing

Why, how now, Orlando, where have you been all this while? You a lover? And you serve me such another trick, never come in my sight more.

ORLANDO My fair Rosalind, I come within an hour of my promise.

ROSALIND Break an hour's promise in love? He that will divide a 35
minute into a thousand parts and break but a part of the thousand part of a minute in the affairs of love, it may be said of him that Cupid hath clapped him o'th'shoulder, but I'll warrant him heart-whole.

ORLANDO Pardon me, dear Rosalind. 40

ROSALIND Nay, and you be so tardy, come no more in my sight – I had as lief be wooed of a snail.

ORLANDO Of a snail?

ROSALIND Aye, of a snail; for though he comes slowly, he carries his house on his head; a better jointure, I think, than you make a 45
woman. Besides, he brings his destiny with him.

ORLANDO What's that?

ROSALIND Why, horns; which such as you are fain to be beholden to your wives for. But he comes armed in his fortune and prevents the slander of his wife. 50

ORLANDO Virtue is no horn-maker, and my Rosalind is virtuous.

ROSALIND And I am your Rosalind.

CELIA It pleases him to call you so, but he hath a Rosalind of a better leer than you.

ROSALIND Come, woo me, woo me; for now I am in a holiday humour 55
and like enough to consent. What would you say to me now and I were your very, very Rosalind?

ORLANDO I would kiss before I spoke.

ROSALIND Nay, you were better speak first, and when you were grav-elled for lack of matter you might take occasion to kiss. Very good 60
orators when they are out, they will spit, and for lovers, lacking – God warrant us – matter, the cleanliest shift is to kiss.

ORLANDO How if the kiss be denied?

ROSALIND Then she puts you to entreaty, and there begins new matter.

ORLANDO Who could be out, being before his beloved mistress? 65

ROSALIND Marry, that should you if I were your mistress, or I should think my honesty ranker than my wit.

ORLANDO What, of my suit?

ROSALIND Not out of your apparel, and yet out of your suit. Am not I your Rosalind? 70

Orlando claims that he will die for love. Rosalind lampoons his claim, telling of famous lovers who died – but not for love. She asks Celia to act as priest and marry her to Orlando.

Characters

Teasing Orlando

Rosalind teases Orlando in lines 92–8 by being deliberately tricky in her replies to his questions and requests.

- How would you stage this exchange and what advice would you give to the actors? Would you want them to bring out Orlando's genuine confusion and Rosalind's slippery contrariness or, alternatively, would you highlight both characters' fun and flirtatious bantering? Write notes in your Director's Journal.

Themes

Marriage: 'Give me your hand' (in pairs)

A 'hand-fast' marriage was a serious betrothal contract between a man and a woman. Although the church made it a legal requirement for marriages to be publicly announced in a church by a priest, 'hand-fast' marriages were thought to be legally binding. The couple held hands, vows were exchanged and this 'hand-fast' marriage was solemnised in a church soon afterwards.

- In line 102, Celia says 'I cannot say the words'. Why? Is she laughing too much because she knows that Ganymede is really Rosalind? Is she shocked because Rosalind has basically proposed to Orlando? Or is she horrified that Orlando has just 'married' Ganymede (a man)?

by attorney by getting someone else to die on your behalf

videlicet namely

love-cause love affair

Troilus (in Classical mythology, a Trojan prince who loved the Greek princess Cressida and was killed by Achilles)

patterns archetypes

Leander (in ancient Greek mythology, he loved Hero and swam the Hellespont strait each night to visit her, but drowned in a storm)

though even if

found it was blamed it on

right true

of this mind think like this

coming-on attractive

Fridays and Saturdays (these were days of fasting)

Go to that's enough, stop it

ORLANDO   I take some joy to say you are, because I would be talking of her.

ROSALIND   Well, in her person, I say I will not have you.

ORLANDO   Then, in mine own person, I die.

ROSALIND   No, faith, die by attorney. The poor world is almost six   75
           thousand years old and in all this time there was not any man died
           in his own person, videlicet, in a love-cause. Troilus had his brains
           dashed out with a Grecian club, yet he did what he could to die
           before, and he is one of the patterns of love; Leander, he would have
           lived many a fair year though Hero had turned nun, if it had not   80
           been for a hot midsummer night, for, good youth, he went but forth
           to wash him in the Hellespont and, being taken with the cramp, was
           drowned, and the foolish chroniclers of that age found it was Hero
           of Sestos. But these are all lies: men have died from time to time –
           and worms have eaten them – but not for love.   85

ORLANDO   I would not have my right Rosalind of this mind, for I
           protest her frown might kill me.

ROSALIND   By this hand, it will not kill a fly. But come, now I will be
           your Rosalind in a more coming-on disposition and, ask me what
           you will, I will grant it.   90

ORLANDO   Then love me, Rosalind.

ROSALIND   Yes, faith, will I, Fridays and Saturdays and all.

ORLANDO   And wilt thou have me?

ROSALIND   Aye, and twenty such.

ORLANDO   What sayest thou?   95

ROSALIND   Are you not good?

ORLANDO   I hope so.

ROSALIND   Why then, can one desire too much of a good thing? –
           Come, sister, you shall be the priest and marry us. – Give me your
           hand, Orlando. – What do you say, sister?   100

ORLANDO   Pray thee, marry us.

CELIA   I cannot say the words.

ROSALIND   You must begin: 'Will you, Orlando –'

CELIA   Go to. – Will you, Orlando, have to wife this Rosalind?

ORLANDO   I will.   105

ROSALIND   Aye, but when?

ORLANDO   Why, now, as fast as she can marry us.

ROSALIND   Then you must say, 'I take thee, Rosalind, for wife.'

ORLANDO   I take thee, Rosalind, for wife.

Rosalind jokes at her own forwardness, then comments on how time sours marriages. She warns of her future giddy behaviour and hints that wives and husbands are unfaithful. She criticises Orlando's proposed absence.

Themes

Love through the year (in pairs)

In lines 114–25, what do the different seasons suggest about the behaviour, motivations and desires of men and women? Discuss what Rosalind means here, then create a tableau that represents your interpretation of these lines.

1 Who's in charge? (in pairs)

The wooing scene is comic because of the role reversals that take place on stage. The added irony on Shakespeare's stage was that Rosalind would have been a boy actor playing a woman dressed as a man. Within the play, Rosalind is also a woman taking the lead in wooing the man she wants to marry.

- Try reading through the script opposite (lines 110–49) in two different ways: in one version, Orlando takes the upper hand and drives the conversation; in the other, Rosalind is the dominant force. Which version seems more plausible? When you have tried both interpretations, stage a third one in which you find a balance between the two characters.

Stagecraft

What is Celia doing?

Celia is present throughout the wooing scene, but says very little until Orlando leaves (line 161). What might she be thinking as she watches the encounter between Orlando and Rosalind?

a Compose stage directions for two points in the script opposite, to advise the actor playing Celia on how she can reveal her thoughts. What actions might Celia use, and where might she stand on the stage so that her feelings can be clearly expressed to the audience?

b Sketch an outline of the stage, and mark on it where you would want the characters to stand, sit and move in relation to one another. You might like to draw arrows and annotate your diagram to show what movement occurs at various points. Keep this plan in your Director's Journal.

commission authority, warrant (Rosalind is addressing the 'priest')

a girl goes before the priest a girl who thinks or acts as if she is married before the priest has actually performed the ceremony

possessed married

April (a month of showers – tears and sighs)

May (a month of merry-making – fun and games)

Barbary cock-pigeon fiercely protective male pigeon

against before

new-fangled amused by novelties

Diana … fountain (possibly a reference to a statue of Diana in a fountain in Cheapside in the late sixteenth century)

waywarder more fickle

Make bar, close firmly

casement window

Wit, whither wilt where are your senses? (an Elizabethan catch-phrase used to mean 'stop talking')

check rebuke

wit could wit have excuse could such behaviour have

one cast away one more woman deserted

ROSALIND I might ask you for your commission, but I do take thee, 110
Orlando, for my husband. There's a girl goes before the priest, and
certainly a woman's thought runs before her actions.

ORLANDO So do all thoughts: they are winged.

ROSALIND Now, tell me how long you would have her after you have
possessed her? 115

ORLANDO For ever and a day.

ROSALIND Say a day without the 'ever'. No, no, Orlando: men are April
when they woo, December when they wed; maids are May when
they are maids, but the sky changes when they are wives. I will be
more jealous of thee than a Barbary cock-pigeon over his hen; more 120
clamorous than a parrot against rain, more new-fangled than an ape;
more giddy in my desires than a monkey. I will weep for nothing,
like Diana in the fountain, and I will do that when you are disposed
to be merry. I will laugh like a hyena, and that when thou art
inclined to sleep. 125

ORLANDO But will my Rosalind do so?

ROSALIND By my life, she will do as I do.

ORLANDO O, but she is wise.

ROSALIND Or else she could not have the wit to do this: the wiser, the
waywarder. Make the doors upon a woman's wit, and it will out at 130
the casement; shut that, and 'twill out at the keyhole; stop that,
'twill fly with the smoke out at the chimney.

ORLANDO A man that had a wife with such a wit, he might say, 'Wit,
whither wilt?'

ROSALIND Nay, you might keep that check for it till you met your 135
wife's wit going to your neighbour's bed.

ORLANDO And what wit could wit have to excuse that?

ROSALIND Marry, to say she came to seek you there: you shall never
take her without her answer unless you take her without her tongue.
O, that woman that cannot make her fault her husband's occasion, 140
let her never nurse her child herself for she will breed it like a fool.

ORLANDO For these two hours, Rosalind, I will leave thee.

ROSALIND Alas, dear love, I cannot lack thee two hours.

ORLANDO I must attend the Duke at dinner, by two o'clock I will be
with thee again. 145

ROSALIND Aye, go your ways, go your ways. I knew what you would
prove – my friends told me as much, and I thought no less. That
flattering tongue of yours won me. 'Tis but one cast away, and so
come, Death! Two o'clock is your hour?

Rosalind warns Orlando not to be late. Celia rebukes Rosalind for her criticism of women, but Rosalind declares she is immeasurably deeply in love. Celia remains sceptical.

1 Rosalind's mood changes

How many mood changes can you identify in Rosalind during this scene? Record exactly where the shifts in mood occur, and think of an action or gesture that the actor playing Rosalind could make at these points to illustrate each emotion. In your Director's Journal, write out these stage directions with their relevant line references.

Characters

Is Celia genuinely upset? (in pairs)

In the early scenes of the play, Celia had quite a large speaking role. Now, as Rosalind plays her love scenes with Orlando, Celia has less and less to say. She was silent in Act 3 Scene 6, and here she only gets the chance to act as 'priest' to 'marry' the lovers. At the scene's end, she has only six lines to express her feelings.

a At the end of this episode, is Celia exasperated or does she speak good-humouredly, using a mocking style that conceals genuine affection? What do Celia's comments below tell us about her at this point in the play?

   • Celia criticises Rosalind for what she has said about women by referencing the proverb 'It is the foul bird that defiles its own nest' (only bad women criticise women) in line 164.
   • When Rosalind tells of her deep love, Celia remarks that her love runs out as fast as it runs in (lines 168–9).
   • To Rosalind's desire to find a shady spot to sigh for Orlando, Celia merely says 'And I'll sleep.' (line 176)

b Take parts as Celia and Rosalind, and read through lines 162–76 several times to explore different versions of Celia's feelings (exasperated, joking, genuinely annoyed, and so on). Does Rosalind listen to Celia at all, or is she completely caught up in her own emotions? Use the script to support your interpretation.

c Imagine Celia is sharing her observations of Rosalind's behaviour with a friend, or pouring her heart out to a counsellor. What would she say about the way things are going in the Forest of Arden? Improvise this imaginary conversation in modern English to further explore Celia's thoughts and feelings.

in good earnest seriously
pretty oaths … dangerous lovers' oaths
jot tiniest part
pathetical pitiable, shocking

gross band entire group
censure criticism
religion devotion, faithfulness

try judge

simply misused completely abused
love-prate prattle about love

many fathom deep infinitely, drowned
sounded measured (in fathoms)

bastard of Venus Cupid
begot of thought fathered in sadness or anxiety
spleen passion
abuses deceives

ORLANDO   Aye, sweet Rosalind.   150

ROSALIND   By my troth, and in good earnest, and so God mend me, and
           by all pretty oaths that are not dangerous, if you break one jot of
           your promise or come one minute behind your hour, I will think
           you the most pathetical break-promise, and the most hollow lover,
           and the most unworthy of her you call Rosalind that may be chosen   155
           out of the gross band of the unfaithful. Therefore beware my cen-
           sure, and keep your promise.

ORLANDO   With no less religion than if thou wert indeed my Rosalind.
           So adieu.

ROSALIND   Well, Time is the old justice that examines all such offend-   160
           ers, and let Time try. Adieu.

                                                                  Exit [Orlando]

CELIA   You have simply misused our sex in your love-prate. We must
           have your doublet and hose plucked over your head, and show the
           world what the bird hath done to her own nest.

ROSALIND   O coz, coz, coz, my pretty little coz, that thou didst know   165
           how many fathom deep I am in love! But it cannot be sounded: my
           affection hath an unknown bottom like the Bay of Portugal.

CELIA   Or rather bottomless, that as fast as you pour affection in, it
           runs out.

ROSALIND   No, that same wicked bastard of Venus that was begot of   170
           thought, conceived of spleen, and born of madness, that blind
           rascally boy that abuses everyone's eyes because his own are out, let
           him be judge how deep I am in love. I'll tell thee, Aliena, I cannot
           be out of the sight of Orlando. I'll go find a shadow and sigh till he
           come.   175

CELIA   And I'll sleep.

                                                                        Exeunt

Jaques proposes that the lord who killed the deer be presented in triumph to Duke Senior. The lords' song claims that it is man's destiny to be a cuckold.

1 How would you present the scene?

Act 4 Scene 2 has been played in many different ways:

- as a celebration of hunting, of masculine strength and unity
- as a nightmare, where Celia dreams of Rosalind being hunted out of the forest
- as a reminder of the role reversals that take place in the Forest of Arden (the 'hunters' are in fact poachers who are not authorised to kill the deer)
- as a continuation of the jokes about cuckoldry and marriage that have been linked to references to 'horns' in the play so far.

How would you stage the scene, and what would you want the audience to take away from it? Write programme notes in your Director's Journal to explain your choice, and to give your audience more information about what they are seeing on stage.

▼ Do you think that the production pictured here is presenting the scene in any of the ways described above? If not, what central interpretation do the costumes, postures and expressions of the actors suggest?

Roman conqueror (crowns of olives were given to Romans who won victories)

branch of victory victory wreath

The rest shall bear this burden all men's destiny is to endure being cuckolds; let everyone carry the dead deer; everybody join in the chorus

Take thou … the horn don't disdain to be a cuckold

crest ere thou wast born destiny before you were born

lusty merry, pleasing

laugh to scorn mock, ridicule

Act 4 Scene 2
A glade in the Forest of Arden

Enter JAQUES *and* LORDS, FORESTERS
bearing the antlers and skin of a deer

JAQUES   Which is he that killed the deer?

FIRST LORD   Sir, it was I.

JAQUES   Let's present him to the Duke like a Roman conqueror – and it
would do well to set the deer's horns upon his head for a branch of
victory. – Have you no song, forester, for this purpose?   5

FIRST FORESTER   Yes, sir.

JAQUES   Sing it. 'Tis no matter how it be in tune, so it make noise enough.

Music

Song

LORDS   What shall he have that killed the deer?
His leather skin and horns to wear.   10
Then sing him home,
The rest shall bear this burden:

Take thou no scorn to wear the horn,
It was a crest ere thou wast born;
    Thy father's father wore it,   15
    And thy father bore it;
The horn, the horn, the lusty horn,
Is not a thing to laugh to scorn.

Exeunt

Celia mocks Rosalind's impatience that Orlando is late. Silvius says that Phoebe's letter contains an angry message. Rosalind seems annoyed and criticises Phoebe.

1 Celia's prose and Silvius's verse (in pairs)

At the beginning of this scene, Celia seems tired of Rosalind and bored with her friend's game of love with Orlando. She speaks of going to sleep.

a Think about Celia's tone and mood here. What words convey her attitude, and how would you speak her lines of prose?

b The script changes from prose to verse with Silvius's entrance. Rewrite at least five lines of Silvius's poetry in prose, then read both versions out loud. Discuss what difference it makes to have Silvius speak in either verse or prose.

c In Shakespeare's plays, it is usually the aristocratic characters that speak in verse and the low-status or comic characters who speak in prose. Here, the pattern seems reversed. Discuss why you think this is, and what effect it might have on the audience.

2 Why is Rosalind so critical?

Silvius's 'Pardon me, / I am but as a guiltless messenger', spoken with an air of wide-eyed innocence, often gets a big laugh from the audience. Yet, after reading the letter, Rosalind calls Silvius a fool and launches an attack on Phoebe.

a Write out some of the insults that Rosalind uses in the script opposite. Then, in role as Rosalind, describe in writing what exactly you mean by these insults. Use the glossary on this page to help you.

b As Rosalind, write a confession to explain why you insulted Silvius and Phoebe so harshly, and why you are so critical of the messenger as well as the writer.

Write about it

An insulting letter

Read through lines 12–28, where Rosalind reacts to the contents of the letter. Write the insulting letter that you imagine Phoebe has sent to 'Ganymede'. Think about the following:

- In line 12, Rosalind says that even the personified figure of patience itself would lose its temper with the letter's author.
- In line 13, she says the letter is written to provoke her to violence.
- In line 19, she accuses Silvius of writing the letter because it is so masculine in its insulting content.

---

much not much
warrant you guarantee that

waspish action fierce or spiteful gesture
tenor message

play the swaggerer fight back

phoenix (a mythical bird that was thought to be the only one of its kind; it lived for five or six hundred years in the Arabian desert, and when it died it was reborn out of the flames that destroyed it and rose again from the ashes)
Her love … I do hunt I don't seek her love
device invention
protest vow
extremity of love most foolish kind of lover
leathern coarse, clumsy
freestone-coloured sandy yellow
hussif housewife
invent compose
invention style

Act 4 Scene 3
The Forest of Arden

Enter ROSALIND (*as* GANYMEDE) *and* CELIA [*as* ALIENA]

ROSALIND   How say you now, is it not past two o'clock? And here much
Orlando!

CELIA   I warrant you, with pure love and troubled brain he hath ta'en his
bow and arrows and is gone forth – to sleep. Look who comes here.

Enter SILVIUS [*with a letter*]

SILVIUS   My errand is to you, fair youth.   5
My gentle Phoebe did bid me give you this:
I know not the contents but, as I guess
By the stern brow and waspish action
Which she did use as she was writing of it,
It bears an angry tenor. Pardon me,   10
I am but as a guiltless messenger.

ROSALIND   [*After reading the letter*] Patience herself would startle at
this letter
And play the swaggerer: bear this, bear all.
She says I am not fair, that I lack manners;
She calls me proud, and that she could not love me   15
Were man as rare as phoenix. Od's my will,
Her love is not the hare that I do hunt –
Why writes she so to me? Well, shepherd, well?
This is a letter of your own device.

SILVIUS   No, I protest, I know not the contents;   20
Phoebe did write it.

ROSALIND   Come, come, you are a fool
And turned into the extremity of love.
I saw her hand, she has a leathern hand,
A freestone-coloured hand. (I verily did think
That her old gloves were on, but 'twas her hands.)   25
She has a hussif's hand – but that's no matter.
I say she never did invent this letter:
This is a man's invention and his hand.

SILVIUS   Sure, it is hers.

Rosalind claims that Phoebe's letter is full of insults. But when she reads the letter, it reveals that Phoebe is passionately in love with Ganymede and wants him to send a secret reply by Silvius.

1 Silvius's reaction (in threes)

Rosalind so passionately denounces the insulting content of Phoebe's letter that Silvius wants to read what she has written. However, when Rosalind reads out the letter, it turns out to be quite different from what the listeners expected. Instead of attacking Ganymede, it describes him as a god who has become a man and conquered Phoebe's heart.

a Discuss why you think Rosalind is offended by the letter.

b Take turns to give a dramatic reading of the letter as if you are:

- the lovesick Phoebe
- the irritated and insulted Rosalind
- the confused Silvius.

c What effect does the revelation of the letter's actual content have on Silvius? Take parts and act out lines 30–62 to show Silvius's reactions to Rosalind's irritation and to the letter itself. Look especially at lines 36–7, 42 and 62.

2 Elizabethan language (in pairs)

Imagine that the actor playing Rosalind wants to cut lines 31–5 because they contain an offensive reference, using 'Ethiop' as a negative adjective to describe Phoebe's words. The director wants to keep these lines, and argues that Shakespeare's words are a reflection of his culture and not an indication that he is racist. In role as the actor or director, argue your case with your partner. Would you cut these lines, or change them, if you were directing the play?

Language in the play
New words

Shakespeare loved making up new words by putting two words together with a hyphen or by using a noun as a verb (and vice versa).

a Find examples of both types of linguistic inventions in the script opposite. Then invent some new hyphenated words of your own – for example, alligator-hungry, dragon-scary, and so on.

b In line 38, Rosalind uses Phoebe's name as a verb: 'She Phoebes me' (meaning 'she insults me in her own typical style'). Invent similar phrases using your own name as a verb. What would your name mean and how would it be used?

boisterous bragging, quarrelsome
challengers duellists, opponents
defies challenges
Turk to Christian (traditional enemies)
drop forth give birth to
Ethiop black (see opposite for discussion of how this Elizabethan usage is now considered offensive)

rail thus use such abusive language

thy godhead laid apart having taken up human shape again
Warr'st thou do you make war

vengeance mischief

eyne eyes

mild aspect gentle looks
chid rebuked

seal up thy mind make up your mind, or send a sealed letter
kind natural affection

make earn

ROSALIND	Why, a boisterous and a cruel style, 30
	A style for challengers. Why, she defies me
	Like Turk to Christian. Woman's gentle brain
	Could not drop forth such giant-rude invention,
	Such Ethiop words, blacker in their effect
	Than in their countenance. Will you hear the letter? 35
SILVIUS	So please you, for I never heard it yet,
	Yet heard too much of Phoebe's cruelty.
ROSALIND	She Phoebes me. Mark how the tyrant writes:
	Reads 'Art thou god to shepherd turned,
	That a maiden's heart hath burned?' 40
	Can a woman rail thus?
SILVIUS	Call you this railing?
ROSALIND	*Reads* 'Why, thy godhead laid apart,
	Warr'st thou with a woman's heart?' –
	Did you ever hear such railing? –
	'Whiles the eye of man did woo me, 45
	That could do no vengeance to me.' –
	Meaning me a beast!
	'If the scorn of your bright eyne
	Have power to raise such love in mine,
	Alack, in me what strange effect 50
	Would they work in mild aspect?
	Whiles you chid me, I did love;
	How then might your prayers move?
	He that brings this love to thee
	Little knows this love in me; 55
	And by him seal up thy mind,
	Whether that thy youth and kind
	Will the faithful offer take
	Of me and all that I can make,
	Or else by him my love deny, 60
	And then I'll study how to die.'
SILVIUS	Call you this chiding?
CELIA	Alas, poor shepherd.

Rosalind rebukes Silvius for being made so feeble by love. Oliver recognises Aliena (Celia) and Ganymede (Rosalind) by their descriptions, and brings a bloody handkerchief from Orlando. He begins his story.

1 Dramatic grammar (by yourself)

Read the script opposite to yourself as you walk around the room. Repeat the grammar activity you did on pages 2 and 106, changing direction and making gestures as you walk to mark the punctuation.

- How might the grammatical structure of the script reflect Rosalind's feelings and experiences? What actions or gestures and what tone of voice might an actress use on stage to capture this?
- In your Director's Journal, write detailed stage directions describing how Rosalind might behave on stage and how Silvius might behave in response.

2 'Enter OLIVER' (in pairs)

Oliver, Orlando's wicked brother, was last seen in Act 3 Scene 1. He was being manhandled by Duke Frederick's officers and was then sent off to capture Orlando, dead or alive. Now he appears again, seemingly a changed man. He brings news of Orlando, along with a bloodstained handkerchief.

- Before you read on in the script, discuss your predictions about how the handkerchief became stained. Make a guess about the part the handkerchief will play in the rest of the story.

Language in the play
The language of love at first sight (in small groups)

Although it is more obvious when you watch the play than when you read the script, Oliver and Celia fall in love at first sight.

a Suggest how you would stage lines 70–85 to give the audience the first hint of their mutual attraction. Does Oliver's and Celia's language hold any suggestion that they are immediately smitten, or will you have to rely on stage business to show this?

b When Oliver enters at line 70, there is an abrupt movement from prose to verse. List any other poetic language features (for example, vocabulary, imagery, and so on) that you can find in the script opposite. Discuss what this shift in language might suggest about Oliver and the effect his sudden appearance might have on the women.

---

make thee an instrument use you

false strains deceitful tunes (tricks)

tame snake harmless worm or drudge

purlieus borders

neighbour bottom nearby valley

rank of osiers row of willows

keep guard

an eye … description I can recognise you by what I've been told

bestows himself behaves, appears

ripe marriageable

low short

napkin handkerchief

Within an hour before too long

Chewing the food of thinking about

fancy love

Lo what befell listen to what happened

threw turned, cast

ROSALIND Do you pity him? No, he deserves no pity. – Wilt thou love
such a woman? What, to make thee an instrument and play false
strains upon thee? Not to be endured! Well, go your way to her – for   65
I see love hath made thee a tame snake – and say this to her: that if
she love me, I charge her to love thee; if she will not, I will never
have her, unless thou entreat for her. If you be a true lover, hence,
and not a word; for here comes more company.

Exit Silvius

Enter OLIVER

OLIVER   Good morrow, fair ones. Pray you, if you know   70
              Where in the purlieus of this forest stands
              A sheepcote fenced about with olive-trees.
CELIA   West of this place, down in the neighbour bottom;
              The rank of osiers by the murmuring stream,
              Left on your right hand, brings you to the place.   75
              But at this hour the house doth keep itself:
              There's none within.
OLIVER   If that an eye may profit by a tongue,
              Then should I know you by description:
              Such garments, and such years. 'The boy is fair,   80
              Of female favour, and bestows himself
              Like a ripe sister; the woman low
              And browner than her brother.' Are not you
              The owners of the house I did enquire for?
CELIA   It is no boast, being asked, to say we are.   85
OLIVER   Orlando doth commend him to you both,
              And to that youth he calls his Rosalind
              He sends this bloody napkin. Are you he?
ROSALIND   I am. What must we understand by this?
OLIVER   Some of my shame, if you will know of me   90
              What man I am, and how, and why, and where
              This handkerchief was stained.
CELIA   I pray you tell it.
OLIVER   When last the young Orlando parted from you,
              He left a promise to return again
              Within an hour and, pacing through the forest,   95
              Chewing the food of sweet and bitter fancy,
              Lo what befell. He threw his eye aside
              And mark what object did present itself.

Oliver relates how Orlando saw an unkempt sleeping man threatened by a snake and lion. Orlando recognised the man as his brother, and killed the lion. Oliver reveals he was the sleeping man.

Stagecraft
Staging the story (in small groups)

The story Oliver tells is improbable and melodramatic. It is an example of the conventions of literary pastoral, in which forests can contain all kinds of exotic animals and give rise to fantastical events.

Work out how you would present Oliver's story on stage, and how you would direct the two women to react. Use the following points to help your preparation:

- To whom does Oliver tell his story: Celia, Rosalind, or both?
- Identify the personal pronoun in line 127 – is it a slip of the tongue or the way by which Oliver tactfully identifies himself?
- How does Celia behave when Oliver reveals his identity?
- Does Oliver listen to Rosalind, or is he completely caught up with Celia?
- How could you use different visual effects to show Oliver's story as he recounts it? For instance, the different events could be acted out by people in costume, shown in silhouette behind a curtain or illustrated by artworks and video clips.

bald leafless
dry antiquity old age

gilded yellow
wreathed coiled

indented glides zigzag movements

with udders all drawn dry hungry because she had fed her cubs
couching crouching

render describe
unnatural cruel, unkind

kindness natural inclination
just occasion legitimate opportunity

hurtling violent struggle
miserable slumber (sleep, or Oliver's spiritual state before his conversion)

contrive plot
do not shame am not ashamed
conversion change to goodness

for what about

	Under an old oak whose boughs were mossed with age,	
	And high top bald with dry antiquity,	100
	A wretched ragged man, o'ergrown with hair,	
	Lay sleeping on his back; about his neck	
	A green and gilded snake had wreathed itself,	
	Who, with her head, nimble in threats, approached	
	The opening of his mouth. But suddenly	105
	Seeing Orlando, it unlinked itself	
	And with indented glides did slip away	
	Into a bush; under which bush's shade	
	A lioness, with udders all drawn dry,	
	Lay couching head on ground, with cat-like watch	110
	When that the sleeping man should stir – for 'tis	
	The royal disposition of that beast	
	To prey on nothing that doth seem as dead.	
	This seen, Orlando did approach the man	
	And found it was his brother, his elder brother.	115

CELIA O, I have heard him speak of that same brother,
And he did render him the most unnatural
That lived amongst men.

OLIVER   And well he might so do,
For well I know he was unnatural.

ROSALIND But to Orlando – did he leave him there,   120
Food to the sucked and hungry lioness?

OLIVER Twice did he turn his back and purposed so.
But kindness, nobler ever than revenge,
And nature, stronger than his just occasion,
Made him give battle to the lioness,   125
Who quickly fell before him; in which hurtling
From miserable slumber I awaked.

CELIA Are you his brother?

ROSALIND   Was't you he rescued?

CELIA Was't you that did so oft contrive to kill him?

OLIVER 'Twas I, but 'tis not I. I do not shame   130
To tell you what I was, since my conversion
So sweetly tastes, being the thing I am.

ROSALIND But for the bloody napkin?

Oliver relates how Orlando fainted, then recovered and sent Oliver with the bloodstained handkerchief to Rosalind. She faints, recovers and pretends her swooning is a pretence.

Stagecraft

Ganymede or Rosalind? (in small groups)

The final moments of Act 4 are rich in comic and dramatic possibilities. While some critics think that Oliver is totally caught up with Celia, with whom he has fallen in love, others think that he sees through Rosalind's disguise and realises she is a woman.

a Talk together about the different comic and dramatic effects that could be achieved if Oliver knows or suspects that Ganymede is really Rosalind in disguise. Use the following questions to guide your discussion:

- At what moments does Rosalind seem close to blowing her cover?
- Does Celia give the game away at line 154?
- Does Oliver begin to suspect that Ganymede is not a boy when he carries out the stage direction 'Raising Rosalind' at line 155?
- Is Oliver's use of Rosalind's name at line 170 a good-humoured signal that he has seen through her disguise?

b Decide what interpretation you think would work best on stage, and make detailed notes in your Director's Journal.

Characters

Oliver's conversion (in pairs)

What conversion did Oliver have? Oliver uses religious language to describe the difference between his shameful past and his converted present (lines 130–2). He also employs religious language when, a few lines earlier, he recounts Orlando's forgiveness and his willingness to suffer harm so Oliver could escape injury.

a What do you think it was that caused such a dramatic change of heart, and character, in Oliver? Was Oliver converted by Orlando's acts of forgiveness and mercy towards him? Or do you believe something else happened before this? Discuss these questions with your partner. Try to support your ideas with evidence from the script.

b Take parts and improvise a conversation between Oliver and Orlando just after the rescue from the lion. How does Oliver describe his conversion to Orlando? How does Orlando respond?

OLIVER   By and by.

When from the first to last betwixt us two,

Tears our recountments had most kindly bathed –   135

As how I came into that desert place –

In brief, he led me to the gentle Duke

Who gave me fresh array and entertainment,

Committing me unto my brother's love,

Who led me instantly unto his cave;   140

There stripped himself and here, upon his arm,

The lioness had torn some flesh away,

Which all this while had bled; and now he fainted,

And cried in fainting upon Rosalind.

Brief, I recovered him, bound up his wound,   145

And, after some small space, being strong at heart,

He sent me hither, stranger as I am,

To tell this story that you might excuse

His broken promise, and to give this napkin,

Dyed in this blood, unto the shepherd youth   150

That he in sport doth call his Rosalind.

                      [*Rosalind faints*]

CELIA   Why, how now? Ganymede, sweet Ganymede!

OLIVER   Many will swoon when they do look on blood.

CELIA   There is more in it. – Cousin! Ganymede!

OLIVER   [*Raising Rosalind*] Look, he recovers.   155

ROSALIND   I would I were at home.

CELIA   We'll lead you thither. – I pray you, will you take him by the arm.

OLIVER   Be of good cheer, youth. You a man? You lack a man's heart.

ROSALIND   I do so, I confess it. Ah, sirrah, a body would think this was well counterfeited. I pray you tell your brother how well I counter-   160 feited. Heigh-ho!

OLIVER   This was not counterfeit: there is too great testimony in your complexion that it was a passion of earnest.

ROSALIND   Counterfeit, I assure you.

OLIVER   Well then, take a good heart, and counterfeit to be a man.   165

ROSALIND   So I do. But, i'faith, I should have been a woman by right.

CELIA   Come, you look paler and paler: pray you, draw homewards. – Good sir, go with us.

OLIVER   That will I. For I must bear answer back how you excuse my brother, Rosalind.   170

ROSALIND   I shall devise something. But I pray you commend my counterfeiting to him. Will you go?

                                       Exeunt

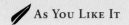

Looking back at Act 4
Activities for groups or individuals

1 Jaques's melancholy – the four humours

In Scene 1, Jaques declares that he has his own, very special melancholy. A popular belief in Shakespeare's time was that personality was determined by four 'humours' (fluids in the human body). These were blood (producing bravery), phlegm (producing calmness), 'yellowe' (producing anger) and black bile (producing melancholy). The belief was that if the four humours were in balance, a person would be healthy and temperate, but if one humour dominated, the result was an unbalanced personality.

◆ Imagine what Jaques would be like if he had an excess of 'blood' or 'phlegm', rather than 'black bile'. What would he say or do at key points in the play if his personality and behaviour were influenced by a different imbalance of humours? How might his language and ideas change?

2 A transitional act?

Act 4, with its three scenes, is the shortest in the play, but it seems to include several key turning points.

◆ What important transitions have taken place in this act? What do you think is the significance of Scene 2 within the action of the play so far?

◆ Imagine that you are writing notes on Act 4 to help a younger student who has also just finished reading the act. They have not had a chance to see a performance of the play, so how would you encourage them to visualise this act's key moments and characters?

3 Oliver's conversion

Oliver's conversion from a vengeful, hateful brother into a kind and thoughtful one is extreme; the actor playing Oliver faces a challenging task in making this change appear credible.

◆ In role as an actor playing Oliver, write out the challenges of making such a change in the way you portray the character. How do you understand the conversion that Oliver has had? How can you make his reformed character believable, and how do you change the way he looks, speaks and moves to show this change of heart?

4 Rosalind's mood changes

Rosalind experiences violent swings of emotion during Scenes 1 and 3.

◆ Find three different ways of visually presenting her shifts of mood – perhaps as a graph, a mime and a trio of drawings. Write notes on each, explaining what it shows and why you chose to use this method of representation.

5 Love is in the air

There are four pairs of lovers in the play so far: Rosalind/Orlando; Touchstone/Audrey; Phoebe/Silvanus; Celia/Oliver.

◆ In pairs, create a tableau for each couple. Try to capture their relationship so that another pair can guess who you are representing each time. When the other pair guesses correctly, stay in role for a minute longer and speak your thoughts and feelings about the other person.

Write an extended piece in which you compare and contrast the different kinds of love that have been explored in the play so far. Include a discussion of other kinds of love in addition to romantic love, such as the sisterly love between Rosalind and Celia or the strong loyalty that Adam has for Orlando.

Audrey regrets that Sir Oliver Martext did not marry her to Touchstone. She denies that William has any claim on her. William enters, and Touchstone begins to mock him.

1 Touchstone's wisecracks (in threes)

Touchstone takes great delight in taunting William, who he thinks is also interested in Audrey. Take parts and read through the script opposite. Discuss the following questions and make notes to help you refine a second reading of this section.

- Does Touchstone speak lines 8–10 to Audrey, to himself or to the audience? What option would you advise the actor to take, and why? How does each variation indicate a different intent?
- What comic business might you make out of the internal stage direction 'cover thy head', which is repeated in lines 14–15?
- William thanks God that he was born in the forest. Touchstone echoes him and agrees, but what else might he mean here? How might he share this joke with the audience or with Audrey?
- The 'saying' Touchstone suddenly remembers in lines 27–8 provides another comic moment. Write out in modern English what Touchstone is really saying. Bear this clearer meaning in mind when delivering – or reacting to – these lines.
- Do you think William would understand what Touchstone is saying on stage?

Write about it

William's role in the play (in pairs)

Why did Shakespeare include William in the play? In the pairings that appear to be shaping up, Touchstone and Audrey already seem committed. To introduce a new character so late in the play, when everyone is apparently coupled up already, seems odd.

a Discuss whether William is there:

- to show who Audrey's 'natural' partner should be, and thus to challenge Touchstone
- to provide yet another perspective on love
- and/or as further fun, to keep the audience amused throughout the final act.

b Improvise a conversation between a director and the actor playing William, to show how each of them understands William's role in the play.

---

gentle kind
the old gentleman Jaques

lays claim to wants to marry
interest in claim on

clown country bumpkin
good wits keen intelligence
shall be flouting are sure to be mocking
we cannot hold we can't help doing it
God ye good ev'n God give you a good evening

ripe fine

so-so average

Act 5 Scene 1
The Forest of Arden

Enter TOUCHSTONE *and* AUDREY

TOUCHSTONE   We shall find a time, Audrey; patience, gentle Audrey.

AUDREY   Faith, the priest was good enough, for all the old gentleman's saying.

TOUCHSTONE   A most wicked Sir Oliver, Audrey, a most vile Martext. But, Audrey, there is a youth here in the forest lays claim to you. 5

AUDREY   Aye, I know who 'tis. He hath no interest in me in the world.

Enter WILLIAM

Here comes the man you mean.

TOUCHSTONE   It is meat and drink to me to see a clown. By my troth, we that have good wits have much to answer for. We shall be flouting; we cannot hold. 10

WILLIAM   Good ev'n, Audrey.

AUDREY   God ye good ev'n, William.

WILLIAM   [*Taking off his hat*] And good ev'n to you, sir.

TOUCHSTONE   Good ev'n, gentle friend. Cover thy head, cover thy head. Nay prithee, be covered. How old are you, friend? 15

WILLIAM   Five and twenty, sir.

TOUCHSTONE   A ripe age. Is thy name William?

WILLIAM   William, sir.

TOUCHSTONE   A fair name. Wast born i'th'forest here?

WILLIAM   Aye, sir, I thank God. 20

TOUCHSTONE   'Thank God': a good answer. Art rich?

WILLIAM   Faith, sir, so-so.

TOUCHSTONE   'So-so' is good, very good, very excellent good – and yet it is not: it is but so-so. Art thou wise?

WILLIAM   Aye, sir, I have a pretty wit. 25

TOUCHSTONE   Why, thou say'st well. I do now remember a saying: 'The fool doth think he is wise, but the wise man knows himself to be a fool.'

Touchstone bamboozles William with impressive-sounding but empty language. He says that he, not William, must marry Audrey, and threatens William with all kinds of punishments.

1 'Country bumpkin'? (in pairs)

The encounter between Touchstone and William is another example of the conflict between court and country. Touchstone is determined to show the superiority of the court, and he talks a good deal of high-flown nonsense in order to get the better of William. He contemptuously refers to ordinary language as 'the vulgar' and 'the boorish' and translates everything into 'common' language so that William can understand.

a Is William cleverer than Touchstone gives him credit for? Would you want Touchstone to be obviously condescending and patronising in this scene, or to hide his sharp wit behind friendly gestures and mannerisms?

b Take parts for a dramatic reading of lines 31–50. Before you begin, prepare by carefully selecting specific words for emphasis and thinking of gestures that will complement your interpretation of each character.

2 Act out the scene

a How would you cast William and how you would advise him to act towards Touchstone? Think especially about how you want the audience to feel towards William. In one production, William stood wide-eyed and open-mouthed – this provoked Touchstone's remark about the heathen philosopher in lines 29–31. In another, as Touchstone finished his threats, William seized him and almost strangled him until Audrey pleaded 'Do, good William.'

b Look at the image on this page, and list the directorial choices that have gone into the production. Beside this list, write what features you would either keep or change if you were directing a production of the play.

learned literate, educated

figure in rhetoric (the formal study of language included 'rhetoric'; this taught the skill of using language in a persuasive way in order to inform and influence people)
consent agree
ipse he himself (Latin)

to wit that is to say
translate change
deal in make use of
bastinado beating with a stick
steel sword-fighting
bandy with thee in faction compete in exchanging insults with you
o'errun overwhelm
policy deceitful scheming

Trip skip, look lively
attend follow

[William gapes]

The heathen philosopher, when he had a desire to eat a grape, would open his lips when he put it into his mouth, meaning thereby that grapes were made to eat and lips to open. You do love this maid? 30

WILLIAM   I do, sir.

TOUCHSTONE   Give me your hand. Art thou learned?

WILLIAM   No, sir. 35

TOUCHSTONE   Then learn this of me: to have is to have. For it is a figure in rhetoric that drink, being poured out of a cup into a glass, by filling the one doth empty the other. For all your writers do consent that '*ipse*' is he. Now you are not *ipse*, for I am he.

WILLIAM   Which he, sir? 40

TOUCHSTONE   He, sir, that must marry this woman. Therefore, you clown, abandon, which is in the vulgar 'leave', the society, which in the boorish is 'company', of this female, which in the common is 'woman': which together is 'abandon the society of this female'; or, clown, thou perishest or, to thy better understanding, 'diest', or, to 45 wit, 'I kill thee', 'make thee away', 'translate thy life into death, thy liberty into bondage'! I will deal in poison with thee, or in bastinado, or in steel! I will bandy with thee in faction, I will o'errun thee with policy – I will kill thee a hundred and fifty ways! Therefore, tremble and depart. 50

AUDREY   Do, good William.

WILLIAM   God rest you merry, sir.

Exit

Enter CORIN

CORIN   Our master and mistress seeks you. Come away, away.

TOUCHSTONE   Trip, Audrey, trip, Audrey. – I attend, I attend.

Exeunt

Oliver confirms that he instantly fell in love with Celia. He promises to give Orlando all his inheritance. Rosalind describes how Oliver and Celia fell in love at first sight and now long for marriage.

Language in the play

The speed of love, the speed of speech? (in threes)

The prevailing theme in the script opposite is the speed of love. Shakespeare provides Orlando, Oliver and Rosalind with a language style that matches the rapidity of falling in love at first sight. All three have speeches that pile item on item, event on event, in rapid succession.

a Take parts and experiment with ways of speaking the three characters' speeches on time (lines 1–3, 4–9 and 23–32). Do you think they should be spoken as quickly as possible, or with distinct pauses between each section? Or perhaps in some other way?

b Identify the following language features in the script opposite, and devise a suitable form of delivery or dramatic gesture for each one:

- **polyptoton** – the repetition of words that are derived from the same root, but have different endings or forms
- **anaphora** – the repetition of the same word at the beginning of successive sentences or clauses
- **alliteration** – the repetition of consonants at the beginning of successive words.

c In role as voice and language coaches for a modern production, write out advice for the actors playing Orlando, Oliver and Rosalind. Help them to understand the meanings and nuances of the words in their speeches at this point then advise on their pronunciation and dramatic delivery.

grant agree to marry you
persevere continue
giddiness suddenness
the poverty of her (she does not have any money, land or goods to bring to the marriage)
sudden hasty
revenue income
estate upon settle on, give to

all's contented followers
all his happy courtiers

scarf sling

1 Does Orlando know Ganymede is Rosalind?

(in threes)

Oliver greets Rosalind as 'fair sister' (line 13) and Orlando says that his brother told him of 'greater wonders' than how Ganymede pretended to faint. Rosalind replies that Oliver is referring to his and Celia's love at first sight. But are these 'greater wonders' the fact that Orlando now sees through her disguise as Ganymede?

a Take parts and act out lines 1–58 in two ways:

- first, as if Orlando is still innocent of the disguises and counterfeits of Rosalind
- second, as if he is fully aware that she has been playing an elaborate game with him.

b Discuss which interpretation feels most appropriate to you at this point in the play, and the implications of each.

I know where you are
I know what you mean

thrasonical boastful

degrees steps
incontinent (line 30) immediately
incontinent (line 31) sexually active
wrath passion
clubs physical force

138

Act 5 Scene 2
The Forest of Arden

Enter ORLANDO *and* OLIVER

ORLANDO Is't possible that on so little acquaintance you should like her, that, but seeing, you should love her, and, loving, woo, and, wooing, she should grant? And will you persevere to enjoy her?

OLIVER Neither call the giddiness of it in question; the poverty of her, the small acquaintance, my sudden wooing, nor her sudden consenting. But say with me I love Aliena; say with her that she loves me; consent with both, that we may enjoy each other. It shall be to your good, for my father's house and all the revenue that was old Sir Roland's will I estate upon you, and here live and die a shepherd.   5

Enter ROSALIND [*as* GANYMEDE]

ORLANDO You have my consent. Let your wedding be tomorrow; thither will I invite the Duke and all's contented followers. Go you, and prepare Aliena, for look you, here comes my 'Rosalind'.   10

ROSALIND God save you, brother.

OLIVER And you, fair 'sister'.   [*Exit*]

ROSALIND O, my dear Orlando, how it grieves me to see thee wear thy heart in a scarf.   15

ORLANDO It is my arm.

ROSALIND I thought thy heart had been wounded with the claws of a lion.

ORLANDO Wounded it is, but with the eyes of a lady.   20

ROSALIND Did your brother tell you how I counterfeited to swoon when he showed me your handkerchief?

ORLANDO Aye, and greater wonders than that.

ROSALIND O, I know where you are. Nay, 'tis true, there was never anything so sudden but the fight of two rams, and Caesar's   25
thrasonical brag of 'I came, saw, and overcame.' For your brother and my sister no sooner met but they looked; no sooner looked, but they loved; no sooner loved, but they sighed; no sooner sighed, but they asked one another the reason; no sooner knew the reason, but they sought the remedy; and in these degrees have they made a   30
pair of stairs to marriage, which they will climb incontinent – or else be incontinent before marriage. They are in the very wrath of love, and they will together – clubs cannot part them.

Orlando says that Oliver's joy at marriage will match his own sadness in not having Rosalind. She claims special powers, and promises he will marry her tomorrow. Phoebe complains about Rosalind's unkind action.

Characters
Orlando's heavy heart

Whether he is aware or not of Rosalind's real identity, Orlando seems to be tiring of the game. Oliver's happiness appears to plunge Orlando into sadness and bitterness.

- How realistic do you think Shakespeare's depiction of Orlando's state of mind is at this point? When others close to you are happy, do you feel yourself reflecting on your own unhappiness? Consider this as you write advice to Orlando to try to lift his spirits.

1 A change of language? (in pairs)

Rosalind wants Orlando to believe she has benign magical powers and will ensure he marries her the next day when Celia and Oliver marry.

a Read lines 40–53 and discuss how you think Rosalind should deliver this speech. Do not worry if you find the third sentence difficult to understand: most people do. It means something like: 'I say that you are intelligent, not to get you to think well of me; the only esteem I want is from helping you, not to improve my own reputation.'

b Take turns to experiment with different styles (mysterious, business-like, serious, provocative, formal, humorous, and so on) of reading out Rosalind's speech. Then write a detailed stage direction at line 46, giving advice to the actor playing Rosalind.

2 A change of pace? (in small groups)

The entrance of Silvius and Phoebe is again marked by a change from prose to verse. The first instance of this, in Act 4 Scene 3, was explored in Activity 1 on page 122.

a Discuss the following questions in groups:

- What do you think the shift from prose to verse, along with the entrance of Silvius and Phoebe, might indicate at this point in the play?
- What do you predict will happen from now until the end of the play?

b Write a paragraph each, describing and explaining what you think will happen from this point on. Think about ideas that other people raised in the discussion and whether or not you agree with them. You should also refer to what Rosalind has just said in lines 55–8.

---

nuptial wedding

turn needs

I speak to some purpose I am in earnest
conceit understanding
insomuch in that

grace me further my own reputation
strange wonderful
art magic
damnable working with devils
gesture appearance
straits of fortune difficult circumstances

in sober meanings seriously
tender dearly hold precious
bid invite

despiteful scornful, cruel
followed pursued

ORLANDO They shall be married tomorrow and I will bid the Duke to
the nuptial. But O, how bitter a thing it is to look into happiness   35
through another man's eyes. By so much the more shall I tomorrow
be at the height of heart-heaviness, by how much I shall think my
brother happy in having what he wishes for.

ROSALIND Why then, tomorrow, I cannot serve your turn for Rosalind?

ORLANDO I can live no longer by thinking.   40

ROSALIND I will weary you then no longer with idle talking. Know of
me, then – for now I speak to some purpose – that I know you are
a gentleman of good conceit. I speak not this that you should bear a
good opinion of my knowledge, insomuch, I say, I know you are;
neither do I labour for a greater esteem than may in some little   45
measure draw a belief from you to do yourself good, and not to
grace me. Believe then, if you please, that I can do strange things.
I have, since I was three year old, conversed with a magician, most
profound in his art, and yet not damnable. If you do love Rosalind
so near the heart as your gesture cries it out, when your brother   50
marries Aliena shall you marry her. I know into what straits of
fortune she is driven, and it is not impossible to me, if it appear not
inconvenient to you, to set her before your eyes tomorrow, human
as she is, and without any danger.

ORLANDO Speak'st thou in sober meanings?   55

ROSALIND By my life, I do, which I tender dearly, though I say I am a
magician. Therefore put you in your best array, bid your friends.
For if you will be married tomorrow, you shall, and to Rosalind, if
you will.

Enter SILVIUS *and* PHOEBE

Look, here comes a lover of mine and a lover of hers.   60

PHOEBE Youth, you have done me much ungentleness
To show the letter that I writ to you.

ROSALIND I care not if I have. It is my study
To seem despiteful and ungentle to you.
You are there followed by a faithful shepherd;   65
Look upon him, love him: he worships you.

141

As Silvius speaks his litany of what it is to love, Phoebe, Orlando and Rosalind echo and endorse his feelings. Rosalind gives orders for them all to meet tomorrow, when their desires will be fulfilled.

At the end of the scene, Rosalind promises to fulfil everyone's desires as long as they keep to their word. Should she deliver these lines in a comic or a serious style?

fantasy imagination

observance
respect, observant care

all trial enduring any hardship

Write about it
'what 'tis to love' (in pairs)

Phoebe's request in line 66 is interrupted until line 78, when Silvius gives his description of what it is to love. Read lines 78–82. Do you agree with his definition of true love? Write your own response to Phoebe's request. Use the same style as Silvius but include your own ideas.

Irish wolves (perhaps because of the monotony of their howling, or an allusion to the belief that the Irish could take the shape of a wolf)

1 Howling of Irish wolves (in fives)

In line 91, Rosalind tells everyone to stop speaking, saying ''tis like the howling of Irish wolves against the moon'. What might be happening on stage to make her say this?

Take parts and read through lines 66–92. Experiment with ways of bringing to life the repetition and language patterns in this part of the script. You should also consider:

fail be missing

- giving each character a different gesture or movement at each echo of the other characters' lines
- having the characters talk over each other or at the same time, like an operatic chorus
- depicting the increasing frustration of Rosalind until her outburst in line 91.

PHOEBE	Good shepherd, tell this youth what 'tis to love.	
SILVIUS	It is to be all made of sighs and tears,	
	And so am I for Phoebe.	
PHOEBE	And I for Ganymede.	70
ORLANDO	And I for Rosalind.	
ROSALIND	And I for no woman.	
SILVIUS	It is to be all made of faith and service,	
	And so am I for Phoebe.	
PHOEBE	And I for Ganymede.	75
ORLANDO	And I for Rosalind.	
ROSALIND	And I for no woman.	
SILVIUS	It is to be all made of fantasy,	
	All made of passion, and all made of wishes,	
	All adoration, duty, and observance,	80
	All humbleness, all patience, and impatience,	
	All purity, all trial, all obedience;	
	And so am I for Phoebe.	
PHOEBE	And so am I for Ganymede.	
ORLANDO	And so am I for Rosalind.	85
ROSALIND	And so am I for no woman.	
PHOEBE	[*To Rosalind*] If this be so, why blame you me to love you?	
SILVIUS	[*To Phoebe*] If this be so, why blame you me to love you?	
ORLANDO	If this be so, why blame you me to love you?	
ROSALIND	Who do you speak to 'Why blame you me to love you'?	90
ORLANDO	To her that is not here, nor doth not hear.	
ROSALIND	Pray you no more of this: 'tis like the howling of Irish wolves against the moon. [*To Silvius*] I will help you, if I can. [*To Phoebe*] I would love you, if I could. – Tomorrow meet me all together. – [*To Phoebe*] I will marry you, if ever I marry woman, and I'll be married tomorrow. [*To Orlando*] I will satisfy you, if ever I satisfy man, and you shall be married tomorrow. [*To Silvius*] I will content you, if what pleases you contents you, and you shall be married tomorrow. [*To Orlando*] As you love Rosalind, meet; [*To Silvius*] As you love Phoebe, meet – and as I love no woman, I'll meet. So fare you well: I have left you commands.	95 100
SILVIUS	I'll not fail, if I live.	
PHOEBE	Nor I.	
ORLANDO	Nor I.	

Exeunt

Touchstone and Audrey look forward to their marriage. The two Pages sing of springtime as the time for young lovers, even though life is brief.

1 Sing it! (in large groups)

The Pages' song seems to have two dramatic purposes:

- first, to mark the passage of time between Scenes 2 and 4 (between Rosalind's instructions to prepare for marriage and the ceremony in the final scene)
- second, to echo the theme of love now that all the lovers are preparing for marriage.

a Choose a new soundtrack for this scene. Which modern songs can you think of that would be appropriate?

b Try singing the original song from the script. Theatre productions of the play often set the song's lyrics to the music below, which was composed in 1600 by Thomas Morley. Play this tune on a piano or keyboard, and perform it to another group. Try to use gestures and actions that relate to the lyrics.

woman of the world
married woman

honest honourable

clap into't roundly
start immediately

hawking throat-clearing

only principal

prologues introductions

like two gipsies on a horse
in unison

ring-time time for ringing wedding bells, exchanging marriage rings, dancing in rings

carol joyful song

Act 5 Scene 3
The Forest of Arden

Enter TOUCHSTONE *and* AUDREY

TOUCHSTONE Tomorrow is the joyful day, Audrey; tomorrow will we
  be married.

AUDREY I do desire it with all my heart, and I hope it is no dishonest
  desire to desire to be a woman of the world?

Enter two PAGES

  Here come two of the banished Duke's pages.   5

FIRST PAGE Well met, honest gentleman.

TOUCHSTONE By my troth, well met. Come, sit, sit, and a song.

SECOND PAGE We are for you; sit i'th'middle.

FIRST PAGE Shall we clap into't roundly, without hawking, or spitting, or
  saying we are hoarse, which are the only prologues to a bad voice? 10

SECOND PAGE Aye, faith, i'faith, and both in a tune like two gipsies on a horse.

FIRST AND SECOND PAGE It was a lover and his lass,
   With a hey, and a ho, and a hey nonny-no,
   That o'er the green cornfield did pass,
    In spring-time,   15
    The only pretty ring-time,
     When birds do sing;
    Hey ding a-ding, ding,
     Sweet lovers love the spring.

   Between the acres of the rye,   20
   With a hey, and a ho, and a hey nonny-no,
   These pretty country folks would lie,
    In spring-time,
    The only pretty ring-time,
     When birds do sing;   25
    Hey ding a-ding, ding,
     Sweet lovers love the spring.

   This carol they began that hour,
   With a hey, and a ho, and a hey nonny-no,
   How that a life was but a flower;   30
    In spring-time,
    The only pretty ring-time,

The pages sing of enjoying the present moment. Touchstone is unimpressed by their singing. Orlando is unsure if Ganymede can deliver his promises. Rosalind makes the Duke and Orlando confirm their agreements.

Themes

Carpe diem – seize the day

The Pages' song highlights the brevity of human life, and advises that present happiness should be seized and enjoyed. The theme of the song is *carpe diem*, a Latin quotation meaning 'seize the day', taken from the Roman poet Horace.

* One of the themes of the play is time and timelessness. Revisit your responses to the activities on page 56, then compare your ideas about this theme with some of the aspects of time that have been evoked in the Pages' song.

Stagecraft

'the note was very untunable' (in pairs)

Why is Touchstone so unimpressed by the song and its sentiments? The Page's response to Touchstone that 'we kept time; we lost not our time' could be simply about their timing in the singing; but it could also refer to their immersion in the moment and their enjoyment of the present time.

* Write either stage directions or asides at various points throughout the song to give more information about what might be happening on stage. Do the Pages really sing in tune, and did Touchstone actually get lost in the song? Or were the singers totally out of tune, and did they interrupt Touchstone's romantic moment with Audrey?

1 Orlando's state of mind (in pairs)

At the beginning of the play's final scene, Orlando still seems unsure about his fate: 'I sometimes do believe and sometimes do not'.

* Imagine Orlando has been discussing his position with Duke Senior and others in Arden since we last saw him. Improvise these conversations, taking turns to play Orlando. Consider what Orlando might say about his thoughts and feelings since last talking to Rosalind. Think about the dreams or visions that have haunted him or inspired him, and the advice that other people have given him.

ditty words of the song
note tune
untunable harsh, discordant
yes indeed you did
mend improve

the boy (Ganymede)

fear they hope fear their hope will not be fulfilled

whiles our compact is urged whilst our agreements are confirmed
bestow her on give her in marriage to

> When birds do sing;
> Hey ding a-ding, ding,
> Sweet lovers love the spring. 35
>
> And therefore take the present time;
> With a hey, and a ho, and a hey nonny-no,
> For love is crownèd with the prime,
> In spring-time,
> The only pretty ring-time, 40
> When birds do sing;
> Hey ding a-ding, ding,
> Sweet lovers love the spring.

TOUCHSTONE Truly, young gentlemen, though there was no great matter in the ditty, yet the note was very untunable. 45

FIRST PAGE You are deceived, sir: we kept time; we lost not our time.

TOUCHSTONE By my troth, yes. I count it but time lost to hear such a foolish song. God buy you, and God mend your voices. – Come, Audrey.

Exeunt

Act 5 Scene 4
Duke Senior's camp in the forest

Enter DUKE SENIOR, AMIENS, JAQUES, ORLANDO,
OLIVER, CELIA [*as* ALIENA]

DUKE SENIOR Dost thou believe, Orlando, that the boy
Can do all this that he hath promisèd?

ORLANDO I sometimes do believe and sometimes do not,
As those that fear they hope and know they fear.

Enter ROSALIND [*as* GANYMEDE], SILVIUS, *and* PHOEBE

ROSALIND Patience once more whiles our compact is urged. – 5
You say, if I bring in your Rosalind,
You will bestow her on Orlando here?

DUKE SENIOR That would I, had I kingdoms to give with her.

ROSALIND And you say you will have her, when I bring her?

ORLANDO That would I, were I of all kingdoms king. 10

Rosalind promises to fulfil every character's wishes. Duke Senior and Orlando remark on Ganymede's resemblance to Rosalind. Touchstone boasts of his skills as a courtier.

1 Promise-keeping (in small groups)

In lines 5–25, Rosalind asks for patience while she gets each character to confirm his or her own promise: that Duke Senior will give his daughter in marriage to Orlando, that Orlando will marry her, and so on.

- List the promises that Rosalind asks each of the characters to confirm. In your Director's Journal, write stage directions for each time that she makes one of these requests. How might her attitude, and therefore her actions and postures, differ in each case? Explain why.
- Use these stage directions as you act out lines 5–25. Think about what additional notes you might write to advise the other actors on stage how to react to Rosalind's speech and actions.

Characters
Reminders of Rosalind

The exchange between Orlando and Duke Senior seems to confirm that Rosalind's disguise as Ganymede is still intact. But is it possible that Orlando has guessed the truth, yet wishes to keep the secret from her father?

- In role as the director of a modern production, write notes in your Director's Journal to advise the actor playing Orlando how to speak lines 28–34. Refer to what he says in lines 3–4 in this scene as you consider what Orlando might be thinking.

2 Touchstone as courtier (in pairs)

In lines 42–5, Touchstone lists the skills that prove he has been a courtier:

- dancing (a 'measure' is a stately dance)
- flattery, diplomacy and deceit ('politic')
- false friendship ('smooth with mine enemy')
- non-payment of bills (he has ruined – 'undone' – three tailors).

a Discuss how Touchstone mocks the life and fashions of the court. Do you think he really was once a courtier?

b Devise gestures to accompany each of Touchstone's criticisms or jokes about the court. Take turns to read lines 42–5 aloud, using these gestures to try to make your partner laugh.

c Prepare and stage an interview with a courtier who would have known a younger Touchstone at court. What was Touchstone like then? Did he criticise the court or did he try to be a popular, fashionable courtier?

make all this matter even straighten everything out
give give away (in marriage)

lively touches lifelike marks
favour features, appearance

rudiments elements, first principles
desperate studies dangerous practices
Obscurèd hidden

flood (Jaques's words recall the story of Noah's flood in the Bible)
toward about to take place

motley-minded crazy-brained

purgation test
measure stately dance

like was likely
ta'en up made

ROSALIND	You say you'll marry me, if I be willing.	
PHOEBE	That will I, should I die the hour after.	
ROSALIND	But if you do refuse to marry me,	
	You'll give yourself to this most faithful shepherd.	
PHOEBE	So is the bargain.	15
ROSALIND	You say that you'll have Phoebe if she will.	
SILVIUS	Though to have her and death were both one thing.	
ROSALIND	I have promised to make all this matter even. –	
	Keep you your word, O Duke, to give your daughter. –	
	You yours, Orlando, to receive his daughter. –	20
	Keep you your word, Phoebe, that you'll marry me	
	Or else, refusing me, to wed this shepherd. –	
	Keep your word, Silvius, that you'll marry her	
	If she refuse me – and from hence I go	
	To make these doubts all even.	25

Exeunt Rosalind and Celia

DUKE SENIOR	I do remember in this shepherd boy	
	Some lively touches of my daughter's favour.	
ORLANDO	My lord, the first time that I ever saw him,	
	Methought he was a brother to your daughter;	
	But, my good lord, this boy is forest-born	30
	And hath been tutored in the rudiments	
	Of many desperate studies by his uncle	
	Whom he reports to be a great magician,	
	Obscurèd in the circle of this forest.	

Enter TOUCHSTONE *and* AUDREY

JAQUES	There is sure another flood toward, and these couples are coming to the ark. Here comes a pair of very strange beasts which, in all tongues, are called fools.	35
TOUCHSTONE	Salutation and greeting to you all.	
JAQUES	Good my lord, bid him welcome. This is the motley-minded gentleman that I have so often met in the forest: he hath been a courtier, he swears.	40
TOUCHSTONE	If any man doubt that, let him put me to my purgation. I have trod a measure; I have flattered a lady; I have been politic with my friend, smooth with mine enemy; I have undone three tailors; I have had four quarrels, and like to have fought one.	45
JAQUES	And how was that ta'en up?	
TOUCHSTONE	Faith, we met and found the quarrel was upon the seventh cause.	

Touchstone declares that he too wishes to be married, because Audrey's roughness conceals inner virtues. He lists the sequence of insults that lead up to a duel, explaining how to avoid it.

1 'amongst … the country copulatives'

Touchstone continues to mock the country ways as well as the court. But he is keen not to be left out of the impending marriages. Unlike Jaques, he wants to be inside, not outside, the action.

a How does Touchstone treat Audrey? Make notes on how you would want to present their relationship to an audience.

b Suggest what Audrey might be doing when Touchstone orders her 'Bear your body more seeming, Audrey.' Write notes in your Director's Journal.

c What is Touchstone's view of marriage (see line 53)? Rewrite it in your own words. Predict how a modern audience might feel about Touchstone's statement.

Write about it

The seventh cause: the etiquette of quarrelling

Touchstone lists how a quarrel develops and how a fight can be avoided by an 'if'. Shakespeare is satirising manuals on correct behaviour for courtiers. Many of these handbooks were about how to behave in a duel when one's honour had been insulted. The table below shows the stages of a quarrel when an insult is repeated.

Name of response	Meaning of reply	Result
1 Retort courteous	Oh, yes it is	Avoid duel
2 Quip modest	It's my affair	Ditto
3 Reply churlish	You are a poor judge	Ditto
4 Reproof valiant	That isn't true	Ditto
5 Countercheck quarrelsome	You lie	Ditto
6 Lie circumstantial	You lie, because …	Ditto
7 Lie direct	You definitely lie	Duel – although it could be also still be avoided!

• Touchstone says 'we quarrel in print, by the book' (line 78). What would a modern rulebook for quarrellers look like? Use the table above to help you create a contemporary version of seven rules for how to avoid a quarrel. Then write a modernised speech for Touchstone that is based upon these new rules.

God'ild … like God reward you and all of you

copulatives lovers

humour whim

swift and sententious quick-witted and full of wise sayings

bolt arrow

dulcet diseases sweet weaknesses

more seeming in a more becoming manner, decently

in the mind of the opinion that

countercheck rebuke

circumstantial (beating about the bush)

durst dared

measured swords checked our swords were of equal length

nominate name

take up settle

as namely

swore brothers promised friendship

JAQUES   How, 'seventh cause'? – Good my lord, like this fellow.

DUKE SENIOR   I like him very well.   50

TOUCHSTONE   God'ild you, sir; I desire you of the like. I press in here, sir, amongst the rest of the country copulatives, to swear and to forswear according as marriage binds and blood breaks. A poor virgin, sir, an ill-favoured thing, sir, but mine own. A poor humour of mine, sir, to take that that no man else will. Rich honesty dwells   55 like a miser, sir, in a poor house, as your pearl in your foul oyster.

DUKE SENIOR   By my faith, he is very swift and sententious.

TOUCHSTONE   According to 'the fool's bolt', sir, and such dulcet diseases.

JAQUES   But, for 'the seventh cause': how did you find the quarrel on   60 'the seventh cause'?

TOUCHSTONE   Upon a lie seven times removed. – Bear your body more seeming, Audrey. – As thus, sir: I did dislike the cut of a certain courtier's beard. He sent me word, if I said his beard was not cut well, he was in the mind it was: this is called 'the retort courteous'.   65 If I sent him word again it was not well cut, he would send me word he cut it to please himself: this is called 'the quip modest'. If again it was not well cut, he disabled my judgement: this is called 'the reply churlish'. If again it was not well cut, he would answer I spake not true: this is called 'the reproof valiant'. If again it was not well   70 cut, he would say I lied: this is called 'the countercheck quarrelsome'. And so to 'the lie circumstantial' and 'the lie direct'.

JAQUES   And how oft did you say his beard was not well cut?

TOUCHSTONE   I durst go no further than the lie circumstantial, nor he durst not give me the lie direct; and so we measured swords, and   75 parted.

JAQUES   Can you nominate, in order now, the degrees of the lie?

TOUCHSTONE   O sir, we quarrel in print, by the book – as you have books for good manners. I will name you the degrees: the first, the retort courteous; the second, the quip modest; the third, the reply   80 churlish; the fourth, the reproof valiant; the fifth, the countercheck quarrelsome; the sixth, the lie with circumstance; the seventh, the lie direct. All these you may avoid but the lie direct, and you may avoid that too with an 'if'. I knew when seven justices could not take up a quarrel but when the parties were met themselves, one of them   85 thought but of an 'if': as, 'If you said so, then I said so.' And they shook hands and swore brothers. Your 'if' is the only peacemaker: much virtue in 'if'.

Duke Senior praises Touchstone. Hymen enters with Rosalind and Celia (undisguised) and asks the Duke to receive his daughter. Rosalind promises to be Orlando's wife. Hymen ordains four marriages.

Stagecraft

'Enter HYMEN' (in small groups)

The entry of Hymen, the Greek and Roman god of marriage, is a great moment of theatre. The episode may have been staged as a masque. Masques were spectacular entertainments that drew imaginatively on Classical mythology to present gods and goddesses. They used elaborate scenery and costumes, and were filled with music, poetry and dance. Masques revelled in visual effects, often using stage machinery and lighting to create striking illusions.

a Discuss your ideas for a masque, and draw up a list to describe the atmosphere you would like to create at the end of a stage production of *As You Like It*.

b Work out a staging of lines 93–134 for a modern production, with all the possibilities of modern set design, machinery, costume, special effects and lighting. Use the following considerations to help you with this plan:

- Will you present Hymen as a god or as a human character?
- Hymen's language is formal and ritualistic and uses rhyming verse. Will you emphasise the rhymes? If so, how?

1 Hymen (in pairs)

a Some directors cut Hymen from the play altogether. Discuss whether the play needs a ritualistic moment at this point, or whether the marriages could be carried out more simply and informally.

b Improvise a conversation between a set designer who wants to include Hymen (because of the opportunities for elaborate special effects) and a director who thinks this character can be cut.

Themes

'If truth holds true contents'

One critic has suggested that line 114 in this scene has at least 168 possible interpretations! One is 'If revealing who Ganymede and Aliena really are brings genuine happiness'. The characters' disguises, shifting moods, changing personalities and uncertain positions make 'the truth' a complex and ambiguous concept.

- Make one or two suggestions for what line 114 might mean. Then write a paragraph on how 'truth' is represented in the play.

stalking-horse (horse trained to conceal hunters as they move towards the animal they are hunting)
Still music solemn and quiet music

mirth joy
made even reconciled
Atone together are reconciled

Peace, ho be silent
bar confusion forbid misunderstandings

Hymen's bands marriage vows

cross troubles, quarrels

accord agree

sure together bound fast

Whiles until

That reason … diminish explanation will reduce your amazement

JAQUES   Is not this a rare fellow, my lord? He's as good at anything, and
          yet a fool.   90

DUKE SENIOR   He uses his folly like a stalking-horse, and under the
          presentation of that he shoots his wit.

Still music. Enter HYMEN, [*with*] ROSALIND *and* CELIA
[as themselves]

HYMEN   Then is there mirth in heaven,
              When earthly things made even
                  Atone together.   95
              Good Duke, receive thy daughter;
              Hymen from heaven brought her,
                  Yea, brought her hither
              That thou mightst join her hand with his,
              Whose heart within his bosom is.   100

ROSALIND   [*To the Duke*] To you I give myself, for I am yours.
              [*To Orlando*] To you I give myself, for I am yours.

DUKE SENIOR   If there be truth in sight, you are my daughter.

ORLANDO   If there be truth in sight, you are my Rosalind.

PHOEBE   If sight and shape be true, why then, my love, adieu.   105

ROSALIND   [*To the Duke*] I'll have no father, if you be not he.
              [*To Orlando*] I'll have no husband, if you be not he.
              [*To Phoebe*] Nor ne'er wed woman, if you be not she.

HYMEN   Peace, ho: I bar confusion,
              'Tis I must make conclusion   110
              Of these most strange events.
              Here's eight that must take hands
              To join in Hymen's bands,
              If truth holds true contents.
              [*To Orlando and Rosalind*] You and you no cross shall part.   115
              [*To Oliver and Celia*] You and you are heart in heart.
              [*To Phoebe*] You to his love must accord,
              Or have a woman to your lord.
              [*To Touchstone and Audrey*] You and you are sure together
              As the winter to foul weather. –   120
              Whiles a wedlock hymn we sing,
              Feed yourselves with questioning,
              That reason, wonder may diminish
              How thus we met and these things finish.

After the song celebrating marriage and fertility, Phoebe accepts Silvius. Jacques de Boys brings news of Duke Frederick's conversion and penitence. Duke Senior orders revelry.

1 Snapshots of the action (in large groups)

a Discuss the questions below, and then write stage directions based on what you decide will work best.

- How does Duke Senior acknowledge Celia? (lines 131–2)
- Does Phoebe accept Silvius grudgingly, willingly or with a different emotion? (lines 133–4)
- How do Oliver and Orlando respond to the sight of their brother?

b Create tableaux that illustrate your stage directions. One member of the group is the photographer, who can call out 'Ready … Snap!' to signal that the moment has been captured.

Juno (goddess of marriage)
board and bed family life
Hymen marriage
High wedlock blessed marriage

Stagecraft

A believable happy ending? (in small groups)

The news of Duke Frederick's conversion is sudden and improbable. But this unlikely surprise is part of the pastoral romance tradition, which Shakespeare was satirising in the play. The tradition delighted in happy endings in which order was restored, with reconciliations, conversions to goodness, forgiveness, marriages, and the prospect of harmony for individuals and society.

a Consider how you would want Jacques de Boys deliver his news (for example, using pauses to add dramatic effect, or moving and gesturing when he recognises his brothers).

b How would you want your audience to respond to the news of Frederick's conversion? How could you convey the satirical edge of Shakespeare's writing, both in the actors' delivery and through other staging decisions? Write notes in your Director's Journal.

resorted to took refuge in
Addressed a mighty power prepared a huge army
conduct leadership

crown sovereignty

Themes

Return to court

In one production, the members of the banished court threw off their country clothes at lines 158–9 to reveal their true court apparel. In a filmed version of the play, the 'rustic revelry' started out as a dance in the forest, then the characters ran through the forest and finished the dance in the very places in the court where the play started.

- In role as director, write notes about how you would stage this final movement from country to court? Would you want to suggest liberation or a return to corruption at the end of the play?

offer'st fairly bring a fine gift
the other myself
at large entire
do those ends realise those intensions
shrewd sharp, harsh
the measure of their states their social status
new-fall'n dignity newly acquired honour (his dukedom)
rustic revelry simple and happy celebrations

Song

                    Wedding is great Juno's crown,   125
                       O blessed bond of board and bed.
                    'Tis Hymen peoples every town,
                       High wedlock then be honourèd.
                    Honour, high honour, and renown
                    To Hymen, god of every town.   130

DUKE SENIOR O my dear niece: welcome thou art to me,
             Even daughter; welcome in no less degree.

PHOEBE   I will not eat my word now thou art mine:
             Thy faith my fancy to thee doth combine.

Enter [JACQUES DE BOYS, *the*] *second brother*

JACQUES DE BOYS Let me have audience for a word or two.   135
             I am the second son of old Sir Roland,
             That bring these tidings to this fair assembly.
             Duke Frederick, hearing how that every day
             Men of great worth resorted to this forest,
             Addressed a mighty power which were on foot   140
             In his own conduct, purposely to take
             His brother here and put him to the sword;
             And to the skirts of this wild wood he came,
             Where, meeting with an old religious man,
             After some question with him, was converted   145
             Both from his enterprise and from the world,
             His crown bequeathing to his banished brother,
             And all their lands restored to them again
             That were with him exiled. This to be true,
             I do engage my life.

DUKE SENIOR   Welcome, young man.   150
             Thou offer'st fairly to thy brothers' wedding:
             To one his lands withheld, and to the other
             A land itself at large, a potent dukedom. –
             First, in this forest, let us do those ends
             That here were well begun and well begot;   155
             And after every of this happy number
             That have endured shrewd days and nights with us
             Shall share the good of our returnèd fortune
             According to the measure of their states.
             Meantime forget this new-fall'n dignity   160
             And fall into our rustic revelry. –

Jaques resolves to join Duke Frederick. He predicts honour and success to all except Touchstone, and declines to join the celebrations. Rosalind asks the audience to approve the play with their applause.

1 Jaques's farewell

Jaques refuses to join in the celebrations, preferring to join Duke Frederick in abandoning court life.

- Why do you think Shakespeare adds this 'serious' episode to the closing festivities? Why might Jaques still be melancholy? Write a stage direction to advise the actor playing Jaques on how to make his farewell.

Stagecraft

Staging the Epilogue (in pairs)

Discuss the following points about the play's **epilogue** (the section at the end of a play or book that concludes or comments on the preceding action), then make notes in your Director's Journal in response.

- **'Exeunt all but Rosalind'** In Shakespeare's day, it was customary for the actor giving the epilogue to remain on stage after everyone else had left it. This is not necessarily the case in modern productions. Decide whether you would have the rest of the cast on view behind Rosalind or whether she should speak to the audience by herself. What effect would each of these two versions have on the audience?
- **Lines 7–8** These lines play on the theme of appearance and reality, which has been complicated by the play's many disguises and role changes. Consider whether Rosalind should stay in role as she speaks the Epilogue, or address the audience as an actor.
- **Line 13** In Shakespeare's time, Rosalind was played by a (usually very young) man. But today, nearly all Rosalinds are female. Consider the effect you would want to achieve with this line, and how you would advise a female actor to deliver it.
- **Lines 13–17** Rosalind teases the audiences by implying that if they don't applaud, they have beards that don't please her, ugly faces and bad breath. How would you expect the audience to respond? How could the actor maximise the audience reaction?

2 Final image (in large groups)

Discuss the final 'stage picture' that you would want the audience to see at the end of your production, and think about what final impression of the play it would give. Stage a tableau of this moment. Script a voiceover that describes the different elements of the tableau and the reasons behind including them.

by your patience wait a minute

thrown into neglect rejected

convertites people converted to a religious life
matter good sense

allies relatives

Is but … victualled has supplies for only two months

pastime fun and games

bush advertisement (wine merchants hung an ivy branch outside their shops)
case state
insinuate with slyly persuade
furnished dressed
become me be appropriate
conjure charm, enchant

simpering silly smiling and smirking
liked pleased
defied disliked
offer (that is, to kiss spectators)
bid me farewell applaud

Play, music – and you, brides and bridegrooms all,
With measure heaped in joy to th'measures fall.

JAQUES   Sir, by your patience. [*To Jacques de Boys*] If I heard you rightly,
The Duke hath put on a religious life   165
And thrown into neglect the pompous court.

JACQUES DE BOYS   He hath.

JAQUES   To him will I: out of these convertites
There is much matter to be heard and learned.
[*To the Duke*] You to your former honour I bequeath: 170
Your patience and your virtue well deserves it.
[*To Orlando*] You to a love that your true faith doth merit.
[*To Oliver*] You to your land and love and great allies.
[*To Silvius*] You to a long and well-deservèd bed.
[*To Touchstone*] And you to wrangling, for thy loving voyage   175
Is but for two months victualled. – So to your pleasures;
I am for other than for dancing measures.

DUKE SENIOR   Stay, Jaques, stay.

JAQUES   To see no pastime, I. What you would have
I'll stay to know at your abandoned cave.   *Exit*   180

DUKE SENIOR   Proceed, proceed. – We will begin these rites
As we do trust they'll end, in true delights.
         [*They dance.*] *Exeunt all but Rosalind who speaks the Epilogue:*

ROSALIND   It is not the fashion to see the lady the Epilogue, but it is no more unhandsome than to see the lord the Prologue. If it be true that good wine needs no bush, 'tis true that a good play needs no Epilogue. Yet to good wine they do use good bushes, and good plays prove the better by the help of good Epilogues. What a case am I in,   5 then, that am neither a good Epilogue nor cannot insinuate with you in the behalf of a good play? I am not furnished like a beggar, therefore to beg will not become me. My way is to conjure you, and I'll begin with the women. I charge you, O women, for the love you bear to men, to like as much of this play as please you. – And I   10 charge you, O men, for the love you bear to women – as I perceive by your simpering none of you hates them – that between you and the women the play may please. If I were a woman, I would kiss as many of you as had beards that pleased me, complexions that liked me, and breaths that I defied not. And I am sure as many as have   15 good beards, or good faces, or sweet breaths will, for my kind offer, when I make curtsey, bid me farewell.   *Exit*

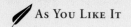

Looking back at the play
Activities for groups or individuals

1 Ending the play

◆ In groups, develop your ideas on the final 'stage picture' you created on page 156 by considering the context (time and place) in which you would want to set the play. This should affect your choice of stage set, music, costume and choreography (dance steps). You could use the images on the page opposite for inspiration.

Imagine you are a team of theatrical experts, preparing a presentation on your vision for the final scene. You will need to answer certain questions:

- **Lighting designer:** what mood would you want to create at the end of the play, and how would you use lighting to enhance this?
- **Sound designer:** some productions of As You Like It end with the whole company on stage singing a song from the play. Which song would you choose?
- **Costume designer:** what colours and styles of costume would you choose for each character at the end of the play?
- **Set designer:** where and when would you want the play to be set? What stage scenery and props could you use to portray this setting?
- **Choreographer:** at which points in the play might a choreographer work with the actors? Write notes for where and how you might want to choreograph a fight scene or a dance sequence in the play.

◆ Develop and prepare your presentation.

2 Did Shakespeare believe it?

Do you think Shakespeare believed in the possibility of a rural utopia where happiness and community spirit reigned? Or was his intention to subvert the notion of that ideal world, showing its impossibility?

◆ In role as Shakespeare, take turns to sit in the hot-seat and answer questions about your ideas of an ideal world in As You Like It.

3 Happily ever after?

Several predictions are made about the couples at the end of the play:

- Jaques says that Touchstone's and Audrey's happiness will not last – they will soon quarrel.
- Hymen says that no troubles will come between Rosalind and Orlando.
- When Phoebe realises that Ganymede is actually a woman, she tells Silvius that his faith (constancy) has finally won her love.
- Rosalind says that Celia and Oliver are so much in love that violence will not part them.

◆ Imagine that the main characters from the play come together for an anniversary party five years after this last scene. What do you think has happened to each of them? Step into role as one of these characters and write your diary entry after the party has taken place. Describe how life is for you and for everyone else, and record some of the things the other characters said and did during the party.

5 A missing scene?

Dr Samuel Johnson, a famous editor and critic of Shakespeare's work, thought that Shakespeare should have taken the opportunity to teach a moral lesson by writing a scene showing Duke Frederick's meeting with the 'old religious man'.

◆ Remind yourself of the report of the meeting (Act 5 Scene 4, lines 138–49). Then write this 'missing scene' in modern English to show what happened to Duke Frederick. Explain his conversion and his decision to withdraw from the world and to renounce all his ill-gotten land and titles.

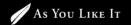

Perspectives and themes

What is the play about?

One way of answering the question 'What is As You Like It about?' is to identify the themes of the play. Themes are ideas or concepts of fundamental importance that recur throughout the play, linking together plot, characters and language. Themes echo, reinforce and comment upon one another and upon the whole play in interesting ways. It would be difficult to write about appearance and reality in the play without referring to the manifestation of evil. It would be equally problematic to write about kingship and masculinity without talking about the themes of loyalty and ambition.

As you can see, themes are not individual categories but a 'tangle' of ideas and concerns that are interrelated in complex ways. In your writing, you should aim to explore the way these themes cross over and illuminate each other, rather than simply listing each of the themes. You might also like to think about the way the themes work at different levels: the individual level (psychological or personal); the social level (linked to society and nation); and the natural level (the natural or supernatural world). For example, in As You Like It you can clearly see how the theme of appearance and reality works across all three of these levels. The following themes can be traced through the play; there are, of course, others – some of which you may have already identified.

Themes

Court versus country

The tradition of pastoral romance (see pp. 165–6) portrayed rural life as an ideal world of innocence and freedom. It was a world into which kings, queens and courtiers could escape, disguised as shepherds and shepherdesses, to enjoy the tranquillity and harmony of country life. On the surface, Shakespeare seems to follow that tradition: As You Like It is full of contrasts between court and country. In the court, brother is set against brother, and ambition, envy and intrigue are commonplace. Duke Frederick has usurped his brother, and he exiles his niece Rosalind on pain of death.

In contrast, the exiles in the Forest of Arden seem to live contentedly as a friendly community. The court appears to be an unnatural and unhappy place, corrupt and artificial; in contrast, the country has a more benign, joyful air of freedom. However, all might not be as clear-cut as it seems.

◆ Devise a dramatic presentation that contrasts life at 'court' with life in the 'country'. Create a series of contrasting tableaux, and set them to a brief narrative voiceover or a suitable musical accompaniment. Try to portray the complexity and contradictory nature of each world beyond its superficial appearance (read through the next section for more ideas).

The Forest of Arden as a utopia

Arden appears to be a refuge from the hypocrisy, deceit and ambition of the court. It seems a place of harmony, free from the anger of fathers and brothers, from envy and malice, and from the false friendship of flattering courtiers. It is an enchanted, innocent world where happiness is truly possible and where community, brotherhood and welcoming hospitality can be found. It apparently fosters regeneration and reconciliation, as characters are changed by their experience, discovering truths about themselves and others. As Charles the wrestler says, Arden is like the 'golden world' of Classical writing (see p. 165) or the simple, egalitarian world of Robin Hood and his merry men.

But the Forest of Arden is not an idealised utopia. It has its own perils: harsh winds, cold weather, low wages, hard masters, dangerous creatures, weariness, hunting and death, hunger and exhaustion. The critic Jan Kott called it 'Bitter Arcadia', and characters in the play refer to it as a 'desert'. The man who employs Corin is a hard taskmaster, and Jaques cynically comments on the foolishness of the man who leaves 'his wealth and ease' for the rough pleasures of the forest. Phoebe cruelly scorns the besotted Silvius, and is quite unlike the idealised shepherdess of the romantic tradition. The native deer are hunted to death by the exiled lords, and snakes and lions threaten people's lives.

◆ Look up some accounts of either the Garden of Eden or the 'golden world' of Classical writings, and compare their features with those of Arden as it is described in the play (particularly at the beginning of Act 2 Scene 1). Write an essay entitled 'What kind of Eden is Arden?' Consider Arden's function in *As You Like It* and look carefully at what happens when the characters bring their issues and problems into this supposedly utopian world.

Love

Love is the driving force of the play. Within a few minutes of her first appearance, Rosalind asks the question 'what think you of falling in love?' and the rest of the play explores love in many of its forms and expressions:

* brotherly love
* love as friendship and service
* self-love
* love as lust
* idealised love
* cruel love
* sincere love
* love at first sight.

As You Like It considers a variety of viewpoints as characters express and criticise the absurdities and contradictions of love. But in spite of (or perhaps because of) all the trials and tribulations of love, the play ends happily in the marriages of the four pairs of lovers.

◆ Find as many examples as you can in the script of the different forms and expressions of love listed opposite. Describe how your example fits each heading. For example:

* **Brotherly love:** Orlando saves Oliver from a lion.
* **Love as friendship and service:** Adam's devotion to Orlando and his late father (and Orlando's compassion towards Adam).

Gender

As You Like It may be a play partly about love, but it is also about gender and sexuality. Rosalind is a young woman who dresses as a young man as she flees from the court. Although she is a woman, it is as Ganymede that she woos Orlando and inadvertently attracts Phoebe. She uses her disguise as Ganymede to encourage Orlando to woo Rosalind, and tricks Orlando into promising to marry her. Through these complicated arrangements, the play shows how Rosalind seems able to subvert traditional gender roles and question the boundaries her society places on sexuality and gender.

Cross-dressing characters are a common feature of Shakespeare's plays, and manifest some of the gender transformations mentioned above. In Shakespeare's time, the sexual ambiguity was heightened in performance: the audience saw a boy actor playing a girl (Phoebe), falling in love with a boy (Ganymede), who is a girl (Rosalind) played by a boy actor! The comedy here might also come from the fact that Rosalind overacts to draw attention to the role reversal. These kind of jokes are **meta-theatrical** in that they draw attention to the play as an illusion and to the conventions of acting that sustain this illusion, even while they break it.

◆ As you can see by looking at the photos of Rosalind in this edition, the appearance of Ganymede can vary dramatically from play to play. Some productions have a more traditionally masculine Ganymede, some aim to blur the distinction between the genders and present a thinly disguised, very feminine Ganymede. Choose which type of disguise you would have in a modern production of the play, and explain why you think it would work best.

Appearance and reality – 'Most friendship is feigning'

Things are not as they seem in *As You Like It*. Oliver deceives Charles about Orlando; Amiens sings of false friendship; the seemingly benign Forest of Arden conceals hardships and dangers. The play sets an ongoing puzzle about the nature of the different types of love it portrays: which are real and which are merely pretence?

The most obvious way in which the play explores the theme of appearance and reality is through disguise. Celia, a princess, disguises herself as a shepherdess called Aliena. Rosalind disguises herself as a youth, the boy Ganymede, and fools the inhabitants of the forest. Most notably, she uses her disguise to conceal and to reveal her true feelings for Orlando. Under cover of her disguise, Rosalind can speak as she really feels and enjoy Orlando's wooing. The dramatic irony of the deception lies in the fact that Orlando does not recognise the truth of what Rosalind says, but the audience does.

◆ Some characters are aware that things are not as they seem, but most are duped by outward appearance. Select four key moments from the play and describe what evidence of false impressions you can find there. How are these moments perceived differently by each of the characters involved? For example, one key moment is where Celia knows that Ganymede is Rosalind in disguise, but Orlando does not.

Order and disorder – 'there begins my sadness'

The play begins with a portrait of disorder. Orlando is rebelling against his cruel treatment by his brother, and Duke Frederick has already disrupted the moral and social fabric of the kingdom by overthrowing his brother and seizing his dukedom. The long middle section of the play then takes place in the apparently peaceful world of Arden. The disorder here is created by the trials of love, as well as the conflict between appearance and reality. The play ends with order restored: Orlando and Oliver are reconciled, four marriages are proclaimed and Duke Senior is returned to his rightful position of Duke.

◆ Some stage productions portray the theme of order and disorder by showing the Forest of Arden as a harsh winter setting that changes to one of high summer for the celebrations of marriage and happiness at the end of the play. How would you use costume, lighting, music and set design to illustrate the theme of order and disorder in a modern production?

Time and change – there's no clock in the forest

Time is discussed in various ways in the play: Rosalind claims that time travels at different speeds, and gives examples of its 'diverse paces'; Jaques remarks bitingly that 'from hour to hour, we rot and rot'. After the hectic speed of the first act, time seems to stand still in the Forest of Arden. The forest itself marks a sort of holiday, a time away from the hurried drama of the court. But holidays don't last forever, and at the end the Duke and his court leave Arden. Jaques's 'seven ages of man' is the play's best-known expression of the passage of time, and the unavoidable changes that accompany it.

As in every Shakespeare play, change is a major theme of *As You Like It*. Celia and Rosalind disguise themselves as Aliena and Ganymede, changing from princesses to a shepherdess and her brother. At the end of the play, both return to their status as princesses. Orlando begins

penniless, a victim of his brother's hatred. He ends the play married to Duke Senior's daughter with the prospect of becoming heir to the dukedom. The 'villains' of Act 1, Oliver and Duke Frederick, are converted to goodness in the final scenes. Only Jaques seems unchanged at the play's end.

◆ In groups, discuss each character in turn. Describe how they change, if at all, over the course of the play (in social status, moral awareness or understanding, knowledge of others/love/themselves). Then take turns in the hot-seat to answer questions from the rest of the group while in role as different characters.

▼ Why do you think Jaques is the only character that remains apparently unchanged at the end of the play?

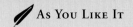

Perspectives

Another way of thinking about the play is to explore the range of interpretations that can be applied to it. Early critics of *As You Like It* were overwhelmingly concerned with Rosalind and with the play as entertainment. Recent criticism has dealt with issues of gender, patriarchy, social hierarchy and personal identity, as you will see below. Of course, there are many other perspectives to the play, and it is up to you to engage with the variety of meanings and to decide what you think the play is about. The following strands of criticism concentrate on particular aspects of the play, and evaluate its meaning based on these primary concerns.

Cultural-materialist criticism

A cultural materialist critique of *As You Like It* argues that the play offers a subversive critique of the social and political beliefs of Shakespeare's time. It looks at the way politics, wealth and power strongly influence every human relationship, and considers how these ideas are thrown into relief by the play's movement from court to country.

Feminist criticism

In feminist readings of the play, gender issues are politicised and critiqued from women's perspectives. This includes looking at the way women and their experiences are represented in literature. In *As You Like It*, the social and symbolic construction of gender, as shown in Rosalind's cross-dressing, allows for exploration of the roles and experiences of women in Shakespeare's time and today.

New-historicist criticism

This strand of criticism places the play firmly in its historical context, to explore ideas about society and power that were current at the time. With regard to *As You Like It*, important factors include the acts of subversion and the way these moments of disorder are contained within the action of the play.

Performance criticism

This approach explores *As You Like it* as a performance text, analysing past and present theatrical productions to consider the changing ways in which the play has been interpreted. In more recent years, this also encompasses film and other moving-image interpretations.

Psychoanalytical criticism

A psychoanalytical critique focuses on currents of desire and repressed sexuality that run beneath the surface of the play and drive its action. It pays particular attention to aspects of cross-dressing and construction of gender that are explored in the play.

None of these readings could be claimed to be the 'correct' one, and at the heart of modern forms of criticism is the belief that all interpretation carries certain assumptions (for example, about society, about what literature is and about political issues referenced in the play).

◆ Working in small groups, devise a short series of tableaux that illustrate some of the themes or possible perspectives of the play. Present your tableaux to other groups, freezing each one for one minute so your audience can guess which theme or perspective you are portraying.

◆ Afterwards, discuss as a class why your group chose to portray those particular themes or perspectives, and try to find links between them. Talk together about whether some of the critical perspectives described above might focus on certain themes, and why that might be. You might like to undertake further research on some of these interpretive approaches to the play in order to understand them more fully.

Contexts and sources

The educated members of Shakespeare's audience would have enjoyed *As You Like It*'s many literary, biblical and Classical allusions. They would have recognised in the play the influence of the books they read for pleasure, picking up its references to the Roman poet Ovid and to the various elements of Classical mythology. They would have also been aware of the elements of pastoral romance in the play, the parody of this type of romance, and the allusions to a story by Thomas Lodge with a similar heroine named Rosalynde.

The pastoral romance tradition

As Shakespeare wrote *As You Like It*, he was greatly influenced by what is now called the pastoral romance tradition. This was made up of two major strands: 'pastoral' and 'romance'.

Pastoral

Pastoral literature and drama idealised nature and rural life. It presented the country as a place of escape, far superior to the city. The country taught moral lessons ('books in the running brooks, / Sermons in stones, and good in everything', Act 2 Scene 1, lines 16–17). In the country, far away from the town, human nature could be changed for the better.

The Greek poet Theocritus (310–250 BC), and other writers of Classical antiquity, imagined a golden world of peaceful and harmonious country life. This rural idyll was peopled by beautiful shepherdesses and shepherds (often aristocrats in disguise as humble country folk) who were poets, philosophers and lovers. Before the French Revolution, Queen Marie Antoinette created her own rural idyll, without dirt or labour, where she and her attendants dressed up as shepherdesses and shepherds.

See pages 46, 98, 100, 128 and 154 for discussion and activities relating to the pastoral tradition.

Romance

The romance tradition largely derives from stories of love and chivalry, which were very popular in the Middle Ages. Famous examples of these are the tales of King Arthur, the 'Chanson de Roland', 'Roman de la Rose' and Chaucer's 'Knight's Tale' in *The Canterbury Tales*. The stories dealt with the trials of young knights, and presented two views of love: courtly and romantic.

Courtly love was sexless. It was the idealised love between a love-struck, languishing man and an unattainable woman whom he worshipped as a goddess. Only by long devotion, many trials and much suffering could a man attract the attention of this woman, the 'fair, cruel maid' of literature.

Romantic love was also idealised, but it included the spontaneous and emotional feature of 'love at first sight', and a happy marriage was seen as its natural result.

See pages 70, 76, 88, 90 and 98 for discussion and activities relating to romantic love.

Pastoral romance

The two earlier traditions described above increasingly merged into pastoral romance as time went on. Pastoral romance literature often included certain major features:

- **Shepherds** Lovesick shepherds yearn for scornful shepherdesses.
- **Forest** In this setting, magical transformations occur and true love flourishes after rigorous testing; it is a place of deposed rulers, 'merry men', kindly outlaws and magicians.
- **Journeys** A young knight leaves court to travel and seek his fortune.
- **Adventures** The knight has many adventures in remote places.
- **Adversity** Misfortune besets the knight and he undergoes many trials, from which he learns.
- **Love** The knight loves a beautiful woman, and she occupies all his thoughts.

- **Faithfulness** Constancy (fidelity) is highly valued.
- **Coincidence** All kinds of improbabilities and coincidences occur.
- **Female beauty** A beautiful woman has a harsh father, and is much prized.
- **Disguise** Mistaken identity and disguise feature in many stories.
- **Happy endings** The knight marries his beloved, and the stories end with forgiveness, reconciliation and the triumph of virtue.

Many members of Shakespeare's audience came to the Globe Theatre with a deep knowledge of pastoral romance literature. They expected to see its themes, characters and conventions portrayed on stage. Shakespeare fulfilled their expectations, but he also gave his audience something radically different. *As You Like It* shows that women can more than hold their own in the battle of the sexes. Rosalind takes the lead, directing and controlling the process of wooing – and falling head over heels in love herself. *As You Like It* also shows that the forest is a place of hardship and suffering as well as one of magical transformations and kindly outlaws.

◆ In pairs, identify how each element of pastoral romance in the list above is represented in *As You Like It*. You should note where any of these elements are contrasted, questioned or parodied in the play. Use the photographs of different interpretations of Arden opposite to prompt your ideas and discussion.

The name 'Arden' would have resonated with Shakespeare on different levels. To begin with it is, as Juliet Dunisberre suggests, a combination of 'Arcadia' and 'Eden' – two imagined sites of earthly paradise and harmony. In addition, 'Arden' is the name of an actual forest in Warwickshire. This ancient woodland lay to the north-west of the Avon River, near the village of Wilmcote where Shakespeare's mother was born. There was also another woodland called Arden, near to where Shakespeare lived as a child. Interestingly, Shakespeare's mother's maiden name was also 'Arden'. You can see why this name would have been significant to Shakespeare!

Shakespeare would certainly have been aware of the pastoral tradition in English folk tales – such as that of Robin Hood and his merry men in Sherwood Forest, fugitives who lived out in the woodland and stole from the rich to feed the poor. It is possible that these stories originated in Warwickshire, where a man called Robin of Loxley became an outlaw and lived in the local woodlands until Richard the Lionheart came back from the Crusades and restored his lands to him. Whether the Robin Hood stories originated near Stratford-on-Avon or further up north, it is clear they made an impact on Shakespeare. In *As You Like It*, Charles likens Duke Senior to Robin Hood:

> They say he is already in the Forest of Arden, and a many merry men with him; and there they live like the old Robin Hood of England. They say many young gentlemen flock to him every day, and fleet the time carelessly, as they did in the golden world.

These side-by-side references to Robin Hood and to the 'golden world' were significant because in Shakespeare's day poets liked to draw comparisons between Queen Elizabeth and the goddess Astraea – a goddess of justice who lived on Earth during the mythical Golden Age, but fled from it due to the increasing wickedness of humans. Many of Elizabeth's supporters believed she had established a new 'Golden Age' in England.

A statue of Robin Hood stands today beside the walls of Nottingham Castle.

Shakespeare finds his story

As pages 165–6 show, the stories and plays of the pastoral romance tradition were very popular in Shakespeare's time. Shakespeare used one of these stories, *Rosalynde, Euphues Golden Legacie* (1590) by Thomas Lodge, as the inspiration for the plot of *As You Like It*. He added the characters of Jaques, Touchstone, Audrey and William, but retained most of the original story.

The following summary of *Rosalynde* shows how closely Shakespeare followed Lodge's tale (the names of Shakespeare's characters are included in brackets the first time they appear):

> *A nobleman dies, leaving three sons. The youngest son, Rosader (Orlando) is kept in poverty by the oldest son, Saladyne (Oliver).*
>
> *Saladyne plots that a wrestler kill Rosader. But Rosader defeats the wrestler. Rosalynde (Rosalind) watches the fight and falls in love with Rosader. She is the daughter of the rightful king, who has been overthrown and now lives in exile.*
>
> *Saladyne again plots to kill Rosader, who flees to the Forest of Arden together with his loyal servant Adam Spencer (Adam). He and Adam receive hospitality from the exiled king.*
>
> *Rosalynde is banished from court. She flees with Alinda (Celia), daughter of the wrongful king, to the Forest of Arden. They disguise themselves as Ganymede and Aliena.*
>
> *They overhear a young shepherd (Silvius) telling an old shepherd (Corin) of his unrequited love for Phoebe (Phoebe), a shepherdess. They give money to the shepherds.*
>
> *Rosader writes love poems to Rosalynde, who, as Ganymede, encourages Rosader to woo her as if she were Rosalynde. Aliena conducts a mock wedding of Rosalynde and Rosader. Phoebe falls in love with Ganymede.*
>
> *Rosader rescues his brother from a lion. Saladyne and Aliena fall in love. Rosalynde drops her disguise as Ganymede.*
>
> *Three marriages are celebrated.*

◆ In Shakespeare's day, plots were borrowed and adapted from many different sources as a normal part of creating a new play. Discuss the difference between using sources in this way and copying other people's work (plagiarising). You might like to research Shakespeare's use of sources as you consider this question.

◆ Step into role as Shakespeare. How would you defend yourself against an accusation of plagiarism? Prepare your argument while your partner thinks of questions to ask you as part of a tough interview.

Characters

A good deal of recent literary theory assumes that the most important aspect of a 'character' is the dramatic function they fulfil within the social and political context of the play and the fact that they exist only whilst on stage within the play's dramatically created world.

In every performance of *As You Like It* a different interpretation of each character is forged. There is no one definitive portrayal of the characters: they are complex, at times ambiguous or riddled with contradictions, and yet always reinvented afresh in each new performance or reading of the play. Keep all these considerations in mind as you explore Shakespeare's characters in the following pages.

Rosalind

Rosalind is one of the longest parts in all Shakespeare: she has more lines than Macbeth or Prospero. Rosalind appears first as a typical court lady, enjoying witty wordplay with her cousin Celia. In her early scenes, she seems to accept a subordinate role to Celia (it is Celia's suggestion that they leave the court and go to Arden). But as the play moves to the forest and she takes up her male disguise as Ganymede, Rosalind takes the initiative more and more. She controls the action, manipulating other characters and exercising her strong sense of humour as she alternately mocks and celebrates love.

In the forest, as Ganymede, Rosalind befriends and tests Orlando, with whom she is head over heels in love. Rosalind displays the range of emotions that one might expect someone in love to feel: she is downcast at Orlando's lateness; she fires a breathless list of questions at Celia, demanding to know who has written poems to her; she delights in hearing Celia talk about Orlando, and relishes the flirting and wordplay in the 'wooing scene' (Act 4 Scene 1, lines 31–161); she expresses sheer exuberance in 'O coz, coz, coz'; and she faints at the sight of a handkerchief stained with her lover's blood.

However, Rosalind's love is also clear-sighted and sceptical. She is not fooled by the bad verses that Orlando writes about her, and she mocks his claim that he will love for ever and a day. There is stark realism in her recognition that 'men have died … but not for love'. Rosalind finally becomes a kind of 'mistress of ceremonies', and arranges the happy ending of multiple marriages.

Below are three comments about Rosalind.

> *Dorothy Tutin plays Rosalind in the disguise scenes with an air of bewildered self-mockery; her comic timing is superb, especially in her deliciously funny attempts to play the man …*
>
> Critic Doreen Tanner

> *[She] never allowed her clothes to distract us from her basic femininity. Her gauche walk, the awkward movement of her hands into her trouser pockets, the timorous way in which she bunched a fist, were there to remind us that she was first and foremost a woman in love.*
>
> Critic Milton Schulman

> *The popularity of Rosalind is due to three main causes. First, she only speaks blank verse for a few minutes. Second, she only wears a skirt for a few minutes … Third, she makes love to the man instead of waiting for the man to make love to her – a piece of natural history which has kept Shakespeare's heroines alive, whilst generations of properly governessed young ladies, taught to say 'No' three times at least, have miserably perished.*
>
> Playwright and critic George Bernard Shaw

◆ How do you see Rosalind? Choose one of the critics' quotes above, then gather evidence from the play to show why you agree or disagree with these comments. Display your evidence in a mind-map, and then perhaps write it up as a few paragraphs of continuous prose.

So we discover immediately that Rosalind is a divided spirit, part of her in exile with her father, and displaced; and that, for Celia, the wounds of the past lie between them, ever present, and can be healed only through the generosity of her affection. There is a sense of urgency about their respective declarations which suggests that the situation for them both is gathering momentum with time, not easing with it.

Actors Fiona Shaw and Juliet Stevenson

◆ **Script an imaginary conversation with the actors quoted above, in which you discuss their interpretation of the characters. Express your own views and consider what they might say in response.**

Celia

Celia is the daughter of the wicked Duke Frederick, and the cousin and best friend of Rosalind. She stands up to her angry father and proposes the plan of escape to Arden, where she disguises herself as a shepherdess. She seems to become more reserved as the play progresses, taking a subordinate role to Rosalind and having less and less to say (she is silent in Act 5).

◆ Discuss Celia in pairs, and ask yourselves: is she genuinely critical of Rosalind in the wooing episode? Does she become increasingly separated from Rosalind, aware that she is losing her best friend?

The friendship and familial bond between Rosalind and Celia is another central 'love' in the play. Fiona Shaw and Juliet Stevenson talk about the strength and humanity of this attachment:

> If the struggle for women is a struggle to be human in a world which declares them only to be female, then this was the territory of As You Like It which most engaged and challenged us. If we even in part gave resonance to the story of Rosalind and Celia, then the struggle was richly rewarded.

Celia and Rosalind's relationship can be interpreted in many ways, and the deep, shifting, complex nature of their connection invites a multi-faceted approach within each different production.

> Deirdre Mullins and Beth Park have charming chemistry as the slapstick duo of Rosalind (Mullins) and Celia. Their on-stage relationship begins with flirtatious play-fighting and solidarity against men (they spit audibly whenever the opposite sex is mentioned) and good-hearted rivalry for Orlando's affections, to a deep appreciation of each other's character.
> Review of a performance at Shakespeare's Globe, Emily Jupp, *The Independent*, 2012

> Samantha Spiro as a fiery, bespectacled Celia was forever eyeing anxiously Rosalind's meetings with Orlando, because from the moment he first appeared it was comically obvious that she also rather fancied him.
> Editors Mike Clamp and Perry Mills, Cambridge School Shakespeare Picture Collection

◆ How would you want to portray Celia on stage to show her character and her relationship with the other characters? In role as a director of a new production, write separate emails to the costume designer and the actor playing Celia. Tell them your ideas about the costume, props and behaviour that you think should be used in bringing Celia's character to life on stage.

Orlando

Just as Rosalind is despised and threatened by her uncle despite her innocence, Orlando is wrongly treated by a close relative who hates him only for his goodness. His eldest brother, Oliver, has denied him education and money, and now plans to murder him. After defeating Charles the wrestler, Orlando flees to the Forest of Arden with Adam, his old servant. In the forest, he plays out the role of a foolish courtly lover, writing bad verses to his beloved Rosalind and hanging them on trees. But Rosalind, in disguise as Ganymede, persuades him to woo her and he discovers true love. Towards the end of the play, he is wounded as he saves his wicked brother Oliver from a hungry lion. At the end of the play, he is set to marry Rosalind and become heir to Duke Senior.

Although he defeats Charles in the wrestling match early in the play, Orlando is portrayed as 'gentle' and 'sweet' – a downtrodden, hard-done-by romantic character, tending to foolishness in his verses – until at the end of the play he rescues his brother from the lion and re-establishes his 'manly', heroic qualities. Orlando's 'gentleness' is more than our present-day associations of 'gentle' with 'kindness' and 'softness'. Rather, he is a gentleman of aristocratic birth (he, like Oliver, is the son of Roland de Boys), with associations of nobility and selflessness.

Several actors who have not themselves played Orlando have yet been struck by the dynamism and complexity of Orlando's character and role in the play:

> The wrestling match is crucially important to the first part of the play because of what it releases in all those attending it … the lid springs off Duke Frederick's latest tyranny, Rosalind's passion, and Celia's grief at her father's wrongs. Orlando finds his heart in love and his life at stake.
>
> Actors Fiona Shaw and Juliet Stevenson

> … a very tricky part, at once full of bullish machismo, then suddenly prancing through the trees in the depths of romantic gooey-ness.
>
> Actor David Tennant

◆ Consider each of the comments above about Orlando. Talk with a partner about which of them you think is most helpful in defining the essence of Orlando's character, and why that is. When you have identified the one that you think gets closest to the truth, present your thoughts to the rest of the class. Be prepared to explain and defend your views with examples from the text.

Oliver

Oliver de Boys ignores his father's dying wishes. He refuses to give Orlando the wealth, status and schooling that is properly due to him. Early in the play, Oliver appears violent and ruthless. He remains relentless, hard and uncompromising in his attitude to his brother and even to Adam, the old servant who served his father for most of his life. Oliver appears to be a usurper similar to Duke Frederick, and in the scenes where the two villains are together we see their greed and violence as they plot to get rid of any contender to their unlawful authority.

However, Oliver undergoes a dramatic change of heart. His journey into the forest starts off with murderous intentions, but away from the corrupt court he experiences a new vulnerability and a new understanding of life and death. When his wronged brother, Orlando, finds him asleep and in danger of being killed by wild forest beasts, he does not choose revenge but selflessly rescues him, incurring injuries of his own. Oliver is swayed by his brother's generosity in saving him from death, and his conversion is complete: he renounces his former way of life and his unjust treatment of Orlando. When Oliver brings news of Orlando's injury to Rosalind, he meets Celia and falls instantly in love with her. He marries Celia, and gives all his lands and possessions to Orlando.

◆ Oliver's perspective is interesting because he undergoes such a dramatic change of heart towards Orlando and the other exiles. What questions would you want to ask him? In groups, put Oliver in the hot-seat: prepare some questions, and then take turns to step into role as Oliver and answer them.

Duke Senior and Duke Frederick

Duke Senior has been deposed by his brother, Frederick, and has escaped into the forest with his loyal courtiers. In the Forest of Arden, they live as outlaws – hiding away from the court, eating the food of the forest and practising hospitality to those they meet there (such as the hungry Orlando and Adam). Their simple lives are contrasted with the corrupt and greedy court, and Duke Senior relishes the lessons that country life can teach. At the end of the play, he is happy to return to court life – perhaps because he has become bored of the simple life of the forest, or maybe because he knows that the lessons he has learnt there will make him a better ruler.

Duke Frederick is the usurper who has seized his brother's dukedom. Injustice and vindictiveness reign in his court, and he is a violent ruler who is always seeking to protect his authority. He threatens Rosalind with death, and in so doing alienates his own daughter, Celia, who sees her cousin Rosalind as her sister and closest friend. Duke Frederick's cruelty and selfishness then leads him to take an army into the Forest of Arden to kill his brother. Surprisingly, he meets an old religious man while in the forest and is condemned for his evil intentions. He undergoes a striking change of mind, gives up all his former wickedness, and resolves to live the simple life of a hermit in the forest rather than the luxurious life of an unlawful ruler. At the end of the play, he is happy to give the dukedom back to his brother.

♦ In pairs, step into roles as Duke Senior and Duke Frederick. Improvise a scene in which each of you tells the story of the play from the point of view of your character. Include any developments that are mentioned in the play but are not seen by the audience. You could also imagine what happens to Duke Senior when he returns to court to rule again, and how Duke Senior fares in the humble life of a country hermit.

Touchstone

Touchstone is the court jester or fool, who joins Rosalind and Celia in their escape to the Forest of Arden. His loyalty to the two exiles and his witty remarks make him a valuable companion in this dangerous journey. When not in disguise, Touchstone would traditionally wear the distinctive costume of a fool, which might include a patchwork coat, colourful breeches, and a hood or cape decorated with donkey's ears or the crest of a rooster. As a fool, he would often carry a short stick – his 'sceptre' – and be accompanied by the jangling sound of the small bells sewn into his costume. This costume was referred to as 'motley' – a word that describes the incongruous colours and diverse fabrics of his outfit. Jaques admires not only the wit of Touchstone, but also his costume: 'O noble fool! A worthy fool! Motley's the only wear.'

Touchstone's role in court was that of licensed fool: to comment on what he saw around him, exposing folly and dishonesty. His name signifies his dramatic function: a touchstone was used to reveal if a metal was true gold. Touchstone similarly tests the genuineness of characters with his sceptical comments. In Act 5 Scene 4, Duke Senior says of Touchstone, 'He uses his folly like a stalking-horse, and under the presentation of that he shoots his wit'. However, as Celia reminds Touchstone, he could also be whipped for speaking the truth.

The clown role in Shakespeare's plays was influenced by two very different actors in his theatre company. William Kempe, who was part of the company from 1594 to 1599 was famous as a clown who performed comic jigs, bawdy tales or satirical songs. Robert Armin, who took over from 1599 (until 1610), was known as a more intellectual fool, contributing to the development of the plot and able to sing and provide music on stage. There is a marked difference in the kind of fools presented by these two actors, and this is reflected in Shakespeare's plays. Kempe's clowning and jigging was not to everyone's taste, and some people preferred Armin's more philosophical and intellectual fool. His witty repartee and critical comment on social superiors was licensed by his status, and he often improvised satirical lines directed at members of the audience as well.

◆ Find out more about William Kempe and Robert Armin, and about the first performance of *As You Like It*. Which actor do you think would have played Touchstone originally? Who would you prefer to see in the role? Can you think of any modern actors or comedians that you think could play the part well?

The flights of ideas, the energy of thought and the inability to shut up are all traits of manic episodes in a bipolar mental illness. It is perhaps an actor's affectation to think of Shakespearean characterisation in this way, but it helped me to make sense of some of Touchstone's less easily motivated moments.

Actor David Tennant, on playing Touchstone

Touchstone, authentically witty, is rancidly vicious, while Jaques is merely rancid … Both of them are in As You Like It *to serve as touchstones for Rosalind's more congenial wit, and she triumphantly puts them in their places.*

Critic and editor Harold Bloom

◆ Can you find examples of where Touchstone tests the genuineness of characters with his sceptical comments and witty remarks, as his name suggests he should?

Audrey

Audrey is a goatherd, and her personality is simple and down to earth. Unlike Phoebe or Celia, she is a 'real' rural character, and on stage she is often played as a dirty, rough country wench.

◆ Draw a prop that you feel would give important information to the audience about Audrey. Make notes on how the actor playing Audrey could use

it for maximum effect – perhaps in multiple ways. Find instances in the script where other characters – for example, Touchstone or Rosalind – could pick up the prop and interact with it themselves. Describe how you would use these moments to show how their personalities differ from Audrey's rustic and unpretentious image.

Jaques – 'They say you are a melancholy fellow'

Today, the melancholy Jaques would probably be called neurotic or unbalanced. He is the malcontent – a familiar role in Elizabethan times: a sardonic observer who comments cynically on everything and everybody around him, seeing only foolishness, absurdities and ingratitude. He has a jaundiced, pessimistic view of the world, and would almost certainly agree with Hamlet's description of it as 'weary, stale, flat and unprofitable'. Duke Senior accuses him of having been 'a libertine' who now wishes to make the world as corrupt as himself.

◆ As you think about Jaques's character, explore possible answers to some of the following questions:

- Is he playing a role to hide his true feelings, and what might these be?
- Why does Duke Senior enjoy his company? Does he have a genuine sense of humour?
- What do you make of his final decision not to take part in the celebrations, but to join Duke Frederick in rejecting court life?
- Audrey calls him 'the old gentleman'. How old do you think he is, and why?
- What is your own attitude towards Jaques?

◆ If Jaques were a real person living today, what do you think he would list as his:

- favourite movie?
- favourite book and/or magazine?
- favourite television programme?
- favourite type of music?
- favourite sport?
- occupation?
- leisure activities?
- views of key current affairs?

◆ Construct a social media profile for the character of Jaques. Include five examples of his 'recent activity' – this could be status updates, comments made on other characters' photos or statuses, or 'liked' pages.

The shepherds: Silvius and Phoebe

Elizabethans would recognise Silvius and Phoebe as stock characters from pastoral literature. Speaking in elegant, polished verse, they are traditional figures of the court in the country. Silvius is the lovelorn faithful shepherd, who suffers the pains of unrequited love. Phoebe is the disdainful shepherdess, the cruel mistress of pastoral literature, whose beautiful face conceals a hard heart. She rejects and humiliates Silvius, but falls for Rosalind disguised as Ganymede. When Rosalind throws off her disguise, Phoebe agrees to marry Silvius.

◆ Think of two actors that you think would work well together as Silvius and Phoebe. Draft a letter asking them to take on the roles in your next production. In the letter, outline your vision for their characters, and for the wider context of the play's setting, and explain why you think they are perfect for this role.

The two old men: Adam and Corin

Adam represents an older world of loyal and faithful service. He gives his life savings to Orlando and goes with him into exile in Arden. He disappears from the play after Act 2: what do you think happens to him? Remember also that actors often played more than one character in Shakespeare's day. What role might the actor playing Adam have taken after Act 2?

Corin is content in his modest life as a shepherd in the forest and calls himself 'a true labourer'. He has served a hard master, but finds better employment with Celia and Rosalind. He counsels Silvius on love, and endures Touchstone's condescension with good humour.

◆ With a partner, discuss whether you think the roles of Adam and Corin should be played seriously, with quiet wisdom and dignity, or as comic characters with exaggerated infirmities and eccentricities. Design costumes and props, and write actors' notes on movement and gestures, for either serious or comic interpretations of both characters.

Visions of the characters

◆ In small groups, make a list of all the 'main' characters in the play. You will have to discuss this, and agree on who you would include or exclude in this category. Take each selected character in turn and look through all the images of them in this edition (including the photo gallery at the beginning). Make notes on what characteristics are emphasised in the various images, making sure you consider age, ethnicity, physical features, facial expressions, clothes and props as appropriate. Then individually decide which photo best fits your idea of how the role should be portrayed, and give reasons for your choice. Which aspects are most important, and which are least important, for each character? Present your choice for each character, along with your reasons, to the rest of the group.

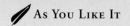

The language of *As You Like It*

Dramatic language

Clues in the script

Shakespeare was writing at a time when theatres could only create a very few special effects, so he used language to establish atmosphere, mood and setting. To set the scene for the audience, he included vivid descriptions in the dialogue; to give actors clues about their actions, embedded stage directions were included in the script. Here are some examples:

> Are not these woods
> More free from peril than the envious court?
> > (Act 2 Scene 1, lines 3–4)

> I pray you bear with me, I cannot go no further.
> > (Act 2 Scene 4, line 7)

> Forbear, and eat no more!
> > (Act 2 Scene 7, line 88)

> In the which hope, I blush, and hide my sword.
> > (Act 2 Scene 7, line 119)

> Welcome. Set down your venerable burden,
> And let him feed.
> > (Act 2 Scene 7, line 167–8)

> Will you dispatch us here under this tree, or shall we go with you to your chapel?
> > (Act 3 Scene 4, lines 49–50)

◆ Consider the lines shown and identify the internal clues given to guide the actors and the audience. In pairs, decide on the actions each character might perform at that point in the script. Try to make the actions appropriate for the character delivering the lines.

Soliloquies and asides

A **soliloquy** is a monologue spoken by a character who is alone (or assumes they are alone) on stage. It gives the audience direct access to the character's mind, revealing their inner thoughts and motives. There are no soliloquies in *As You Like It*, although Orlando's reflections at the end of Act 1 Scene 2 and in Act 3 Scene 2 come close. Instead, there are many monologues in which characters develop their thoughts while addressing others on stage, such as when Jaques gives his explanation of the 'seven ages of man' in Act 2 Scene 7, or when Phoebe talks about Ganymede in Act 3 Scene 6.

An **aside** is a brief comment or address to the audience that gives voice to a character's inner thoughts, unheard by other characters on stage. The audience is taken into this character's confidence, or can see deeper into their motivations and experiences. Asides can also be used for characters to comment on the action as it unfolds. Although not marked as such, Jaques's lines at the start of Act 3 Scene 4 are generally performed as asides.

◆ Identify some of the play's monologues and asides. Choose one and speak it to a partner. Then write notes on how you would perform it on stage to maximise its dramatic effect. Remember to comment on how the other characters on stage might react to the speech.

◆ Choose one of the photographs in this book and use it as inspiration to write your own aside for one of the characters. This brief comment should reveal the character's thoughts at a particular point in the play, and should be accompanied by appropriate gestures and/or expressions.

◆ Write a soliloquy for one of the characters at a key point in the play, when the audience would benefit from finding out more about their inner feelings and intentions.

Imagery

As You Like It abounds in **imagery**. Imagery is created by using vivid words and phrases to conjure up mental pictures and associations. It provides insight into character and helps the audience use its imagination to transform a bare stage into Duke Frederick's court or the 'golden world' of the Forest of Arden. It deepens the dramatic impact of particular moments, and helps to create distinctive atmospheres and themes.

As You Like It contains a wide range of imagery, particularly that of animals, country life, hunting and theatre. On every page of the play you will find at least one example of imagery, and there are often many more.

Recurring imagery

Animals

There is a wealth of animal imagery in the play. For example, Duke Senior says: 'Sweet are the uses of adversity / Which like the toad, ugly and venomous, / Wears yet a precious jewel in his head' (Act 2 Scene 1, lines 12–14). In Act 4 Scene 1, Rosalind 'had as lief be wooed of a snail' (line 42) and 'will laugh like a hyena' (line 124). It is not so much that animals appear in the Forest of Arden or elsewhere in the play's imagined settings, but more that animal references are used to comment on human nature and various characters' actions and attributes. For an extended example of this, see Act 4 Scene 3, lines 93–115.

Hunting

Images of hunting, particularly of the deer in the Forest of Arden, are prevalent in the play. Celia compares Orlando to a hunter ('furnished like a hunter', Act 3 Scene 3, line 205), and Rosalind pictures 'the pursuit that will be made / After my flight' (Act 1 Scene 3, lines 126–7). But Rosalind is not just Orlando's quarry; he describes her as possessing a 'huntress' name' (Act 3 Scene 2, line 4), too. Many of the characters in the forest are both hunted and hunter. Duke Senior and his court have taken refuge there away from the corruptions of the city court, and their own hunting of the deer ('Come, shall we go and kill us venison?', Act 2 Scene 1, line 21) is symbolic of their new-found power and their part in nature.

Nature's bounty and wisdom

In a play that draws strongly on the pastoral tradition (see pp. 165–6), there are inevitably many images of nature – and connections and comparisons between nature and humanity are often made. In Act 3 Scene 3, Celia says of Orlando that she 'found him under a tree like a dropped acorn' (line 196), and Orlando's poems are hung in trees. Touchstone, in criticising Orlando's verse, remarks that 'Truly, the tree yields bad fruit.' Rosalind's response continues the metaphor of trees and fruit, revealing her wit and mastery of language: 'I'll graft it with you, and then I shall graft it with a medlar; then it will be the earliest fruit i'th'country, for you'll be rotten ere you be half ripe, and that's the right virtue of the medlar' (lines 94–6). (Grafting has the technical sense of splicing one type of tree with another to make a hardier version, and also means to work hard.)

That nature should judge the actions of humans is one of the abiding themes of later Shakespeare plays, and this idea is often contrasted with the corruptions of the city court. As is often the case, wise words on this subject are placed in the mouth of the fool, Touchstone.

Wrestling

Other images that appear in the play are those of sport ('sport for ladies', Act 1 Scene 2, line 109) – in particular, wrestling. The significance of Orlando defeating Charles early in the play is about more than Orlando proving his manhood and attractiveness to Rosalind. Wrestling is court entertainment (of a fairly brutal nature, in this play), and also suggests the complicated moves that Rosalind makes throughout the play to secure her victory – not just in winning Orlando, but also in teaching him how to truly love. Wrestling is both a sport and a deadly serious activity, in which one can be gravely injured. Love is presented as a similarly multi-faceted endeavour, bringing joy and witty frivolity but also pain and anxiety to the play.

The theatre

Shakespeare's preoccupation with the theatre is evident throughout *As You Like It*. The play is full of acting and playing, particularly for those in disguise – like actors, these characters take on new costumes and identities. The many monologues scattered throughout the play, and the different roles portrayed by the characters (romantic lover, melancholic misanthrope, reformed oppressor) remind the audience of other popular dramatic traditions. As Rosalind says of Phoebe and Silvius, 'I'll prove a busy actor in their play'. The theatre is also the central metaphor used by Jaques in his famous reflection on the stages of life:

> *All the world's a stage*
> *And all the men and women merely players:*
> *They have their exists and their entrances*
> *And one man in his time plays many parts,*
> *His acts being seven ages.*
>
> (Act 2 Scene 7, lines 139–42)

◆ Many of the examples of imagery given above are from Acts 1–4. Look at Act 5 to identify the imagery Shakespeare uses there, and how it contributes to the meaning of the play as a whole.

◆ In small groups, list what you think are the key images of the play. Create a collage on a large sheet of paper, using images that you have collected from magazines and pictures that you have drawn yourselves. You can combine images and words, and include pictures from any other sources you come across. Present your collage to other groups, explaining its content by referring closely to the script.

◆ Look at Act 3 Scene 6, lines 8–27, where Shakespeare gently mocks the use of imagery. He gives Phoebe twenty lines, in which she ridicules the imagery based around the idea that a lover's disdainful eyes could inflict cruel wounds. Look closely at these lines, then write your own parody of some of the imagery that Shakespeare uses in this play. Use modern English, and try to identify some of the limitations of the imagery used in the play.

Metaphor, simile and personification

Shakespeare's imagery uses **metaphor**, **simile** or **personification**. All of these language devices are comparisons. A simile compares one thing to another by using 'like' ('creeping like snail / Unwillingly to school') or 'as' ('my age is as a lusty winter'). A metaphor does not use 'like' or 'as', but suggests that two dissimilar things are the same. Examples are Rosalind labelling Silvius 'a tame snake', Orlando calling himself 'a rotten tree' and Touchstone insulting Corin as 'worms' meat'. Personification is a particular type of imagery. It imagines things or ideas as people ('the good housewife Fortune'), giving them human feelings or body parts ('the swift foot of Time'). Jaques and Orlando use personification to bid each other a mocking farewell as 'Signor Love' and 'Monsieur Melancholy'.

◆ Compile a list of metaphors, similes and personification from the script. What do they add to your understanding of the characters or the events of the play?

Verse and prose – 'Didst thou hear these verses?'

Most of the verse in the play is **blank verse** (unrhymed verse with a five-beat rhythm known as iambic pentameter). Each ten-syllable line has five alternating unstressed (×) and stressed (/) syllables, as shown in the line below:

× / × / × / × / × /

Because that I am more than common tall

This rhythmic pattern is what distinguishes verse from prose, rather than rhyming lines. Prose is different from blank verse: it is everyday language with no specific rhythm, metric scheme or rhyme. Shakespeare uses prose to break up the verse in his plays, to signify characters' madness or low status, to draw attention to changes in plot or character, and for other less consistent and obvious reasons (see below for more discussion of this). It is easy to tell the difference: verse passages begin with a capital letter and the lines do not reach the other side of the page, whereas prose passages have lines that reach both sides of the pages and only use capital letters at the beginning of sentences.

◆ To experience the rhythm of iambic pentameter, read a few lines aloud from any of the verse speeches in the play. Pronounce each syllable very clearly, as if it were a separate word. As you speak, beat out the five-beat rhythm by clapping your hands or tapping your desk.

◆ The songs, Orlando's poems, Phoebe's letter and Hymen's blessings are all in verse, but not in the five-beat rhythm of iambic pentameter. Speak a few lines of each aloud to discover their distinctive rhythms.

◆ Invent a few lines of blank verse to describe your response to the play. Make sure that it has the correct structure and rhythm of iambic pentameter.

Over half of *As You Like It* is in prose: almost 1300 lines against just over 1100 lines of verse. How did Shakespeare decide whether to write in verse or prose? In his time, the play-writing convention was that high-status characters spoke in verse and that prose was used for comedy or by low-status characters. However, Rosalind and Celia are high-status characters (they are both the daughters of dukes), yet much of their language is in prose. Silvius and Phoebe, the shepherd and shepherdess (low status), speak in verse.

It may be that as he wrote *As You Like It*, Shakespeare used prose or verse depending on whether he felt the situation to be 'comic' or 'serious'. But even this is not always the case: Oliver uses prose as he urges Charles the wrestler to harm Orlando (a 'serious' episode).

◆ Look through the play to discover which characters speak only in verse or in prose, and which use both forms of speech. Then select one act and work through it, identifying where prose switches to verse, or verse to prose. Explain why you think Shakespeare decided to use prose and verse in this way, referring to specific examples in the script.

Repetition

Shakespeare uses repetition to give dramatic force to his language. Lines that incorporate this language device are rich in the repeated sounds of rhyme and the hypnotic effects of rhythm. At various points in the play, repeated words, phrases, rhythms and sounds add to the emotional intensity of a scene. This repetition can occur on many levels: sounds, words, phrases and rhythms, and patterns across sentences or clauses.

Repetition of sounds

Alliteration is the repetition of consonant sounds at the beginning of words:

> *Time travels in diverse paces with diverse persons*

Assonance is the repetition of vowel sounds (in the middle of words):

> *Take thou no scorn to wear the horn,*
> *It was a crest ere thou wast born*

Rhymes (which are repeated sounds) are most obvious in songs, Orlando's poems, Phoebe's letter and the rhyming couplets that often end long speeches or signal the end of a scene. These repetitions are opportunities for actors to intensify emotional impact and draw attention to changes in character or action.

Now go we in content,
To liberty, and not to banishment.

Repetition of words

Sometimes the same word is repeated several times in rapid succession, in order to increase pace and tension:

O Phoebe, Phoebe, Phoebe!

More, more, I prithee more

O wonderful, wonderful, and most wonderful wonderful,
an yet again wonderful…

Repeated phrases and rhythms

One example of the use of repeated phrases and rhythms to underscore a particular moment is when the three lovers repeat Silvius's litany of love, 'And so am I for Phoebe' (Act 5 Scene 2, lines 67–90); and when Rosalind promises to satisfy the wishes of each lover, 'I will help you, if I can' (Act 5 Scene 2, lines 92–100). At other times, particular phrases and rhythms are repeated throughout a passage so that an idea can be developed or extended. Examples of this are Silvius's refrain 'Thou hast not loved' (Act 2 Scene 4, lines 27–36), and the echoing exchange between Orlando and Duke Senior: 'If ever you have looked on better days'.

Repetition of patterns

Anaphora is the repetition of the same word or phrase at the beginning of successive sentences or clauses:

I'll tell you who Time ambles withal, who Time trots withal,
who Time gallops withal, and who he stands still withal

Epistrophe is the repetition of the same word or phrase at the end of successive sentences or clauses:

Live a little, comfort a little, cheer thyself a little.

A lean cheek, which you have not; a blue eye and sunken, which you have not; an unquestionable spirit, which you have not; a beard neglected, which you have not.

◆ Look at one or two of the seven songs in this play:

- 'Under the greenwood tree' (Act 2 Scene 5)
- 'If it do come to pass' (Act 2 Scene 5)
- 'Blow, blow, thou winter wind' (Act 2 Scene 7) 'O sweet Oliver' (Act 3 Scene 4)
- 'What shall he have that killed the deer?' (Act 4 Scene 2)
- 'It was a lover and his lass' (Act 5 Scene 3)
- 'Wedding is great Juno's crown' (Act 5 Scene 4)

Identify all the ways in which Shakespeare uses repetition in these songs.

◆ **Read through the last two lines of each scene. See how many of these closing lines are rhyming couplets, and suggest why Shakespeare chooses to end scenes in this way.**

Lists

Shakespeare liked to accumulate many words or phrases at certain moments in the script, rather like a list. He knew that 'piling up' item on item, image on image, view on view, can intensify description, atmosphere, character and dramatic effect.

The most famous example is Jaques's 'seven ages of man' speech, and there are many other points in the play where lists are used to great effect. A few of the longer ones are:

- Corin's list of his contentments (Act 3 Scene 3, lines 53–6)
- Rosalind's breathless list of questions about Orlando (Act 3 Scene 3, lines 185–8)
- Rosalind's ten 'marks' of a man in love (Act 3 Scene 3, lines 312–18)
- Rosalind's many ways of having 'cured' a lover (Act 3 Scene 3, lines 336–46)
- Jaques's description of different kinds of melancholy (Act 4 Scene 1, lines 9–16)
- Silvius's list of what it is to love (Act 5 Scene 2, lines 67–82)
- Touchstone's repeated catalogue of how to avoid a duel (Act 5 Scene 4, lines 62–83).

◆ Choose an example of how this listing technique is used in the script, either from the examples given here or from elsewhere in the play. Take turns with a partner to speak the lines in a way that maximises the impact of the repetition. Think about how you can use gestures and expressions as well as your voice.

Antithesis

Antithesis, the use of contrasting words or phrases within the same sentence or short section of text, is used to bring out oppositions and express conflict. Although *As You Like It* is a comedy, it is full of conflict: brother versus brother, court versus country and lover against lover.

Antithesis is most clearly seen in the verse sections of the play. The first time that verse is spoken, Duke Frederick says to Orlando: 'The world esteemed thy father honourable / But I did find him still mine enemy' (Act 1 Scene 2, lines 177–8). Here 'world' opposes 'I', and 'honourable' contrasts with 'enemy'.

◆ Working through the play, collect ten examples of antithesis. Write an essay in which you show how antithesis helps create a sense of conflict in *As You Like It*. You might like to base your discussion on the following statement: 'Much of the conflict in *As You Like It* is created through language.'

Puns and wordplay – 'How now, wit, whither wander you?'

People in Shakespeare's time loved wordplay of all kinds, and **puns** were especially popular. A pun is a play on words where the same sound or word has different meanings. Rosalind puns on 'hart' (female deer) when, hearing that Orlando is dressed like a hunter, she cries 'he comes to kill my heart'. However, the most intriguing wordplay comes when Rosalind (disguised as Ganymede) persuades Orlando to woo her/him.

◆ Take parts and read aloud the 'wooing scene' (Act 4 Scene 1, lines 31–161). Orlando thinks he is speaking to a boy, but Rosalind revels in the ambiguity that her disguise gives. She can speak as herself without Orlando knowing it. After you have read through the scene, take it in turns to speak only Rosalind's lines: every time she uses a personal pronoun (I, me, myself, and so on), pause and say whom she might have in mind.

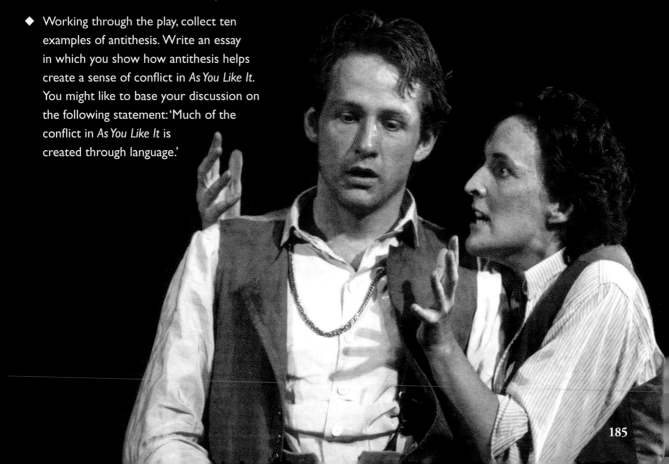

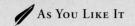

Critics' forum

Use the following quotations from a range of critics to explore your own responses to the play. As you read through them, think about its usefulness to you in your understanding of As You Like It. Remember, you do not have to agree with any of them, but you should be able to justify your own interpretation.

It is the most ideal of any of [Shakespeare's] plays. It is a pastoral drama in which the interest arises more out of the sentiments and characters than out of the action or situation … Caprice and fancy reign and revel here, and stern necessity is banished to the court.

William Hazlitt, 1817

As You Like It is a criticism of the pastoral sentiment, an examination of certain familiar ideas concerning the simple life and the golden age … The result is something very curious. When Rosalind has made her last curtsy and the comedy is done, the pastoral sentiment is without a leg to stand on, and yet it stands; and not only stands but dances. The idea of the simple life has been smiled off the earth, and yet here it is, smiling back at us from every bough of Arden … The doctrine of the golden age has been as much created as destroyed.

Mark Van Doren, 1939

The pastoral region is a place of refuge and the dominant symbol of relief from danger, weariness, want, every ill … And what is Arden but a pastoral region where lost children are found, parted lovers reunited, dispossessed men come to their own again, and repentance and reconciliation grow like leaves on the trees?

Mary Lascelles, 1959

Shakespeare is not interested in a comforting pastoral dream. From the dark corridors of the duke's palace, the forest has all the inviting warmth of the escape world of the Golden Age. But those who make the journey find 'a desert inaccessible', where the wind bites shrewdly, and food is only to be had by hunting. Expecting a womb, they are faced with a challenge. The forest only helps those who help themselves.

David Jones, 1968

The play shows us not a court made simple, but a simple place made courtly.

D. Nuttall, 1972

Behind Rosalind's disguise … lies the great Renaissance wish-dream of harmony between the masculine and feminine principles.

Anne Barton, 1973

[The play's] aristocratic protagonists formulate and enact an ideology: they express the particular interests of their own class as if these were identical with universal interests, with the interests of the whole society.

Elliot Krieger, 1979

[Rosalind's] disguise as Ganymede permits her to educate him about himself, about her, and about the nature of love. It is for Orlando, not for Rosalind that the masquerade is required; indeed the play could fittingly, I believe, be subtitled 'The Education of Orlando.'

Marjorie Garber, 1986

Elizabeth's court by the end of the sixteenth century was increasingly adopting Duke Frederick's style of arbitrary and personalised decision-making. Thus the many angry comments by Rosalind, Orlando, Adam and others about the 'fashion of these times', as well as Jaques' desire to 'cleanse the foul body of the infected world', must have held an extraordinary power over an audience caught up in a whirlwind of change, social disintegration and ultimately Civil War.

Stephen Unwin, 1994

With Orlando what you see is what you get. Rosalind on the other hand needs to be freed from the feminine role that projects so pale a version of the resourceful, noisy, energetic person she really is before she can love Orlando with all her might … He has no wish to be cured; it is she who needs to replace bad poetry and stereotyped reactions by true love and loyalty and these she draws from him in the person of a boy.

Germaine Greer, 1996

The forest people in As You Like It do not, actually, 'fleet the time carelessly'. They have hierarchy, property and money, and give little serious thought to living without them … [They] are not outside the state system; they are a government in waiting. The play presents a conflict within the ruling elite: which faction is to control the state and its resources?

Alan Sinfield, 1996

Feminist thought has highlighted the audacity and originality of Shakespeare's conception of Rosalind, analysing the ways in which the play participates in an Elizabethan questioning of attitudes to women.

Juliet Dunisberre, 2006

As You Like It is poised before the great tragedies; it is a vitalizing work, and Rosalind is a joyous representative of life's possible freedoms.

Harold Bloom, 2009

The place of 'banishment' turns out to be the home of 'liberty' – free from the constraints of court hierarchy and customary deference, Arden is where you can play at being someone different and find out who you really are. It's where you learn to live alongside people who come from very different backgrounds from your own. And where, in the end, you all come together for a big party in celebration of multiple mixed marriages that cut across the traditional social order.

Jonathan Bate, 2010

◆ **Choose three of the quotations above and make notes on them. Decide whether you agree or disagree with the view expressed in each one, using examples and direct quotations from the script in order to justify your decision.**

◆ **Afterwards, use your notes to write your own extended response to these three perspectives on the play. Structure your response in the form of a formal essay, with an introduction, paragraphs giving your perspective on each view you chose (one view per paragraph), and a conclusion.**

As You Like It in performance

Shakespeare probably wrote *As You Like It* around 1600, perhaps in response to the popularity of pastoral plays at that time. It is traditionally believed that this was the very first play acted at the Globe Theatre on London's Bankside, and that Shakespeare played Adam in the production. Another claim is that *As You Like It* was performed before King James I in 1603. However, no one knows for sure if these stories are true. There is no record of a performance during Shakespeare's lifetime.

Performance on Shakespeare's stage

In Shakespeare's time, plays staged in outdoor amphitheatres such as the Globe Theatre were performed in broad daylight during the summer months. So, at 2.00 p.m. people would assemble with food and drink to watch a play with no lighting and no rule of silence for the audience. There were high levels of background noise and interaction during performances, and audience members were free to walk in and out of the theatre.

In the Globe Theatre, the audience was positioned on three sides of the stage: the 'groundlings' stood in the pit around the stage, while those who paid more were seated in three levels around the pit. Actors would see around three thousand faces staring up or down at them. The positioning of the audience made it difficult for everyone to hear all that was going on. Inevitably, the actors would have their backs to sections of the audience at times. The best place for an actor to stand, especially for a soliloquy or an aside, was at the front of the stage – so that he could directly address almost all of the audience. However, it would be tedious if all the action occurred in this area of the stage.

Shakespeare's use of repetition helped to overcome the problem of addressing the different sections of the audience. There are times when the same idea is stated or developed in three ways in order to allow an actor to address each section in turn. These repetitions were never simply word-for-word repeats but were used to create rhythm, accumulate details and build on an idea

through different metaphors and imagery (see 'Repetition' on pp. 183–4). If you spot significant repetition, it may be a clue that Shakespeare intended the character to move around the stage and engage with different parts of the audience.

In Shakespeare's time, where a character was placed on stage gave the audience clues about their role or authority in the play. Characters that were absorbed in their own lives, or characters that played out literary or conventional stereotypes, were often placed centre-stage or upstage (furthest away from the audience). Characters that had a comic role, that performed many roles, or that commented on the action on stage, were often placed downstage (closer to the audience) and were sometimes at the edge of the stage. In this way, these comic characters straddled the divide between the play and its audience.

◆ Look at the images opposite, which give an idea of what the Globe Theatre and its surrounding area would have looked like in Shakespeare's time. A faithful modern recreation of the Globe now stands on the same site, and it is called Shakespeare's Globe. Use the library or the Internet (the Shakespeare's Globe website may be helpful) to research what kind of experiences Elizabethan theatregoers – both rich and poor – would have had watching one of Shakespeare's plays at the Globe.

◆ Actors at Shakespeare's Globe often comment on how effectively its stage layout can be made to work dramatically. They particularly praise the way in which the theatre's design encourages a close rapport with the audience. What parts of *As You Like It* do you think would work well on a stage where the audience is so close to the actors, and why? What parts do you think it would be difficult to stage convincingly, and why?

The exterior and interior of Shakespeare's Globe have been designed to look just like the original Globe Theatre that stood on the same site beside the Thames hundreds of years ago.

Performances after Shakespeare

The first historical record of a performance since Shakespeare's time is of an adaptation of the play in 1723, which was called *Love in a Forest*. This version cut all of the lower-class characters, such as Touchstone, Audrey, Phoebe, Silvius and Corin. It also replaced the wrestling match with a bout of fencing with rapiers (thin swords), and it included lines, songs and characters from other Shakespeare plays. Jaques married Celia, and the mechanicals from *A Midsummer Night's Dream* performed their 'Pyramus and Thisbe' play.

In 1740, the play was performed largely as Shakespeare had written it, and from then on it became one of the most popular and frequently performed of all his plays. In the eighteenth and nineteenth centuries, many leading actresses played Rosalind, and the success of a production was largely judged on who played the part. The popularity of *As You Like It* was also in part due to the audience's enjoyment at the sight of a woman dressed in breeches and showing off her feminine ankles and legs. Around this time, Shakespeare's comedies rose in popularity compared to the tragedies and histories, and they were seen as opportunities for songs, dances and comic episodes.

In the last half of the nineteenth century, and early in the twentieth century, many productions of *As You Like It* were staged outdoors and attempted to create a realistic Forest of Arden on stage. These forests included running streams, real trees, logs, grass, leaves and ferns. Some productions brought live animals on stage, and sheep and rabbits were common. One staging, in Manchester, presented a whole herd of deer, while another used leaves that covered the stage up to the actors' ankles!

For many years, annual productions of *As You Like It* at Stratford-upon-Avon included a stuffed deer from nearby Charlecote Park. Shakespeare was supposed to have poached deer from this park, and consequently fled to London to escape the wrath of the landowner. In 1919, the director of that year's production refused to include the stuffed deer. Many local people were outraged at the break with tradition and the director was insulted in the street.

◆ Create a list of props for your production of *As You Like It*. You might want to take ideas from the list below, which includes some different props that have been used by directors in the past. Annotate your prop list, explaining the significance and intended use of each prop you have chosen. You should also think about the practical considerations of including certain props.

- a clock that does not tick (time is not measured and controlled as it is at court)
- mirrors (a reflection of the audience?)
- real grass or leaves on the stage
- animals such as sheep and deer
- sheets of white silk for different, magical effects
- a bare tree with a few apples on it
- a boar spear for Rosalind
- a rabbit, dead or alive (a dead rabbit was skinned and beheaded on stage by Corin in an RSC production in 2009)

More recent productions

By the second half of the twentieth century, the earlier emphasis on the play as a vehicle for the actor playing Rosalind had given way to 'company productions', in which all the actors contributed significantly to the success of each performance. More recent productions have often been bold in identifying a theme or perspective on the play that sheds new, sometimes glaring light on it.

Adrian Noble's production for the Royal Shakespeare Company in the 1980s focused on the idealism of the forest, but with a new emphasis on feminism. It explored the liberal, feminist notions of gender – in particular, Rosalind's switching of gender and her cross-dressing. In this production, the concept was to see Arden as an imaginative landscape rather than as a real place to which the courtiers had escaped. The characters' escape from Duke Frederick's court was like an extended dream, and Jaques's world-weary cynicism appeared to be that of someone disappointed by a dream unfulfilled.

Social issues have also been more prominently stressed in more recent productions, with the emphasis both on the harsh political realities of Duke Frederick's court and on the exploitation of the natural world by the exiled court. A 1992 film version of As You Like It set Arden in a modern urban wasteland, to bring home messages about social deprivation to contemporary audiences. This transposition of a green, pastoral, ecologically vital England to a background of despair and dereliction gave the play a darker tone, especially when contrasted with the extravagance and wealth of the court scenes. Banishment from the court meant exile from the good life to a bleaker world in Arden, as if the utopian dreams projected in other productions were transformed into a dystopia in this one.

Such social commentary upset many viewers, who thought the movie had lost much of the joyous, comic exuberance of the play. Rosalind became a boyish Ganymede in jeans, parka and hat, and her interplay with Orlando was cut down. There was also a good deal of doubling in the movie, with the lovers looking much like each other by the end of the play, and the city court being mirrored by the court in Arden. Such doubling, which is easier to achieve on film than on stage – challenges you to think about the structure, the characters and the significance of the play as a whole.

▲ The 1992 film version of As You Like It used a contemporary setting and style of dress to to address issues in modern society.

As You Like It is a popular play outside the UK, too. Salvador Dalí once designed surrealist sets and costumes for a lavish 1948 production in Rome, choosing to represent the Forest of Arden as a single large apple painted on the backdrop behind the stage. Before the reunification of Germany, a famous 1977 production in Berlin implied that the Forest of Arden (a 'free' place) was like West Berlin surrounded by the socialist German Democratic Republic.

A 1990s Cheek by Jowl production featured an all-male cast in modern dress. By revisiting this single-gendered approach, which was exclusively used for performances in Shakespeare's time, the director invited a modern reappraisal of how the play represents gender. Rather than a female actor stepping into the female role of Rosalind and then 'acting like a man' when disguised as Ganymede, in this production a male actor had to realistically embody a female character and then interrogate what it meant to be a man in order to self-consciously act like one when required. Adrian Lester played Rosalind and was widely praised for his grace, humour and sensitivity in the role.

Some productions have focused on the festive and romantic elements of the play. Lucy Bailey's 1998 Shakespeare's Globe production flirted with the idea of street theatre by bringing the wrestling match between Charles and Orlando off the stage and into the central pit of the theatre, thus immediately placing the action right in the heart of the audience. Rosalind was played as a woman whose femininity was emphasised so that when she was disguised as Ganymede, the disguise was superficial. Beneath Ganymede's exterior, there was clearly a young woman with a strong passion for Orlando. In this production, there was a renewed focus on the joy and earnestness of the script.

In a 2006 production directed by Louisa Fitzgerald for Castle Theatre Company at Durham University, the emphasis was on colour in a garden setting. The production seemed, indeed, like a garden fête – with a bandstand of musicians providing accompaniment, a wrestling match arranged in a hastily erected ring, and the pastoral seeming to overpower the forest and the court. The audience sat on chairs on the lawn, and the action surrounded them. There was both a sense of the surreal, prompted by the garish colours of Touchstone and some deckchairs, and a real sense of the outdoors being essential to the Englishness of the play. The production as a whole had the feeling of a glorious romp: a youthful, concentrated exploration of love, society and the breaking of convention.

▼ **Adrian Lester and Simon Coates as Rosalind and Celia in the widely praised Cheek by Jowl production.**

An Australian production in 2011 was described as 'cheeky', 'accessible', 'hilarious' and 'tightly paced' in theatre reviews. The world of the corrupt Duke Frederick was full of social injustices that were easily recognised by the local audience, but all this was quickly swept away as the play moved into the forest. Here, the musically talented cast performed song and pantomime routines in a rollicking, fun-filled performance of the play.

An RSC production in 2011 was considered by some to be similarly gloomy. The anger and discontent at the beginning of the play created a harsh atmosphere that was followed by a focus on the trials and tribulations of love in all its forms. Even Rosalind and Celia embarked on their adventure to the forest with a sense of dismal woe. However, as winter turned to spring in the forest, the focus changed to the transformative power of love and there was 'love, and jokes, and pleasure' for the rest of the play.

Other recent productions have tempered the fun and festive aspects of the play with more serious and melancholic overtones. Sam Mendes's 2010 production of the play, with a mixed cast of American and British actors, presented a cold and unfriendly Arden full of adversity and melancholy. In this production, Orlando seemed to border on deep despair; and Adam, despite his assertions that he was still young and healthy, died as he and Orlando journeyed into the forest. The hardships and difficulties encountered by the characters were reflected in the intensity of some of the dramatic scenes, as well as in the stage set for the forest — which was covered at times by drifts of snow, before gradually blossoming as the play moved through its final scenes.

In 2013, a vibrant and youthful performance of the play by the RSC evoked the atmosphere of an English summer music festival, complete with lots of mud that Rosalind and Orlando smeared all over each other at the end. Arden was a place of escape and joyous freedom, rather than the site of arduous trials and eventual redemption as in the productions described above.

Staging Shakespeare

Any script by Shakespeare should be read as a blueprint (plan) for a live performance, so it is essential that you think about how it can or should be staged. There is no substitute for seeing a live performance of the play at the theatre (or a filmed performance of such a production) in order to gain an appreciation of the play as a script that has been brought to life.

When creating sets for specific theatres, professional set designers often produce three-dimensional models of the stage, and reproduce the key features of the set in miniature to see how all the components will work together and with the space.

◆ In groups, have a go at creating this kind of model, perhaps by using a shoebox as the basic structure. Compare your set designs with those of other groups in the class. How different do you think the audience's response will be to the different sets? (See images of the sets from other productions in this book.)

Programme notes that are sold at performances of the play sometimes include information on how the stage set links to the director's interpretation and characterisation.

◆ In role as a director, write your own programme notes on how the key features (themes, setting, tone, and so on) of your interpretation and vision for the production have informed the set design and other staging decisions such as casting choices, costumes, sound design and lighting.

Film versions

In 1936, a film version of *As You Like It* was released, starring Laurence Olivier (in his first Shakespeare film) as Orlando and the Austrian actress, Elisabeth Bergner, as Rosalind. Bergner, who was Jewish, had played Rosalind on the stage in Germany more than 500 times, but she had to leave the country when the Nazis took power there.

She had a strong German accent, which confused some of the movie's viewers, while others thought she was too small and slight to play the robust Rosalind. Despite this, she was one of the most sprightly, vivacious and flirtatious Rosalinds that most people had seen.

Olivier was not as famous as Bergner when he took on the role of Orlando, but by the time the movie was released his name was in large letters on all the publicity posters. His Orlando was both poetic and impressively athletic, taking on a wrestler who was twice his size. Interestingly, this was the only Shakespeare role for which Olivier did not receive an award, and he did not count his performance as a personal success.

The film was an extravagant production with a forest set over 90 metres long (the largest ever made for a film studio) and a cast of famous actors, many of whom were star performers in their own right. A number of animals were also included in the movie: swans and ostriches were seen in scenes at the court, and in the Forest of Arden, pigs, cows, sheep and even a serpent and lioness, made appearances.

In 1978, a production of *As You Like It* was filmed for the BBC at Glamis Castle in Scotland. It starred Helen Mirren as Rosalind. It was famed for the lush greenery of its Arden Forest. Although the director, Basil Coleman, wanted to film the changing seasons over the course of the year, he was unable to do so and had to complete most of the filming in May. The action therefore takes place in a summer climate, while the characters speak incongruously of the winter weather and their harsh life in the forest.

In 1992, Christine Edzard directed a film version of *As You Like It* with young, unknown actors as Rosalind and Orlando. The same actor played Orlando and Oliver, and the two characters were never in the same shot together. The Welsh comedian and TV personality Griff Rhys Jones was cast as Touchstone. Edzard set the play in an urban wasteland where the exiled Duke Senior and his courtiers live like homeless people, in tents and cardboard boxes, hiding from a violent overlord. Rosalind and Celia live in a taxi shelter and Audrey runs a café from her caravan. The characters are dressed in modern clothes, with Rosalind wearing a jumper and jeans, and Orlando writes his love poems to Rosalind using an aerosol can. Despite this setting, and the urban noise that was part of the movie's soundtrack, all Shakespeare's references to life in the forest – including animals, trees and weather – remained in the script.

Kenneth Branagh's 2006 film version of *As You Like It* sets the play in Japan. The graphics at the start of the film indicate 'a dream of Japan', with associations of exotica, formality and the distant 'Orient'. As in some productions in the theatre, as well as on film, Duke Senior and Duke Frederick are played by the same actor – their respective costumes indicate that they are extreme opposites in character. The movie starts in a court, with Duke Senior and his followers, including Celia and Rosalind, enjoying a Kabuki theatre performance. The courtiers' costumes are from nineteenth-century Japan, and Duke Senior bases his court on Japanese culture and ceremony.

An attack by the usurping court abruptly disturbs this tranquillity. Duke Frederick and his entourage appear like samurai warriors – or like Darth Vader and his stormtroopers from *Star Wars*. The movie depicts the

moments in which Duke Frederick usurps his brother and, with his ninja warriors, takes control. The new rulers' sinister presence broods over the court, while Duke Senior and his courtiers are chased into the forest, to be followed later by the banished Rosalind and Celia. In the court of Duke Frederick, Orlando and Oliver engage in a full-scale fight rather than just the mutual threats of one. In keeping with the formal Japanese setting, Charles is a sumo wrestler.

In this film, Arden appears as a kind of paradise. It is a place where meditation, soft-spoken exchanges and gentleness (in the sense of gentility and nobility, as well as softness) are the order of the day. Jaques is the principal source of humour in the movie, and his changing moods, his melancholy observations and his love of the forest are all emphasised in this production. Interestingly, the minor characters in the pastoral romance – such as Silvius, Corin and Phoebe – are given prominence and status, as if their way of life is seen as equally heroic and important to the play as a whole. Indeed, it is they who seem to be the centre of moral power and goodness in the movie, rather than any character from the court.

◆ Plan a movie pitch. Imagine that you are making the pitch to a group of investors. They have the money to finance a new film version of the play – if you can convince them of the merits of your concept. Work through the following points to create your presentation, and remember that your production can be big-budget!

◆ Consider your audience: why would people go to see this movie, and why would it appeal to a modern audience?

◆ How will your movie begin? Where (and when) will it be set? What music or sound effects will you use? What atmosphere are you seeking to create? Will you want to reorder/cut the script? Storyboard the opening of the play. If you have access to cameras, film the opening three or four minutes and share the video with other groups in your class. Which group's video do you like best, and why do you think it is the most successful?

◆ Summarise the storyline in approximately 500 words, and include a list of characters.

◆ Describe the setting and time – this could be any place at any point in the past, present or future. Suggest a series of locations, matched to specific scenes, within your chosen setting. Add further ideas about how lighting, costume and music could contribute to the overall effect.

◆ Cast your production with known actors, comedians or other celebrities, and explain your choices. Then identify several speeches that you think are particularly important, and write instructions on how they should be delivered.

◆ Draw some costume designs, or use pictures taken from magazines or the Internet to create collages of the costumes.

◆ Design a DVD cover with the title, strapline and production photo(s) on the front and a short promotional 'blurb' on the back.

◆ Create a publicity poster. What elements of your movie will you emphasise in order to persuade people to see it? Will you include a quotation as a 'slogan'? Which image from the play, and which character, will you give most prominence to? Or will you use an abstract image that ties in with a particular theme? For inspiration, look at the promotional posters opposite.

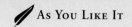

Writing about Shakespeare

The play as text

Shakespeare's plays have always been studied as literary works – as words on a page that need clarification, appreciation and discussion. When you write about the plays, you will be asked to compose short pieces and also longer, more reflective pieces like controlled assessments, examination scripts and coursework – often in the form of essays on themes and/or imagery, character studies, analyses of the structure of the play and on stagecraft. Imagery, stagecraft and character are dealt with elsewhere in this edition. Here, we concentrate on themes and structure. You might find it helpful to look at the 'Write about it' boxes on the left-hand pages throughout the play.

Themes

It is often tempting to say that the theme of a play is a single idea, like 'death' in *Hamlet*, or 'the supernatural' in *Macbeth*, or 'love' in *Romeo and Juliet*. The problem with such a simple approach is that you will miss the complexity of the plays. In *Romeo and Juliet*, for example, the play is about the relationship between love, family loyalty and constraint; it is also about the relationship of youth to age and experience; and the relationship between Romeo and Juliet is also played out against a background of enmity between two families. Between each of these ideas or concepts there are tensions. The tensions are the main focus of attention for Shakespeare and the audience; this is also how the best drama operates – by the presentation of and resolution of tension.

Look back at the 'Themes' boxes throughout the play to see if any of the activities there have given rise to information that you could use as a starting point for further writing about the themes of the specific play you are studying.

Structure

Most Shakespeare plays are in five acts, divided into scenes. These acts were not in the original scripts, but have been included in later editions to make the action more manageable, clearer and more like 'classical' structures. One way to get a sense of the structure of the whole play is to take a printed version (not this one!) and cut it up into scenes and acts, then display each scene and act, in sequence, on a wall, like this:

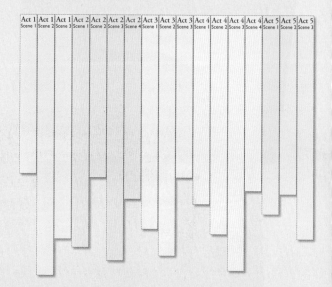

As you set out the whole play, you will be able to see the 'shape' of each act, the relative length of the scenes, and how the acts relate to each other (such as whether one act is shorter, and why that might be). You can annotate the text with comments, observations and questions. You can use a highlighter pen to mark the recurrence of certain words, images or metaphors to see at a glance where and how frequently they appear. You can also follow a particular character's progress through the play.

Such an overview of the play gives you critical perspective: you will be able to see how the parts fit together, to stand back from the play and assess its shape, and to focus on particular parts within the context of the whole. Your writing will reflect a greater awareness of the overall context as a result.

The play as script

There are different, but related, categories when we think of the play as a script for performance. These include stagecraft (discussed elsewhere in this edition and throughout the left-hand pages), lighting, focus (who are we looking at? Where is the attention of the audience?), music and sound, props and costumes, casting, make-up, pace and rhythm, and other spatial relationships (for example, how actors move around the stage in relation to each other). If you are writing about stagecraft or performance, use the notes you have made as a result of the Stagecraft activities throughout this edition of the play, as well as any information you can find about the plays in performance.

What are the key points of dispute?

Shakespeare is brilliant at capturing a number of key points of dispute in each of his plays. These are the dramatic moments where he concentrates the focus of the audience on difficult (sometimes universal) problems that the characters are facing or embodying.

First, identify these key points in the play you are studying. You can do this as a class by discussing what you consider to be the key points in small groups, then debating the long-list as a whole class, and then coming up with a short-list of what the class thinks are the most significant. (This is a good opportunity for speaking and listening work.) They are likely to be places in the play where the action or reflection is at its most intense, and which capture the complexity of themes, character, structure and performance.

Second, drill down at one of the points of contention and tension. In other words, investigate the complexity of the problem that Shakespeare has presented. What is at stake? Why is it important? Is it a problem that can be resolved, or is it an insoluble one?

Key skills in writing about Shakespeare

Here are some suggestions to help you organise your notes and develop advanced writing skills when working on Shakespeare:

- Compose the title of your writing carefully to maximise your opportunities to be creative and critical about the play. Explore the key words in your title carefully. Decide which aspect of the play – or which combination of aspects – you are focusing on.
- Create a mind map of your ideas, making connections between them.
- If appropriate, arrange your ideas into a hierarchy that shows how some themes or features of the play are 'higher' than others and can incorporate other ideas.
- Sequence your ideas so that you have a plan for writing an essay, review, story – whichever genre you are using. You might like to think about whether to put your strongest points first, in the middle, or later.
- Collect key quotations (it might help to compile this list with a partner), which you can use as evidence to support your argument.
- Compose your first draft, embedding quotations in your text as you go along.
- Revise your draft in the light of your own critical reflections and/or those of others.

The following pages focus on writing about *As You Like It* in particular.

Writing about *As You Like It*

Any kind of writing about *As You Like It* will be informed by your responses to the play. Your understanding of how characters, plot, themes, language and stagecraft are all interrelated will contribute to your unique perspective. This section will help you locate key points of entry into the play, so that your writing will be engaging and original. The best way to capture your reader's attention is to take them with you on a journey of discovering a new pathway into *As You Like It*.

But first, how do you find your unique perspective? You may want to start with the title *As You Like It*, and think about Shakespeare's hints as to the play's meaning. *As You Like It* may be Shakespeare saying to his Elizabethan audiences: 'whoever you are, whatever your social background and interests, there's something here for you'. All kinds of meanings and interpretations are possible in the play, and there is something in it for everyone – whether you like spectacle, some violent action, songs, clowns and jokes, disguise, lots of talk about love, or the silliness of people in love.

The title may have also promised Elizabethan audiences that they would find many reminders of their own world. In Jaques they would see the malcontent – the world-weary cynic who was such a familiar figure in Shakespeare's London. They would recognise certain figures from society in Jaques's 'seven ages of man' speech: brave soldiers, justices who accepted bribes, and so on. Despite containing reminders of the audience's own world, the Forest of Arden that lies at the heart of this play is a world of its own. It is a place of escape, an illusion of perpetual holiday and freedom where time stands still. This contented 'Never-Never Land' of make-believe exists under many names: Utopia, Xanadu, Arcadia, the Land of Cockaigne, the Golden Age, Shangri-La and Camelot. These are festive worlds of romance, full of magical possibilities, where anything can happen: disguises are adopted and all kinds of confusions, errors and mistakes occur. But the end result is marriage and happiness because these are places where dreams come true and harmony can be restored.

At this point, you may think about Rosalind – the character who seems to orchestrate events to make sure her dream (and everyone else's) comes true! Like Rosalind, who is disguised as Ganymede for much of the play, life in the forest is not always what it seems. It is full of people with their own agendas, and it also has its own hardships and injustices. And yet, in this world that is set apart from the everyday formality of the court, there is a special freedom that allows Rosalind (as Ganymede) to take on different roles in order to shape events in general and woo Orlando in particular. Shakespeare's use of theatrical metaphors and imagery reminds the audience of the play's central theme of illusion, and at the same time sets Rosalind apart as a character who can play on the border between illusion and reality. Indeed, Shakespeare gives Rosalind the very last word, as she talks directly to the audience in the epilogue.

While thinking through the range of possible perspectives on the play, you might find that reflecting on the performance possibilities offered in the play script is helpful. Your own perspective on the play will begin to develop as you think about what you are interested in, and allow yourself to make connections between the dramatic, contextual, linguistic and thematic features of the play.

Creative writing

At different times during your study of *As You Like It*, and during assessments and examinations, you will write about the play and your personal responses to it. Creative responses to the play, such as those encouraged in the activities in this book, can allow you to be as imaginative as you want. This is your chance to develop your own voice and to be adventurous as well as sensitive to the words and images in the play. *As You Like It* is a rich, multi-layered play that benefits from many different approaches, both in performance and in writing. Don't be afraid of larger questions or implications that cannot be reduced to simple resolutions. It is often the problematic and complex issues, for which you do not have easy answers, that can be the most interesting.

◆ Duke Frederick's usurpation of Duke Senior takes place 'off stage', before the play opens. Imagine how this rebellion might have taken place and how Duke Senior could have been overthrown. Write the missing scene.

◆ What happens to Silvius and Phoebe or Touchstone and Audrey after the play has finished? Choose one of the characters and write their story, extending it to cover the times before and after they appear in the play. You might like to write this as a monologue or a diary entry. You could also compose a scene showing one of the couples after five years of married life.

Essay writing

Other types of written response to the play, such as essays, have a set structure and specific requirements. Writing an essay gives you a chance to explore your own interpretations, to use evidence that appeals to you, and to write with creativity and flair. You can approach the play from a number of critical perspectives and with a focus on various different themes. Don't forget to consider the social, literary, political and cultural contexts of the play, both in Shakespeare's day and when it is experienced today.

Your essay should present a strong, reasoned argument, using evidence and structural requirements to persuade your readers that you have an important perspective on the play. You will need to integrate evidence from the script into your own writing by using embedded quotations and by explaining the significance of each quotation and reference to the play. Some people like to remember the acronym PEA to help them here. P is the POINT you are making. E is the EVIDENCE you are taking from the script, whether it is a direct quotation, a summary of what is happening, or a reference to character, plot and themes. A is the ANALYSIS you give for using this evidence, which will reflect back on the point you are making and also contain your own personal response and original ideas.

The following are typical examination essays on *As You Like It*:

• Choose two or three central themes and explain how each is developed linguistically and dramatically through the play.

• Write about an aspect of language that interests you in *As You Like It*.

• The pastoral romance tradition is parodied throughout *As You Like It*. Discuss the effect this has on your understanding of characters and events in the play.

• 'Although, in the Forest of Arden, women seem to be temporarily empowered, male dominance is re-established at the end of the play.' Consider the events of the play in the light of this comment.

• How does Rosalind's disguise help her to orchestrate the events leading up to the marriages at the end of *As You Like It*? Write about the significance of her disguise at different points in the play.

• 'The Forest of Arden is a setting where simple, natural love is able to develop.' To what extent do you agree with this view?

◆ Pick at least two of the essay titles above, and sketch out an essay plan for each. Swap plans with two other students in your class, giving constructive feedback and making suggestions for improvements.

◆ Select the two essay titles that you think are the most difficult to answer. Try to pinpoint what aspects of the questions you find most challenging, then get together with a partner and share ideas about how to address these challenging aspects of each question.

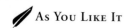

William Shakespeare
1564–1616

1564	Born Stratford-upon-Avon, eldest son of John and Mary Shakespeare.
1582	Marries Anne Hathaway of Shottery, near Stratford.
1583	Daughter Susanna born.
1585	Twins, son and daughter Hamnet and Judith, born.
1592	First mention of Shakespeare in London. Robert Greene, another playwright, described Shakespeare as 'an upstart crow beautified with our feathers'. Greene seems to have been jealous of Shakespeare. He mocked Shakespeare's name, calling him 'the only Shake-scene in a country' (presumably because Shakespeare was writing successful plays).
1595	Becomes a shareholder in The Lord Chamberlain's Men, an acting company that became extremely popular.
1596	Son, Hamnet, dies aged eleven.
	Father, John, granted arms (acknowledged as a gentleman).
1597	Buys New Place, the grandest house in Stratford.
1598	Acts in Ben Jonson's *Every Man in His Humour*.
1599	Globe Theatre opens on Bankside. Performances in the open air.
1601	Father, John, dies.
1603	James I grants Shakespeare's company a royal patent: The Lord Chamberlain's Men become The King's Men and play about twelve performances each year at court.
1607	Daughter Susanna marries Dr John Hall.
1608	Mother, Mary, dies.
1609	The King's Men begin performing indoors at Blackfriars Theatre.
1610	Probably returns from London to live in Stratford.
1616	Daughter Judith marries Thomas Quiney.
	Dies. Buried in Holy Trinity Church, Stratford-upon-Avon.

The plays and poems

(no one knows exactly when he wrote each play)

1589–95	*The Two Gentlemen of Verona, The Taming of the Shrew*, First, Second and *Third Parts* of *King Henry VI, Titus Andronicus, King Richard III, The Comedy of Errors, Love's Labour's Lost, A Midsummer Night's Dream, Romeo and Juliet, King Richard II* (and the long poems *Venus and Adonis* and *The Rape of Lucrece*).
1596–99	*King John, The Merchant of Venice*, First and *Second Parts* of *King Henry IV, The Merry Wives of Windsor, Much Ado About Nothing, King Henry V, Julius Caesar* (and probably the Sonnets).
1600–05	***As You Like It***, *Hamlet, Twelfth Night, Troilus and Cressida, Measure for Measure, Othello, All's Well That Ends Well, Timon of Athens, King Lear*.
1606–11	*Macbeth, Antony and Cleopatra, Pericles, Coriolanus, The Winter's Tale, Cymbeline, The Tempest*.
1613	*King Henry VIII, The Two Noble Kinsmen* (both probably with John Fletcher).
1623	Shakespeare's plays published as a collection (now called the First Folio).

Acknowledgements

Cambridge University Press would like to acknowledge the contributions made to this work by Rex Gibson, Richard Andrews and Perry Mills.

p. 171 extract from a review of a performance of As You Like It at Shakespeare's Globe by Emily Jupp, 10 September 2012, reproduced courtesy of The Independent.

Picture Credits

p. iii & 69 top: Courtyard Theater 2011, © Chicago Shakespeare Theater (photo by Liz Lauren, dir. Gary Griffin, actors pictured are Philip James Brannon, Chaon Cross and Kate Fry); p. v top: Curve Theatre 2009, © Donald Cooper/Photostage; p. v bottom: Bath Theatre Royal 2003, © Donald Cooper/Photostage; p. vi top: Royal Shakespeare Theatre 1992, © Donald Cooper/Photostage; p. vi bottom: Bath Theatre Royal 2003, © Donald Cooper/Photostage; p. vii top: Shakespeare's Globe 1998, © Donald Cooper/Photostage; p. vii bottom: Bath Theatre Royal 2003, © Donald Cooper/Photostage; p. viii Wyndham's Theatre 2005, © Donald Cooper/Photostage; p. ix top: Shakespeare's Globe 1998, © Donald Cooper/Photostage; p. ix bottom: Royal Shakespeare Theatre 1985, © Donald Cooper/Photostage; p. x top: Royal Shakespeare Theatre 1992, © Donald Cooper/Photostage; p. x bottom: Old Vic 2010, © Nigel Norrington/ArenaPAL; p. xi top: Wyndham's Theatre 2005, © Donald Cooper/Photostage; p. xi bottom: Bath Theatre Royal 2003, © Donald Cooper/Photostage; p. xii: Royal Shakespeare Theatre 1992, © Donald Cooper/Photostage; p. 4: Curve Theatre 2009, © Donald Cooper/Photostage; p. 10: Illustration from John Lydgate's Siege of Troy, showing the Wheel of Fortune held by the Queen of Fortune; p. 12 Shakespeare's Globe 2009, © Robbie Jack/Corbis; p. 14: Barbican 2001, © Donald Cooper/Photostage; p. 16: Regent's Park Open Air Theatre 2002, © Donald Cooper/Photostage; p. 18: Barbican 2001, © Donald Cooper/Photostage; p. 26: Curve Theatre 2009, © Donald Cooper/Photostage;

p. 33: Regent's Park Open Air Theatre 2002, © Donald Cooper/Photostage; p. 38: Still from 2006 As You Like It film directed by Kenneth Branagh, © REX/Moviestore Collection; p. 44: Royal Shakespeare Theatre 2007, © Donald Cooper/Photostage; p. 50: Shakespeare's Globe 1998, © Donald Cooper/Photostage; p. 58: Wyndham's Theatre 2005, © Donald Cooper/Photostage; p. 60: Royal Shakespeare Theatre 2007, © Donald Cooper/Photostage; p. 64: Bath Theatre Royal 2003, © Donald Cooper/Photostage; p. 66: Bath Theatre Royal 2003, © Donald Cooper/Photostage; p. 69 bottom left: Regent's Park Open Air Theatre 2002, © Donald Cooper/Photostage; p. 69 bottom right: Shakespeare's Globe 1998, © Donald Cooper/Photostage; p. 74: Royal Shakespeare Theatre, © Donald Cooper/Photostage; p. 80: Old Vic 2010, © Donald Cooper/Photostage; p. 88: Bath Theatre Royal 2003, © Donald Cooper/Photostage; p. 94: Royal Shakespeare Theatre 1992, © Donald Cooper/Photostage; p. 102: Shakespeare's Globe 2012, © Donald Cooper/Photostage; p. 109 top: Royal Shakespeare Theatre 2007, © Donald Cooper/Photostage; p. 109 bottom: Clywd Theatre 2012, © Clark Nobby/ArenaPAL; p. 114: Lyric 2000, © Donald Cooper/Photostage; p. 120 Royal Shakespeare Theatre 2000, © Donald Cooper/Photostage; p. 128 Regent's Park Open Air Theatre 2002, © Donald Cooper/Photostage; p. 133 top: Swan Theatre 2003, © Donald Cooper/Photostage; p. 133 bottom left: Bath Theatre Royal 2003, © Donald Cooper/Photostage; p. 133 bottom right: Royal Shakespeare Theatre 2000, © Donald Cooper/Photostage; p. 136: Royal Shakespeare Theatre 1992, © Donald Cooper/Photostage; p. 142: Swan Theatre 2003, © Donald Cooper/Photostage; p. 159 top: Old Vic 1989, © Donald Cooper/Photostage; p. 159 bottom: Bath Theatre Royal 2003, © Donald Cooper/Photostage; p. 161: Bath Theatre Royal 2003, © Donald Cooper/Photostage; p. 163: Bath Theatre Royal 2003, © Donald Cooper/Photostage; p. 166: Statue of Robin Hood in Nottingham, © Deniskelly/Dreamstime; p. 167 top: Rose of Kingston 2011, © Donald Cooper/Photostage;

Produced for Cambridge University Press by White-Thomson Publishing
+44 (0)843 208 7460
www.wtpub.co.uk

Project editors: Alice Harman and Sonya Newland
Designer: Clare Nicholas
Concept design: Jackie Hill